Patron Gods *and* Patron Lords

Patron Gods *and* Patron Lords

The Semiotics of Classic
Maya Community Cults

JOANNE P. BARON

UNIVERSITY PRESS OF COLORADO
Boulder

© 2016 by University Press of Colorado

Published by University Press of Colorado
245 Century Circle, Suite 202
Louisville, Colorado 80027

All rights reserved
First paperback edition 2019

 The University Press of Colorado is a proud member of the Association of University Presses.

The University Press of Colorado is a cooperative publishing enterprise supported, in part, by Adams State University, Colorado State University, Fort Lewis College, Metropolitan State University of Denver, Regis University, University of Colorado, University of Northern Colorado, University of Wyoming, Utah State University, and Western Colorado University.

ISBN: 978-1-60732-517-8 (cloth)
ISBN: 978-1-64642-004-9 (paperback)
ISBN: 978-1-60732-518-5 (ebook)

Library of Congress Cataloging-in-Publication Data

Names: Baron, Joanne, author.
Title: Patron gods and patron lords : the semiotics of classic Maya community cults / Joanne P. Baron.
Description: Boulder : University Press of Colorado, [2016] | Includes bibliographical references.
Identifiers: LCCN 2016019946| ISBN 9781607325178 (cloth) | ISBN 9781646420049 (pbk)| ISBN 9781607325185 (ebook)
Subjects: LCSH: Mayas—Religion. | Mayas—Mythology. | Mayas—Politics and government. | Mayas—Guatemala—Politics and government. | Mayas—Guatemala—Religion. | Semiotics—Religious aspects.
Classification: LCC F1435.3.R3 B37 2016 | DDC 972.81—dc23
LC record available at https://lccn.loc.gov/2016019946

Cover image copyright: © Museum der Kulturen Basel.

For Steve

Contents

	List of Figures	*ix*
	List of Tables	*xiii*
	Acknowledgments	*xv*
1	The Classic Maya and Their Political System	3
2	Words and Things: Semiotics and the Archaeological Record	19
3	Semantics: Defining Patron Deities	45
4	Pragmatics: Using Patron Deities	75
5	Patron Deity Introduction at La Corona, Guatemala	117
6	The Classic Maya Polity	165
	Appendix: Patron Deities of Classic Maya Sites	*173*
	References Cited	*189*
	Index	*219*

Figures

1.1. Map of the Maya area showing sites mentioned in this book ... 7
1.2. Timeline of major periods in Mesoamerican archaeology ... 8
3.1. The *k'uh* glyph ... 48
3.2. The "water group" ... 49
3.3. The *k'uh* glyph rendered with the sign for "eat" ... 50
3.4. Patron Deity Introductory Glyph ... 54
3.5. Reconstructions of identifiable patron deity temples drawn at same scale and orientation ... 64
4.1. Lintel 3 of Tikal Temple I, showing the victorious ruler Jasaw Chan K'awiil with the captured god Yajaw Maan of Calakmul ... 81
4.2. Lintel 2 of Tikal Temple I, showing Jasaw Chan K'awiil with the Teotihuacan war god, Waxaklajun Ubaah Kaan ... 83
4.3. Lintel 3 of Tikal Temple IV, showing ruler Yihk'in Chan K'awiil after his victory over El Peru ... 85
4.4. Lintel 2 of Tikal Temple IV, showing Yihk'in Chan K'awiil with a captured patron deity from Naranjo ... 86

4.5.	Timeline showing references to the patron god GI-K'awiil and political changes in the Petexbatun region of Guatemala	89
5.1.	Map of the Coronitas group	121
5.2.	Lineages of La Corona rulers	126
5.3.	North profile of Structure 13R-5 showing stages of construction and Burial 1	127
5.4.	South profile of Structure 13R-2 showing stages of construction and Burial 6	129
5.5.	Vessel forms recovered from three middens and on the shared front terrace of Structures 13R-2, 13R-3, and 13R-4	130
5.6.	Schematic representation of the Muk Stage back terraces of Structures 13R-2, 13R-3, and 13R-4	132
5.7.	Marine shell recovered from Burial 6	133
5.8.	Ceramics recovered from Burial 6	134
5.9.	Impression of a woven mat left on the fill above Burial 6	135
5.10.	Right side of La Corona Panel 6, showing the arrival of Lady Naah Ek' in 520	138
5.11.	Hieroglyphic Stairway blocks mentioning the patron god Ikiiy	141
5.12.	Polychrome ceramics with royal titles recovered from the patio of Structure 13R-10 and the lower fill of Structure 13R-9	145
5.13.	Hieroglyphic Stairway block (Element 39) describing a ritual dance by K'inich [?] Yook "in the year of Yaxal Ajaw"	147
5.14.	Hieroglyphic Stairway block (Element 23) describing K'inich [?] Yook drinking and giving pulque	148
5.15.	La Corona Panel 1, recovered from the Ub Stage of Structure 13R-5	149

5.16. Plan of the front terraces of Structures 13R-2 and 13R-3 showing Unen Stage features 153

5.17. Unen Stage plaster decoration on the front of Structure 13R-3 154

5.18. Plan of the back terraces of Structures 13R-4 and 13R-5 showing Unen Stage features 155

Tables

3.1.	Terms analogous to *luut* in Mayan languages	55
4.1.	Terms related to "gathering together" in some Mayan languages	77
5.1.	Construction on the Coronitas temples	123
5.2.	Important historical dates in La Corona texts	124

Acknowledgments

This book came into existence because of the support of many friends, colleagues, and organizations. Fieldwork at La Corona was supported by grants from the Wenner-Gren Foundation and from the University of Pennsylvania via the Sylvia Brown Travel Grant, the Sorenson Research Grant, and the Lisa Lynn Brody Foley Research Grant. I am grateful for their generosity. I am also grateful to the project directors of the La Corona Regional Archaeological Project, Marcello Canuto and Tomás Barrientos. Not only did they give me the opportunity to work for five years at this beautiful archaeological site, their leadership has created an environment where ideas and friendships flourish in the middle of the jungle.

Out of those friendships and ideas came great collaborations, and this book is an example. The work of my colleagues Mary Jane Acuña, Kike Fernández, Jocelyne Ponce, Antonieta Cajas, and Divina Perla added to my interpretations of the Coronitas temples. The artifacts I recovered wouldn't have told their story without the analyses of Carry Parris, Erin Patterson, Diana Fridberg, and Clarissa Cagnato. The inscriptions of the site would be more cryptic without the work of David Stuart and Stan Guenter. I could never have moved all that dirt without the excellent excavators Nelwin Herida, Antonio Obando, Luis Ernesto Saquij, and José Balarmino Quixchan, as well as many assistants from Paso Caballos, Dolores, and San Andrés, Peten.

And I would not have stayed happy and sane without the camaraderie of all of the La Corona project members.

The book grew out of my dissertation at the University of Pennsylvania and has benefited from the input of my mentors there. I am grateful to Bob Sharer, who advised me through every stage of my field research, though he never got to see the finished product. Richard Leventhal has added great theoretical insights to my ideas on ancient power structures. Asif Agha introduced me to the world of semiotic anthropology, changing the way I understood human culture. And Simon Martin guided me through the challenging process of learning how to read Maya hieroglyphic writing and how to use it to understand political relationships. Finally, to all the participants in weekly Maya coffee hour, I am grateful for your ideas and support.

In addition to these mentors, others have helped me improve and refine the ideas that went into this book. Robert Preucel has ceaselessly supported my foray into archaeological semiotics and offered helpful commentary about my work. Richard Parmentier's comments on an earlier paper for *Signs and Society* brought my use of Peircian semiotics to a new level. Christian Prager's review of an earlier draft of this book greatly improved the manuscript. And various anonymous reviewers of article submissions, this book's prospectus, and the first draft have allowed me to refine my thinking and fine-tune my writing about Maya patron deities.

Many friends and loved ones have also helped me see this work through. I am grateful to Sarah Kurnick for many discussions that helped me conceptualize Maya political authority. All my Penn anthropology friends have been there through the joys and sorrows of academic life. My parents have always supported my somewhat dubious life choice to pursue archaeology. And my husband Steve, though not an anthropologist, has listened attentively as I talk about metapragmatics and patron deity effigies.

Finally, I would like to thank everyone at the University Press of Colorado, especially Darrin Pratt and Jessica d'Arbonne, for their assistance at every stage of this book, from prospectus, to writing, to press.

Patron Gods *and* Patron Lords

1

The Classic Maya and Their Political System

When Chakaw Nahb Chan acceded as ruler of the small Classic Maya kingdom of La Corona in the mid-seventh century, he immediately began his reign by commissioning three temples. Dedicated a month after his accession, these temples housed three deities—"Firstborn Lord," "Yellow Rain God," and "Red Dreamer Rain God." The rapid completion of this building project, recorded in hieroglyphic inscriptions, draws attention to these gods. What was their significance? Why did Chakaw Nahb Chan make their temples a top priority? Archaeological and epigraphic evidence at La Corona paints a picture of a protracted power struggle within the kingdom, in which these temples played an important role. But La Corona was not the only Classic Maya community to possess such local patron gods, and Chakaw Nahb Chan was not alone in sponsoring the building of temples for them. Many Maya rulers wielded rituals and narratives of patron deities as political tools in order to influence their peers and subjects. This book explores Classic Maya patron deity cults and how they were used in power relationships within and between communities.

THE EXCEPTIONAL MAYA?

In the mid-twentieth century, it was widely held that the ancient Maya were a unique and exceptional civilization. Other early societies built populous cities, engaged in military conquest, and intensively farmed

DOI: 10.5876/9781607325185.c001

fertile soils. But the Maya, the story went, had low populations living in dispersed hamlets around vacant religious centers where priests recorded esoteric calendar rituals on carved monuments. They rarely fought one another except for religious purposes, and they supported their low numbers with slash-and-burn agriculture in a marginal jungle environment (see Becker 1976). Over the course of the late twentieth and early twenty-first century, new ideas about Maya society have replaced those of Maya exceptionalism. Decades of excavation and mapping have revealed the high populations of Maya sites. The decipherment of Maya writing has shown that carved monuments recorded historical narratives about political leaders. And new insights into the Maya economy have revealed intensive farming techniques that allowed them to thrive in a diverse tropical landscape.

Anthropological archaeologists have also contextualized the ancient Maya within theoretical scholarship about the nature of pre-modern political evolution. In the 1960s and 1970s the "New Archaeology" championed evolutionary and cross-cultural models of chiefdoms and archaic states, and Mayanists looked for comparisons with other ancient civilizations. Should the Maya be considered a chiefdom-level or a state-level society? And, since the general consensus came out on the side of the state, what kind of state did the Maya constitute? How centralized and integrated? In spite of this turn toward scientific and anthropologically-based approaches to the past, the Maya have continued to provoke public and scholarly fascination with their seemingly exceptional accomplishments. Their sophisticated writing system, complex calendar, exquisite art, and breathtaking architecture are all immediately recognizable cultural traits. And their political system continues to inspire heated debates among archaeologists and epigraphers.

Were the Maya unique? Was their political organization different from that of other ancient societies? Were their governing institutions distinct from those of other pre-modern peoples? The answer, I argue in this book, is yes. But this claim is not as outlandish as it may appear at first blush. Over the past few decades, a number of archaeologists have shown dissatisfaction with the evolutionary models of ancient polities that were developed in the 1960s and 1970s (e.g., Pauketat 2007; Smith 2003, 2011; Yoffee 2005). Do traditional definitions of chiefdoms and states, they ask, actually obscure the differences between early social systems? Might it not be more useful to look at how authority was actually constituted in different cultural contexts? Or how historically contingent circumstances contributed to the rise of political institutions? Might the concept of a cross-culturally applicable definition of a chiefdom or a state actually be a delusion? Instead, these archaeologists are increasingly looking at the ways that politics in all ancient societies (not just the Maya) were shaped by unique cultural and historical factors.

But how to systematize this vast collection of uniqueness? Does this approach diminish the comparative project of anthropology? In this book I argue that a semiotic approach offers a mode of analysis and a common vocabulary with which cultural and historical factors can be explained and compared without reducing them to a set of universal typologies. Semiotic anthropology—born from the philosophy of Charles S. Peirce and developed by linguists, ethnographers, and archaeologists—examines how human beings mediate social relationships through signs. These signs can be linguistic or material in nature, ephemeral or highly durable. And their social effects can be felt long after the moment of their use. Semiotic anthropology breaks apart culture—that familiar tool of anthropological analysis—like splitting the atom to reveal its constituent parts. Its methodologies allow archaeologists to describe culturally and historically contingent circumstances in ways that are intelligible to colleagues working in other parts of the world.

This is a book about the ancient Maya. It offers new data and interpretations of Maya deity cults and should therefore be of interest to scholars working in that area. But I wrote this book for all archaeologists interested in studying ancient complex societies. And although I claim that the Maya were unique, they were no more unique than any other human society studied by archaeologists and anthropologists. In chapter 2 I describe what I believe are the most useful insights of semiotic anthropology for archaeologists. Over the course of the book I apply this model to the study of Maya religious practices and offer a new look at Maya political relationships. It is my hope that by demonstrating the utility of this approach to my own work, I encourage other archaeologists to use it as well.

But first I must provide some background on the ancient Maya. Who were they? What is the state of knowledge about their religion and political organization? And what questions still remain that a semiotic approach can address?

ETHNIC ORIGINS OF THE MAYA

The Maya are one of many groups considered part of a wider phenomenon known to scholars as "Mesoamerica." This region consists of parts of Mexico and Central America, where indigenous peoples shared certain cultural traits such as religious beliefs, artistic styles, and political institutions (Kirchoff 1943). Throughout their history, the Maya visited, exchanged, and borrowed from other Mesoamerican groups and vice versa. Nevertheless, they are recognizably distinct as an ethnic group, particularly by their languages.

The word "Maya" was originally the indigenous place-name for the northern Yucatan Peninsula at the time of Spanish contact (Zender and Skidmore n.d.). The term may have derived from the name of the city of Mayapan, a late Postclassic capital near modern-day Merida.[1] Spanish colonists eventually adopted "Yucatan" as the name of the province, but "Maya" stuck as an ethnic designator for the indigenous inhabitants, their language, and their immediate ancestors. As anthropologists and archaeologists began to investigate the history of the region, they noted clear linguistic similarities to other indigenous groups in Guatemala, Belize, Honduras, El Salvador, and the Mexican states of Tabasco and Chiapas. Originally calling these languages "Mayoid" and later "Mayan," the scholarly community began to conceptualize the Maya as a single family of related ethnic groups spread out across this region. Not only do they share linguistic features, they also have many cultural traits in common, such as religious practices and material culture. The ancient Maya also shared these linguistic and cultural characteristics and were the ancestors of today's modern Maya groups. But the use of a single ethnic designator for all these modern communities as well as the entire history of Maya civilization can artificially obscure the diversity that in fact characterizes the ancient and the modern Maya.

The area that is today inhabited by speakers of Mayan languages is composed of diverse landscapes, ecological zones, and natural resources (Figure 1.1). The Yucatan Peninsula—also called the northern lowlands—has a low elevation and hot, humid climate. Although there is comparatively less rainfall here, the Maya of the Yucatan were able to practice rain-fed agriculture just as their southern neighbors. The southern lowlands—stretching across Tabasco, Campeche, Quintana Roo, northern Guatemala, and Belize—have more rain and can support higher tropical forest. To the south of these are the highlands, a band of mountains running through Chiapas, southern Guatemala, Honduras, and El Salvador. This region is cooler and is home to many valuable mineral commodities such as obsidian, jade, and volcanic ash used to temper pottery. Finally, a hot, humid strip of land hugs the Pacific Coast, a premier region for growing chocolate.

Today Mayan language speakers inhabit all of these regions, though this was not always the case. These groups originally emerged from a smaller population of Proto-Mayan speakers and spread out to absorb or displace Archaic populations. The origins and spread of the Maya have been traced linguistically and archaeologically. Kaufman (1976) proposes that the Proto-Mayan homeland

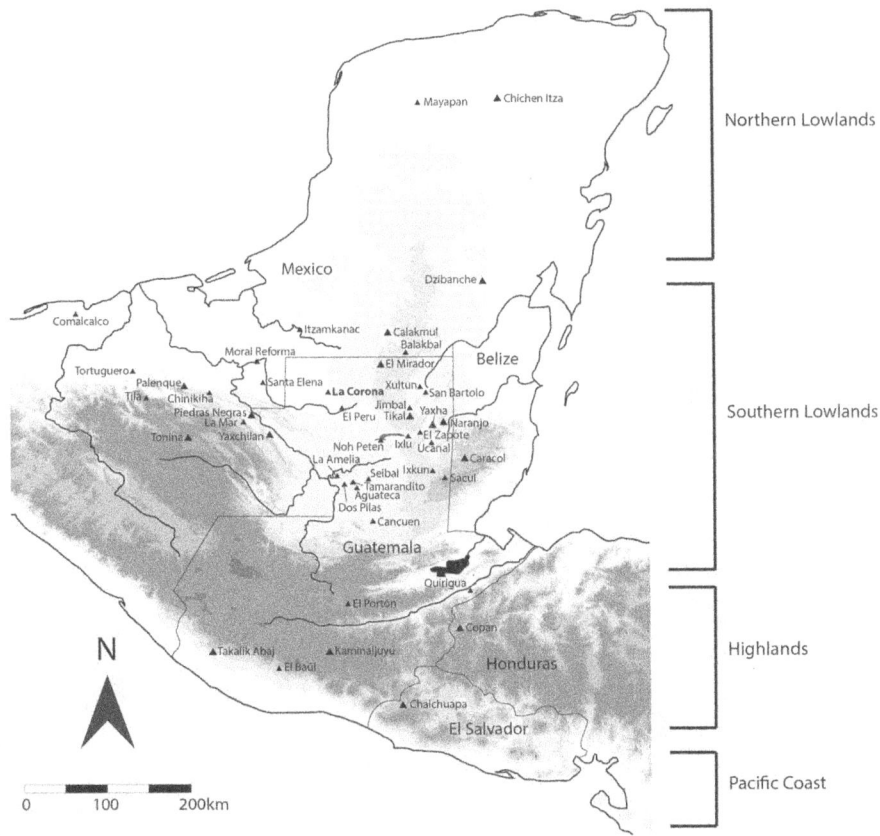

FIGURE 1.1. *Map of the Maya area showing sites mentioned in this book*

may have been in the Cuchumatan Mountains of southwestern Guatemala. Using glottochronology, he suggests that this language broke up at the end of the Archaic period or Early Preclassic period, around 2000 BCE. Greater Tzeltalan, one of the branches of the Mayan language family, may have spread into the lowlands around 1000 BCE (Figure 1.2). He also proposes that this linguistic dispersal corresponds archaeologically to the appearance and spread of the Mamom ceramic tradition, which replaced earlier ceramics in the lowlands. Of course, as archaeologists long ago realized, it is dubious to assume an absolute one-to-one correlation between a particular language group and a particular feature of material culture like ceramics (Andrews 1990:2).

By the Late Preclassic period (400 BCE to 250 CE) many of the most celebrated features of Maya material culture had emerged across the whole

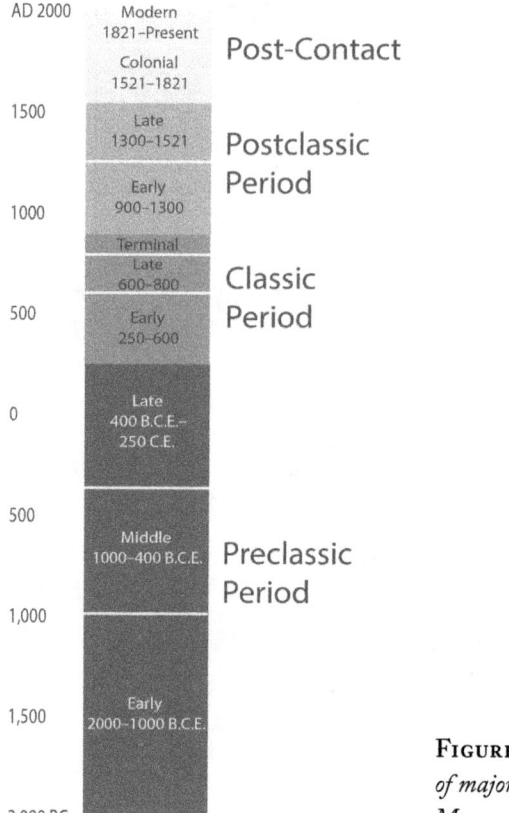

FIGURE 1.2. *Timeline of major periods in Mesoamerican archaeology*

region (Freidel and Schele 1988). These include carved monuments with the famous long count. This calendrical notation recorded the amount of time that had elapsed since the mythical beginning of the world in 3114 BCE. The earliest examples of the long count on Maya monuments come from the highland and Pacific sites of Tak'alik Ab'aj, Chalchuapa, and El Baúl during the first centuries BCE/CE. The lowland site of San Bartolo records the earliest legible Maya hieroglyphs, dating to around 200–300 BCE (Saturno, Stuart, and Beltran 2006). Maya-style monumental architecture, which had emerged in the earlier Middle Preclassic period, reached a grand scale at sites like Kaminaljuyu in highland Guatemala and El Mirador in lowland Guatemala. Political institutions like hereditary rulership are also evident in the archaeological record, with depictions of enthroned rulers. Ideological narratives justifying the ruler's power can also be traced back to this period, in particular on the murals of San Bartolo, where the accession of the site's ruler is framed as part of mythical cycle involving the birth of the Maize God.

THE CLASSIC PHENOMENON

The Classic period is so named because of scholars' admiration for the cultural achievements of the Maya of this era, which they equated to classical Greece and Rome. It was once defined as the period in which the Maya carved long count dates on stone monuments from 292 to 909 CE. Of course, earlier long count dates have now been identified on Preclassic stelae, and archaeologists have acknowledged that the institutions and material culture of the Classic period are an outgrowth of Preclassic developments. Nevertheless, the Classic period was a circumscribed chronological era.

One reason for this is that the Classic Maya themselves saw their era as different from what came before. Martin (2003:5) notes that in addition to stylistic changes in architecture and iconography, Classic Maya dynasties traced their origins to founders who lived in the first few centuries CE. Archaeological evidence shows that the end of the Preclassic period corresponded to a series of demographic shifts. El Mirador, the largest Maya city ever built, saw a dramatic decrease in population, as did the highland city of Kaminaljuyu, though it eventually recovered. Classic period hieroglyphic inscriptions contain sparse historical references to this time of change, remembering a place called "Maguey Grinding Stone" and a person epigraphers have nicknamed "Foliated Ajaw" (Stuart 2003, 2014).

In addition to being chronologically circumscribed, the Classic Maya phenomenon was also geographically circumscribed. To be sure, Mayan-speaking groups inhabited the entire Maya region for the duration of the Classic period. However, the southern lowlands were characterized by a unique suite of features. This included a particular elite artistic and architectural style. It also included a fluorescence of hieroglyphic writing, which, though present at some other Maya sites, was concentrated in the southern lowlands. Not only did these sites share a set of orthographic conventions, they also recorded the same specific language, known today as Classic Ch'olti'an (Houston, Robertson, and Stuart 2000). Still unclear is whether the Classic Maya of the southern lowlands were linguistically homogenous, or whether this language constituted an elite lingua franca among a more diverse commoner population. Finally, in addition to these similarities, the Classic Maya of the southern lowlands shared a common geopolitical system that integrated their communities into a single large network. So while this region clearly engaged in economic and cultural exchanges with other Mayan and Mesoamerican groups, its synchronized historical trajectory and the inward-looking geopolitical focus reflected in its historical records allow it to be treated as distinct from other areas.

The beginning of the Classic period saw a proliferation of small kingdoms across this southern lowland area. It is likely that this political landscape in fact represented a fragmentation of the more consolidated Preclassic polities (Martin 2003). Classic period kingdoms were centered on the royal court, which consisted of the residence of the ruler, religious structures, and administrative buildings. The court was surrounded by homes of lower-class individuals, most of whom engaged in maize farming. Each of these courts had its own hereditary nobility, though they often intermarried. Many of these kingdoms produced carved hieroglyphic monuments, demonstrating that they had their own unique historical and mythological narratives, creating an emic distinction between the different polities.

The Classic period ended in a dramatic fashion with the famous Maya collapse. During this period, the southern lowlands were largely abandoned, though they had seen their highest populations shortly earlier. This demographic shift seems to have been precipitated by an abrupt event just after 800 CE, after which many sites ceased to record hieroglyphic inscriptions. This was followed by a slower decline over the next century, in which lower-class populations gradually left their homes.

During this period of decline, called the Terminal Classic (800–900 CE), sites elsewhere in the Maya area saw greater populations and an increase in wealth and political influence, especially in northern Yucatan. One of these was Chichen Itza. Archaeological evidence and later written chronicles indicate that it was probably founded around 750 or 800 CE. During the first century of its occupation, the nobility of Chichen Itza commissioned monumental architecture that showed both continuities with typical Classic Maya sites as well as inspiration from other Mesoamerican groups in Central Mexico. The hieroglyphic writing of Chichen Itza was also dramatically different from that of the southern lowlands, with a less ornate style. It also records the Yucatec Mayan language rather than Classic Ch'olti'an. However, these inscriptions are still legible and thus constitute a continuation of the orthographic system in use during the Classic period. They also reflect political institutions of hereditary rulership similar to those of the southern lowland Classic sites (Boot 2005). Most relevant for this book, these inscriptions also discuss devotions to patron gods. For these reasons, I have included Chichen Itza in my analysis of Classic Maya patron deity cults.

After the Terminal Classic the Maya area saw changes in political institutions, the distribution of ethnic groups, and economic relationships with the rest of Mesoamerica. Other Maya kingdoms rose and fell, even in the now sparsely populated southern lowlands. The historical rupture brought about by the Classic collapse makes it impossible to identify any specific modern Maya group as direct descendants of the Classic Maya of the southern lowlands. Linguistically, the closest relation to Classic Ch'olti'an would be Ch'orti', spoken today in eastern Guatemala and western Honduras (Houston, Robertson, and Stuart 2000). But it is likely that the population dispersal at the end of the Classic period sent southern lowlanders all over the Maya area, to be absorbed into local populations and adopt local languages. Thus, in a general sense, today's many modern Maya ethnic groups can be considered inheritors of the Classic phenomenon. As I will demonstrate in chapter 4, these cultural continuities make historical and ethnographic information about these groups invaluable for reconstructing the religion and politics of the Classic period.

Classic Maya Political Organization

The nature of Mesoamerican politics is a theme that has occupied many archaeologists and scholars (see Kurnick 2016). In particular, the political organization of the Classic Maya has been the subject of intense debate over the past several decades. Already in this chapter I have referred to Maya sites as "kingdoms," "polities," and "communities," an ambiguity that reflects both the unique aspects of Maya political organization and the lack of scholarly consensus on what Maya politics entailed. So far I have also avoided using the term "state," given its association with problematic evolutionary models (Smith 2003). However, much of the literature takes it as given that the Classic Maya constituted a "state-level" society and focuses on what kind of state they represented. Were they strong or weak states? Large or small? Centralized or decentralized? Were they segmentary states like those observed in Africa or theater states like those of Southeast Asia?

Early attempts to model Maya states focused on the size and architecture of Maya sites. Bullard (1960) classified sites by the number and size of buildings and plazas and the presence or absence of inscriptions and ballcourts. He suggested that these differences might reflect a political hierarchy, with larger and more ornate sites representing the highest levels of political control. Similarly, Adams (1980; Adams and Jones 1981) counted the number of courtyards at different sites to propose hierarchies. Hammond (1974) recommended using Thiessen Polygons to estimate the size of the "realm" controlled by Classic

Maya sites. This geometric exercise involves the assumption that the boundary between two hierarchically equivalent sites should be equidistant between them. Of course, without an independent way of judging whether two sites are in fact equal in the political hierarchy, this methodology is problematic and even circular. Especially in areas of high population density, using Thiessen Polygons in this way simply produces a model of small polities (Adams 1980).

Although the Maya writing system was not well understood until the 1990s, researchers in the mid-twentieth century used epigraphic data to model political organization. Berlin (1958) first recognized "emblem glyphs," hieroglyphic signs seemingly associated with particular sites. These signs can now be read as titles of Maya rulers (see chapter 3), but at the time Berlin proposed that they might correspond to the place-name, patron deity name, or dynastic name of each site. Barthel (1968) noted that two inscriptions (Copan Stela A and Seibal Stela 10) both recorded a set of four emblem glyphs, which at Copan were associated with the four cardinal directions. He suggested that these four emblem glyphs corresponded to four regional states and that it might be possible to identify the area of political control of each of them by looking for references to its emblem glyph at smaller nearby sites. Marcus (1973; 1976) built upon Barthel's observations, suggesting that a subordinate site might mention its capital's emblem glyph in its inscriptions, but never the other way around. She made a systematic attempt to identify the areas of regional control of each of the four proposed Maya capitals. But since few glyphs could actually be read at the time, her initial model was eventually replaced.

Mathews and Justeson (1984) realized that part of the emblem glyph read *ajaw*, meaning "lord" or "ruler."[2] They also noticed other titles in the epigraphic record and proposed that there was a hierarchy of titles, each associated with a particular kingdom. Stuart (1984a) recognized one of these titles, which he read as *cahal* (now read *sajal*). He demonstrated that individuals with this title were nobles who often controlled minor sites but were never rulers with emblem glyphs. He observed that the word *sajal* could be grammatically possessed by a person of higher rank, indicating a political hierarchy. But *sajal*s remained in office even after the death of the original *ajaw* who "owned" them. This suggests a degree of autonomy, as if *sajal*s were hereditary or appointed for life. The implication of these new glyphic readings, as interpreted by Mathews (1985; 1991), was that all sites with emblem glyphs (i.e., ruled by *ajaw*s) were hierarchically equal to one another, while they controlled subsidiary sites with lower-ranked nobility such as *sajal*s. And because numerous Classic Maya sites recorded emblem glyphs—including the *ajaw* title—in their inscriptions, he argued that Maya states were relatively small and weak. This was in direct contrast to earlier proposals by Barthel and Marcus that there were four large regional states. Mathews instead saw twenty-three small states spread over the southern lowlands by 790 CE.

During the 1990s most Maya scholars were divided between these two "strong state" and "weak state" models. Most proponents of the weak state agreed with Mathews, arguing that glyphic evidence demonstrated that Maya polities were not particularly stable or powerful beyond their immediate capitals. Sanders and Webster (1988), for example, argued that Maya sites had low populations and small hinterlands. Rulership was based on family relationships, and the entire court could be seen as an extended household. The activities of lesser nobility mirrored that of the ruler in a disguised form of mechanical solidarity (534). They called this system a "segmentary state," a term borrowed from African anthropology (Southall 1956). Demarest (1992), borrowing from Tambiah's (1976) model of the "galactic polity" of Africa and Geertz's (1973a, 1980) model of the "theater state" in Southeast Asia, claimed that the Maya state was centered on rituals performed by the ruler. This, he argued, made the state inherently weak, since the same functions performed by the ruler were mimicked at lower hierarchical levels. Other scholars (e.g., Ball and Taschek 1991; Hammond 1991; Houston 1993) concurred with these African and Asian parallels.

But the other camp saw evidence for more centralized Maya states. Chase, Chase, and Haviland (1990) pointed to evidence of high population densities as well as public works like roads, raised fields, and earthworks as evidence of strong central authority. They argued that large Maya sites like Tikal and Caracol had political control over smaller surrounding communities with an efficient system of administration not accounted for by weak state models. Culbert (1988:73) concurred, suggesting that the sophistication of intensive agricultural systems, craft specialization, and regional trade point to some degree of centralized coordination. He also pointed out (Culbert 1991) that just because *ajaw* was the most evident political title in hieroglyphic inscriptions, this did not preclude some higher order of political organization. Indeed, he noted, some site with emblem glyphs seemed to express fealty to other sites with emblem glyphs, belying the argument that all *ajaw*s were politically equal.

Martin and Grube (1994; 1995; 2000) expanded on this point with their development of the "superstate" (a.k.a. "hegemonic") model. They used epigraphic analysis to show that while many Maya rulers were nominally equal to one another and used the *ajaw* title, a higher order of political organization structured their relationships with one another. Marcus (1998:63) argues that the term "superstate" is unnecessarily hyperbolic, as if the Classic Maya represented a state on steroids. The term, however, was not meant to imply a new step in the evolution of social complexity, but rather a political structure above the level of the individual royal court. Specifically, the rulers of Tikal, Calakmul, and a few other sites were able to control networks of allies and vassals to create power blocs that acted in concert. Because of the advances in epigraphic decipherment, Martin and Grube also recognized that these blocs were not geographical regions, as Barthel and Marcus had proposed, but rather spread amorphously across the southern lowlands. Individual *ajaws* of different sites held important decision-making powers, however, and frequently shifted their loyalties.

In recent years this "suprastate" model has become widely accepted among scholars of the Classic Maya. It is acknowledged that Tikal and Calakmul were exceptionally powerful polities, which controlled the affairs of client kingdoms over several generations and whose bitter rivalry shaped many of the historical events of the Classic period. But Maya politics cannot be fully comprehended by looking at political organization alone. That is why many scholars have also debated Maya political strategies, both at the level of the local polity and the suprapolity network.

Classic Maya Political Strategies

A number of scholars of the ancient Maya and Mesoamerica have examined strategies used by rulers to establish and maintain political relationships with their subjects. Blanton et al. (1996), for example, propose that these can be broken into two categories. Network strategies are those in which individuals attempt to gain political power by monopolizing resources such as contacts with leaders in other polities, esoteric knowledge, and exotic commodities. Corporate strategies, in contrast, emphasize interdependence and reciprocity between social groups such as lineages or economic classes. Blanton et al. conceptualize these as two poles on a spectrum and argue that, while a polity may display varying degrees of one or the other, either a network or a corporate strategy usually predominates.

This dual-processual theory has proven useful for many Mesoamerican archaeologists as a heuristic for considering the nature of ancient polities. Blanton et al. themselves applied it to the study of ancient Mesoamerica, though the model is intentionally general enough that it can be applied to the study of any complex society. Indeed, the authors drew upon examples from all over the world when formulating their arguments. It has been critiqued, however, as a simple one-dimensional typological axis rather than a means of truly elucidating the complex nature of political action (Kurnick 2016; Smith 2011:419). In other words, while dual-processional theory places political actions into certain categories, it cannot offer an *explanation* of why a particular strategy was adopted at any given place or time, nor can it predict whether or why such strategies were successes or failures. This is because it simply does not address the unique cultural and historical circumstances that would contribute to political variability. The authors themselves recognize the importance of such contingencies, noting, "whatever its source, power is always exercised in a culture-laden social situation. Materials and symbols are powerful only to the extent that they move people" (Blanton et al. 1996:3). Thus, in order to move beyond a generalizing typology, archaeologists must explore these very cultural factors to determine why and how materials and symbols contribute to political dynamics.

An area of particular emphasis by scholars of the ancient Maya has been the relationship between political power and religious beliefs and ritual (this book is no exception). The phrase "divine kingship" is frequently used to describe the Classic Maya system of rulership, not least of all because the most common royal title, *k'uhul ajaw*, can be translated as "divine king" (but see chapter 3). However, the foundational literature on Classic Maya divine kingship, produced in the 1980s and 1990s, generally does not consider the subject in relation to the extensive literature on sacred kings in the Old World (but see Fields 1989; Fields and Reents-Budet 2005:21). Instead, these authors explore the topic in relation to cross-cultural literature on shamanism. Central to this concept was the work of Eliade (1964), who defined shamanism as the ability of a ritual specialist to undergo a trancelike change of mental state in which the soul journeyed to other places to communicate with powerful spirits. Furst (1976) expanded on this work, building a model of shamanism in the Americas. Believing that a definition of shamanism relying solely on altered states of consciousness was not always appropriate for Native American societies, he instead focused on specific ideological features of Native American religion. For Furst, shamanism was associated with a three-tiered universe and an axis mundi connecting these levels, often surmounted by a supernatural bird. It also included beliefs in an animistic universe, in which supernatural forces were personified, and the ability of humans to transform into animals. These features are indeed common in Native American beliefs. As a consequence, Furst's definition of shamanism became circular—common American religious beliefs defined shamanism, and therefore most Native American groups must be shamanic by definition (Klein et al. 2002:388–89).

Furst applied his model of shamanism to the study of Olmec figurines, concluding that they depicted shamans engaged in transformation into jaguars as part of a trance ritual.

Other scholars argued that in hierarchical Mesoamerican societies hereditary rulers must have appropriated shamanic powers as a path to political authority (e.g., Coe 1972; Guernsey 2006:20; Joyce and Winter 1996; Masson and Orr 1998; Reilly 1994). For the Maya, this idea was championed by Schele and Freidel and their students (e.g., Freidel and Schele 1988; Freidel, Schele, and Parker 1993; Schele and Freidel 1990; Fields 1989; Fields and Reents-Budet 2005). They argued that in the Preclassic period village-level ritual specialists (shamans) used their personal charisma to intercede with gods and spirits on behalf of community members through ritual transformation. This power became institutionalized in the Late Preclassic and Classic periods, such that Maya rulers were seen as shamanic specialists, through which they derived their power. This political strategy, they argued, was apparent in features such as rulers' royal regalia, which resembled the World Tree/axis mundi. They also pointed to glyphic references to *wahy* creatures, which they interpreted as shamanic familiars.

Others have been critical of the shamanic approach (e.g., Klein et al. 2002; Stuart 2005; Zender 2004). Zender (2004), for instance, refutes the evidence that Maya rulers embodied the axis mundi or that they made shamanic journeys. He believes that Schele and Freidel misinterpreted certain iconographic contexts and that the *wahy* glyph represents a more complex concept than originally supposed. On theoretical grounds he also contrasts the shamanic model to a cross-cultural model of a priestly hierarchy. Shamans, he argues, tend to command and threaten divine forces while priests merely plead with them. Shamans serve individual clients on a case-by-case basis while priests serve the whole community. The shaman works in his or her own home or in that of a client, while the priest operates in a temple or official religious building. Shamans are recruited through their personal charisma or spiritual power, while priests are recruited from particular families or social classes.

But the debate about whether Maya rulers were more priest-like or shaman-like, and even the very definition of shamanism itself, obscures the most valuable contributions of this scholarship on Maya religion. Neither of these cross-cultural models adequately describes the relationship between Maya politics and religious practices. Instead, archaeologists and epigraphers have to do the careful work of reconstructing the actual claims to political authority made by rulers through their ritual practices and discourses and the extent to which their followers found these claims plausible (Kurnick 2016).

Research has revealed the myriad connections between the complex systems of Classic Maya religious belief and politics. For example, Stuart (1996) showed that Maya stelae, often carved with images of Maya rulers, were considered actual embodiments of rulers themselves. Furthermore, since these monuments were carved and dedicated to commemorate significant junctures within the Maya calendar, rulers and their carved images were, by extension, manifestations of time's passage. McAnany's (1995) analysis of Maya ancestor veneration has revealed the importance of "living with the ancestors" in claims to inherited rights and privileges, not just of rulers but of other community members as well. Houston and Stuart's (1996) study of Classic Maya gods revealed the role of deities in Classic Maya politics—rulers were named for gods, impersonated them, and cared for their images. They propose that Maya rulers were not so much themselves considered gods, but that they served "a central role in communications between gods, humans, and, frequently, royal ancestors" (290). This is particularly significant, they argue, because the ruler's interpretation of divine will would be equally applicable to all of his subjects. Houston et al. (2003) extend this observation, noting that, as intermediaries with gods, rulers embodied the ethnicity of the polity and served as the hub of a "moral community."

This important research on religion-based political strategies has mostly focused on the level of the individual polity or community. In other words, it has examined how the *ajaw* (ruler) acquired and maintained authority over his local subjects. What remains to be seen, however, is the extent to which suprapolity political strategies of network and alliance building also had religious aspects. Evidence points to the importance of intermarriage, gift-giving, tribute payments, and warfare in the creation and maintenance of these power blocs. But Sabloff (2015) has recently challenged scholars of the Maya to explore the cultural specificities of Maya politics more aggressively. Neither a peer-polity nor a superstate model is sufficient, he argues, to explain the Classic Maya phenomenon, nor is it enough to say that Calakmul, Tikal, or other large sites controlled client kingdoms. What did that "control" actually entail, since it did not seem to have involved outright military occupation? What did warfare actually achieve? What was the Classic Maya polity?

Patron Gods

This book cannot fully solve the questions posed by Sabloff, but it takes a step. Classic Maya political strategies were extremely complex, and even those we would call religious are too numerous to explore in one volume. Here I focus on just one of the many overlapping and intertwined sets of ideological discourses and practices through which the Classic Maya enacted social relationships and power differentials. This book explores the phenomenon of patron deities of particular Maya communities. I will show that each kingdom had its own local pantheon of gods that were believed to inhabit physical effigies. Though the evidence suggests that these gods were believed to protect all people living in a given place or region, rulers loudly proclaimed their own obligations to care for their effigies. These gods were considered important players in the political machinations between different polities. Not only did they bring success in war, they also represented the local kingdom in its dealings with allies and vassals. And, in fact, some powerful polities such as Calakmul and Tikal experimented with political strategies involving the patron deities of their clients and enemies.

In the chapters that follow, I will turn to the extensive evidence of patron deity veneration from Classic period hieroglyphic inscriptions. I will contextualize it within the archaeological evidence for temples and rituals for these gods as well as the obvious continuities of these practices in later periods of Maya and Mesoamerican history. I will also explore the role of patron deities in the politics of the kingdom of La Corona, a site with valuable epigraphic and archaeological information about its tumultuous dynastic history. But first I will turn to an exploration of semiotic anthropology. By applying a semiotic approach to the archaeological study of ancient societies, I believe scholars can simultaneously recognize the contingent cultural and historical factors—like patron deity veneration—that shaped political action in the past, while still employing a set of concepts and terms that are applicable cross-culturally. And in the end I believe a semiotic orientation toward the study of Maya patron deity veneration will provide a partial answer to some of the persistent questions about the nature of Maya politics.

NOTES

1. Interestingly, the *-pan* ending of the word Mayapan means "banner" in Nahuatl, a language of Central Mexico. Whether the word "Maya" was also borrowed from Nahuatl is unclear.

2. Lounsbury (1973) had previously argued that this sign was of highland origin and read *ahpop* or "lord" and that it was adopted by lowland Maya and read as *ajaw*. While his conclusion (that the sign reads *ajaw*) was ultimately correct, his explanation was not.

2

Words and Things

Semiotics and the Archaeological Record

Mayanists are fortunate to study an ancient society that left historical records on monuments, portable objects, and books. Since the decipherment of this writing system in the 1970s through 1990s, an abundance of new information has become available about many different aspects of Maya politics and society. However, some archaeologists treated this new data with skepticism or open hostility at first (e.g., Marcus 1992; Ruz Lhuiller 1977). These skeptics correctly pointed out that historical data from these texts might not be fully representative of all aspects of Classic Maya society. They were commissioned by elites, produced by elites, and dealt with elite matters, almost never even acknowledging the existence of the nonelite population. Furthermore, they are found in a limited set of contexts such as building dedications and labels on high-status portable artifacts. Texts that may have addressed other topics, such as accounting, administration, or even literature, have not survived from the Classic period. If they existed at all, it was probably on paper, which has long since disintegrated.

Eventually, Mayanists became more comfortable incorporating hieroglyphic texts into their analyses of the past. Research projects began to explicitly use archaeology and epigraphy together. Investigators at Copan, for example, called this the "conjunctive approach" and successfully used archaeology to give detail and context to epigraphic narratives (Bell et al. 2004; Bell et al. 1999; Buikstra et al. 2004; Fash and

DOI: 10.5876/9781607325185.c002

Sharer 1991:166, 170; Sharer, Fash, et al. 1999; Sharer, Traxler, et al. 1999). In the years that followed, the integration of archaeological and epigraphic data has become more and more common on projects studying the Classic Maya.

But some argue that the pendulum has swung too far the other way (Carrasco and Valencia 2013; Chase, Chase, and Cobos 2008). Hieroglyphic texts are taken at face value, they claim, and archaeology is used merely to confirm the historical record or to fill in gaps where it is lacking. But what if history and archaeology do not agree? Should the investigator believe the written record, with its obviously propagandistic intent, or the hard evidence of the artifacts in the ground?

These debates are linked to wider questions about the nature of archaeological evidence: are archaeological data more reliable than other types of data? Should history and ethnography be used to interpret the archaeological record or do they inappropriately skew understandings of the past? Should archaeological theory necessarily follow social theory developed in the context of modern ethnographic societies or should archaeology develop its own theory focused on material culture? Addressing these questions, Pauketat (2007:2) echoes many scholars in arguing that archaeological evidence in the form of artifacts, spaces, and places provides archaeologists with direct access to what people did and how they experienced the world in the past, since these acts and experiences had a material and spatial component. He contrasts this favorably to historical and ethnographic information: "[some] archaeologists now claim explanatory priority with respect to the cultural processes that reside not in the mind alone but in the interface of the human body and external world." This claim to explanatory priority has two implications: first, that ethnographic and historical studies do *not* study material culture or spatial components of society and, second, that the processes studied by cultural anthropologists are primarily mental phenomena. While these critiques are justified in the case of much classical anthropological theory, semiotic approaches to human society in fact frequently incorporate material culture into their analyses. And they see culture not as that which resides in the in the mind but in perceivable social action (e.g., Agha 2007; Geertz 1973b).

Semiotic approaches have enjoyed widespread circulation in American linguistic anthropology. A growing number of archaeologists have adopted them as well (e.g., Bauer 2013; Coben 2006; Crossland 2014; Fogelin 2014; Gardin 1992; Joyce 2007, 2008, 2012; Knappett 2005; Lele 2006; Preucel 2010; Preucel and Bauer 2001; Pugh 2013; Watts 2008), but by and large the discipline of

American archaeology has not used them to their full potential. This is unfortunate, since semiotic theory can illuminate the ways in which the meanings of material objects that archaeologists study became established and disseminated in ancient societies. My own anecdotally collected evidence suggests that archaeologists have some reasonable objections to the approach. To begin, the vocabulary of semiotic anthropology can be unintelligible to the outsider, leading some curious readers to express annoyance or dismay. Others ask how the approach is really any different from Saussurian semiology and the structuralist and poststructuralist approaches that followed—isn't this unfamiliar vocabulary just a new way of restating a more familiar theory? And even if this approach is different and insightful, they ask, how is it useful in archaeology? Isn't this mostly a theory about language and mental phenomena, beyond the reach of archaeologists?

In this chapter I will address these misgivings that have been expressed to me by archaeological colleagues. I will describe what I believe to be the most useful insights of semiotic anthropology. I will also define some of its dense vocabulary and explain how these terms are not simply restatements of more familiar theories. Finally, I will discuss the ways archaeologists can incorporate this perspective into their interpretive processes.

ACCOUNTS OF THE SIGN

Saussure and His Legacy

Probably the most well known account of the sign among archaeologists is the Saussurean model (sometimes called *semiology*), which eventually gave rise to the structuralist and poststructuralist intellectual movements. Saussure was a historical linguist who wrote in the late nineteenth and early twentieth centuries. His *Course in General Linguistics* was collected and published posthumously by his students (Saussure 1966). Though acknowledging a wider body of nonlinguistic signs, Saussure was primarily concerned with language and how it signified meaning. He saw the linguistic sign as a two-part phenomenon: it consisted of a *signifier* (like the word "tree"), which was linked to a *signified* (the idea of a tree produced in the mind). Neither the signifier nor the signified in this example is an actual tree, because Saussure's account of the sign was intentionally divorced from the real-world context in which people might speak about trees. Saussure saw all linguistic signs as forming an abstract system called *langue*, which was separate from their actual context of use, which he called *parole*. He believed that the study of *parole* was beyond the scope of the field of linguistics.

According to Saussure, the relationship between signifiers and signifieds is largely conventional—nothing about the word "tree," for example, resembles either an actual tree or the image of the tree in the hypothetical mind. The only thing that motivates the relationship between signifier and signified is that the signifier is in some way distinct from all the other signifiers in use in the same system. In other words, "tree" has communicative capacity because it is different from "rock" or "grass."

In the social sciences, Saussure's most famous follower was Claude Levi-Strauss, who carried Saussure's account of the sign into the realm of nonlinguistic cultural phenomena. Levi-Strauss reasoned that language is just the tip of the iceberg when it comes to human social action. But it is an easily observable and analyzable system whose basic rules, he believed, had been worked out by Saussure (Levi-Strauss 1963). Thus, just as linguistic signs are conventional and convey meaning through opposition to other linguistic signs, other phenomena such as kinship relations and myths must follow similar rules. Levi-Strauss set about to analyze these cultural behaviors as sets of conventional oppositions divorced from their context of use. He called this analysis "structuralism," with *structure* the nonlinguistic equivalent of *langue*.

Later poststructuralist thinkers, of whom the most influential in American archaeology are perhaps Bourdieu (1972) and Giddens (1979, 1984), saw the exclusive focus on structure as a fault in structuralist theory. Looking again to Saussure for inspiration, they proposed shedding new light on *parole* and its nonlinguistic equivalent, *practice*. In the poststructuralist account, structure, much like *langue*, makes up rules of human conduct. These rules are instantiated in practice—everyday behavior. This behavior, in turn, transmits the rules without explicitly stating them, as people subconsciously follow them. But such transmission is imperfect and can lead to changes in structure.

Though these accounts move beyond Saussure to examine the actual use of linguistic signs and other cultural behavior, they remain wedded the Saussurean account of the sign (Preucel and Bauer 2001). This account is problematic for several reasons. First, the relationship between signifier and signified is assumed to be arbitrary or conventional. But Saussure did not adequately address how these conventional meanings become established, nor did he explore other motivations for the connections between signifier and signified. Furthermore, the Saussurean account of the sign is limited to signifieds—ideas that are produced in the minds of hypothetical interlocutors. It does not explore how these ideas are transmitted in social actions and relationships. Thus, in poststructuralist accounts this process is often described as automatic, subconscious, and unconnected to communicative events. As a result of these deficiencies, the structuralist and poststructuralist traditions cannot adequately describe the mechanisms through which structure actually shapes practice or they ways in which practice reinforces or changes structure.

PEIRCIAN SIGNS

The philosopher Charles S. Peirce was a contemporary of Saussure, though the two did not refer to one another in their work. He looked beyond language, believing signs to be a general property of the universe. According to Peirce, a sign is that which communicates something to someone in some capacity. Signs are therefore mediators—they link some object or idea out in the world to an interpreter who then takes action (or inaction) in response to the sign. Peirce recognized three important elements to this semiotic process: the *object*—that thing or idea out in the world; the *sign*—that which represents the object; and the *interpretant*—someone's interpretation of the sign and resulting thoughts or actions (Peirce 1998:478, 289–99). This account of the sign differs from the Saussurean account in two crucial ways: first, it sees the sign as a three-part rather than a two-part phenomenon. Whereas the Saussurean sign "tree" is composed of the word (the signifier) and the corresponding idea produced in the hypothetical mind (the signified), the Peircian sign relationship includes the actual tree to which a speaker might refer. Second, Peirce did not separate signs from their context of use as Saussure had done. On the contrary, he proposed to study signs empirically—by observing their use and relationships with one another.

Crucial to Peirce's account is the observation that an interpretant can become a new sign. For example, a fire in the kitchen (an object) produces smoke (a sign). Given my previous experience that fire comes from smoke and that fire can be dangerous, I interpret this smoke to mean that there is a dangerous fire in the kitchen and I yell "fire!" (an interpretant). Everyone else in the house hears "fire" (now a sign) and interprets it to mean that that they should leave immediately, which they all do (an intrepretant). The next-door neighbor sees both the smoke (a sign), hears "fire!" (another sign), and sees people fleeing the house (now another sign as well) and interprets these to mean that she should call the fire department (an interpretant), and so on. As interpretants become new signs, semiotic events are linked to one another in long chains, often stretching across time and space at different scales, a process called *semiosis* (Eco 1979:68–69; Parmentier 1997:8). Nobody fleeing a burning building stops to consider the properties of the objects, signs, and interpretants that led them to take that action, of course. But this semiotic chaining in fact happens constantly in all social relationships all the time. The implications of this process are profound for the study of human behavior.

Peirce's scholarly inquiry explicated the properties of signs and their relationships to objects and interpretants (Peirce 1998:289–99). Signs, he reasoned, came in three major categories: signs can be general types, such as a flag conventionally representing a nation. These general types presuppose and are made up of specific instances or tokens, such as a particular flag in a particular place. And each specific token is made up of qualities, such as the color red, which can't exist physically apart from other co-occurring qualities.

In the most famous of his typologies, Peirce also determined that the relationship between the sign and its object can also fall into three main categories: it can be *iconic*, in other words, a sign and an object can share some kind of perceived physical similarity. For example, a drawing of a tree can iconically represent a tree through a perceived physical similarity to its trunk, branches, and leaves. The relationship can be *indexical*, which is to say that object and sign are related because of a co-occurrence in space or time. For example, a wedding ring indexically represents the marital status of the wearer through co-occurrence with the person's hand. The relationship can be *symbolic*, or based on convention. For example, letters symbolically represent sounds of a language. A sign-object relationship can also incorporate two or all three of these categories. For example, a fire escape plan posted in a building represents a hypothetical plan of action. It often includes iconic properties by means of a map physically resembling the plan of the building; indexical properties by being posted near an escape doorway or indicating "you are here"; and symbolic properties through conventional use of written words or symbols.

Finally, Peirce also examined the relationship between the sign and the interpretant. Predictably, he reasoned that there were three main categories to this relationship as well: the sign could merely produce a recognition of existence in the mind of the interpreter, as in the case of a loud noise that startles. The sign could convey specific information leading to a conclusion, as in the case of a proposition or smoke in the kitchen meaning an immediate threat. Or the sign could formulate for the interpreter a general law or norm, which is supposed to operate on multiple occasions. For this last kind of sign he used the familiar term *argument*. Arguments are especially relevant for the study of large-scale cultural phenomena.

To each one of these trichotomies Peirce assigned special vocabularies, and he argued that they combined to form ten major types of object-sign-interpretant relationships. Although his terminology can be difficult to master, Peirce's observations offer insights useful to archaeologists and social scientists more generally. Signs come in different forms and produce different interpretants depending on their use and context. Semiosis takes place constantly as signs co-occur, overlap, reinforce, contradict, and form long chains of linked interpretants across time and space. Signs can occur in infinite possible combinations. It follows that human societies, since they are mediated by signs, don't fall into a small number of discrete formations but in an infinite number of possibilities. Therefore, evolutionary models of social complexity must be discarded in favor of historical ones (Pauketat 2007; Smith 2003).

Contrary to what some might believe, Peircian semiotics does not primarily concern itself with mental phenomena. In fact, Peirce believed that the only way to understand the meaning of signs was to observe their practical results—the interpretants that follow. He referred to this doctrine as *pragmatism* (Peirce 1998:400–401) and claimed that it relied on an experimental methodology in which people's ongoing reactions to signs were observed. Some interpretants are indeed mental phenomena, in that they consist of internal reactions to signs. But in order for them to be studied by Peirce's experimental methodology, interpretants must be outwardly observable. They include a wide array of actions—from startling, to running from a burning building, to articulating complex counterarguments—that human beings perform when responding to signs. This empirical nature of signs lends them to study by archaeologists, who have long debated our relative ability to observe cognitive processes (e.g., Flannery and Marcus 1996; Hawkes 1954; Johnson 1999:85–97; Renfrew 1994).

Semiotic Anthropology

The Peircian semiotic tradition can be contrasted to the structuralist and poststructuralist traditions by its recognition that signs exist only in the context of their use—there is no decontextualized *langue* or structure that they draw from. Instead, individual sign tokens are linked back to previous signs tokens in the long semiotic chains of signs and interpretants recognized by Peirce. And each new token of a sign and its resulting interpretant models future sign use by those who are aware of it. This means that large-scale patterns of human conduct, such as language or political institutions, must be analyzed by studying these multiple overlapping semiotic chains and the individual semiotic events that compose them.

The study of semiotics has also illuminated the relationships between linguistic and nonlinguistic signs to a far greater extent than the structuralist and poststructuralist traditions. Levi-Strauss and those who followed him saw language as the perfect model for all cultural phenomena. This approach found its way into archaeology as well, where theorists continue to contemplate the similarities and differences between language and the material objects left by ancient people (Deetz 1967; Hodder 1982a, 1982b, 1987, 1989, 1992; Miller 1982; Olsen 2003; Preucel 2010; Preucel and Bauer 2001; Shanks and Tilley 1987; Tilley 1991; Wylie 1982; Wynn 1993). But Michael Silverstein (1976), a linguistic anthropologist, made the insightful observation that the purely symbolic sign mode—the one that the Saussurean tradition used as the model for all cultural behavior—is in fact unique to language alone. In linguistics this purely symbolic referential use of language is called its *semantic* function. It is the function of language that is easiest to grasp: strings of phonemes (like words) represent particular things in the world through a purely conventional understanding. Such semantic functions do not exist for nonlinguistic signs. The meaning of nonlinguistic signs is always at least partially contextual and therefore relies at least partially on iconic and indexical sign modes.

Just as it is easy to grasp the importance of symbolism (the semantic function) in language, it is easy to grasp the importance of indexicality when considering material objects as signs. Hodder (1992:204) uses the example of wallpaper, which "may provide an appropriate setting, evoke the 'right' atmosphere, but it does not have a specific [semantic] meaning in the same way that words or sentences do." In other words, through spatial and temporal contiguity, wallpaper indexes something about a room and its inhabitants. Hodder mistakenly concluded from this observation that indexicality is more important for material signs than it is for linguistic signs. But Silverstein (1976), drawing on the linguist Roman Jakobson (1990), pointed out that indexicality is in fact fundamentally important in language as well, since language is used to characterize things in the world that co-occur with language use. Pronouns, for example, point to specific people and things, while an accent gives information about the geographic origin or status of a speaker. Following Peirce, Silverstein called these indexical functions of language *pragmatic* functions, since they have practical consequences in human behavior and social relationships. Both linguistic and nonlinguistic signs have pragmatic functions through their co-occurrence with their objects. And all signs, whether linguistic or not, have practical social consequences, just as Peirce observed. The semantic function of linguistic signs can be thought of as a small subset of the larger world of pragmatic functions, one that happens to be unique to language (Silverstein 1976:20). Therefore, to understand the relationship between language and material culture it is necessary to examine the pragmatic—or indexical—functions of each.

Finally, Silverstein (1976:48) reasoned that there is a category of behavior called *metapragmatics*, whereby people characterize or comment on these pragmatic functions of language. This turns out to be absolutely essential to human social behavior. For example, interrupting another speaker during conversation is sign of poor manners. It is an indexical (pragmatic) sign because it has meaning through its co-occurrence with the interrupter. The phrase "it's rude to interrupt" is an explicit metapragmatic sign that states this pragmatic meaning of speaking out of turn. Metapragmatic signs can also be implicit (Silverstein 1993). For example, the question "who put you in charge?" implicitly suggests an inappropriately authoritative tone on the part of a speaker.

The definition of metapragmatics can also be extended to include discourses that comment upon the indexical function of material objects (Agha 2007:254; Silverstein 1993:36). To take Hodder's wallpaper example again, linguistic activities such as compliments on the lovely wallpaper or pleasant names given to wallpaper colors like "Ocean Spray" are all metapragmatic signs. They characterize and comment on the indexical meaning of the wallpaper as appropriate, inappropriate, masculine, fashionable, edgy, and so forth. In fact, it is these metapragmatic signs that establish this indexical meaning in the first place. The meaning of a particular wallpaper color in relation to the inhabitants of a room is not inherent in the wallpaper itself but the result of long chains of metapragmatic activity, in which wallpaper is discussed and characterized.

These kinds of metapragmatic activities are highly effective in both formulating norms and socializing people to those norms. They are responsible for many of the regularities of behaviors observable within human societies, especially when metapragmatic signs are linked to one another in the long semiotic chains observed by Peirce. The implication for the study of human societies is that large-scale social institutions, such as political formations and religious beliefs, are not spontaneously generated large-scale phenomena, nor are they fundamentally the same cross-culturally. Instead, they are formed one semiotic event at a time, as signs and interpretants gradually accumulate in long semiotic chains. The links on these chains are often metapragmatic discourses and behaviors. The semiotic events and chains that formed a political institution in one cultural context are not the same as those of a different cultural context. Therefore, in order to study large-scale social phenomena—as archaeologists do—it is necessary to examine the individual metapragmatic events that shaped them.

SOCIAL NORMS AND SOCIAL MODELS

Many approaches to the study of human society see human behavior as governed by rules, often called "structure," thought to constrain what a person can say or do into a set of only one or a few alternatives. However, a semiotic account holds that these supposed rules are in fact simply norms that have been shaped through metapragmatic activity over time (Agha 2007:7). These norms serve as points of reference for human actions, even when the norms are not followed. Individuals have a reflexive grasp of these norms and are able to consider questions such as "what is the norm?"; "for whom is it a norm?"; "when does it apply?"; and so on. Such a reflexive grasp becomes the basis for communicating with others, even if those messages are in fact contrary to the norm. The bucking of a norm can be a message itself (Agha 2007:8–9). For instance, a "structural rule" that one person should show deference to another person of higher status (through the use of honorific speech, averted gaze, or other actions) is in fact simply a standard of behavior against which actual behavior can be measured. By adhering to the standard, a person appropriately shows deference. By failing to show deference, the person has communicated something else (such as contempt or humor) (Agha 2007:282–83).

Agha (2007:15–16) argues that there are two major inquiries to studying social norms: the first is to examine the process by which norms come about and how they spread throughout a society or segments of it. The second is to understand how specific individuals become socialized to norms. How do social actors develop the ability to manipulate them effectively for their own communicative purposes? The answers to these two questions vary broadly depending on the society and the norm in question. But I will discuss some processes that are important to the case study described in this book. In order to examine the first question, I will look at social institutions and the ways in which these institutions create and disseminate norms among the social community. Next I will examine the second question in terms of social asymmetries. No individual is able to evaluate norms and respond appropriately in all social situations. These asymmetries of interpretive capacity have important implications for asymmetries of power within society.

Institutions

As discussed above, human beings use metapragmatic activity to characterize the indexical meaning of signs (Silverstein 1976). The interpretants of metapragmatic signs (and of all signs) can themselves become new signs in long semiotic chains extending across time and space. These chains can eventually form widespread social models of particular types of activities, often called "institutions." Such social models appear to be powerful and enduring because they are characterized as such through metapragmatic activity. In our own society an example of an institution is the justice system. While it appears as a unitary, self-evident entity, the justice system can be analytically broken down into many constituent parts, including (1) a series of individuals (judges, attorneys, prison wardens, etc.) whose roles and authority to act are linked to specific semiotic events such as classes and exams in law school, swearing-in ceremonies, etc.; (2) a series of places (courtrooms) whose official nature is established through patterns of furniture placement, objects signifying authority such as a flag or state seal, and perhaps ceremonial events such as ribbon cuttings; and (3) prior metapragmatic events (case law) that establish whether particular conduct is deemed criminal, the appropriateness of certain behaviors within a courtroom, and the social entitlements of the accused, victims, jurors, and others.

Social theorists in the functionalist tradition tend to see institutions as reflective of society-wide models of conduct that are generated almost automatically through collective will. For example, Durkheim (1933:84) saw political systems as functioning for the greater good of society. He referred to the government as the "social brain" and argued that the law was in fact an expression of collectively sanctioned conduct. Thus, legal punishment, he argued, is meted out by society itself (68–69). In fact, however, institutions such as the justice system may not necessarily reflect the will of the entire social body and are actually produced one semiotic act at a time, not in large chunks.

The reason that social institutions are often perceived in this way has to do with the nature of semiotic chains linking signs and interpretants across time and space. In the modern world of mass communication, a single semiotic act can be perceived by millions of people, who each produce their own reactions. These reactions (interpretants) immediately become new signs, rapidly forming chains radiating out from the original event. Mass media is thus highly effective at creating largely uniform social norms rapidly. But semiotic chains can also form widespread social models through face-to-face interaction, as they did in the ancient past. Consider Agha's (2007:66–69) example of the process by which a name becomes attached to an individual. This starts with some sort of "baptismal event." This event can literally be a baptism, in which a ritual is performed for close family and friends in which a religious authority officially names the individual. In other cases, it may be the simple act of new parents deciding on a name for their child among themselves or the act of filling out a birth certificate. From this time forward, a potentially infinite number of semiotic acts serve to make this name widely known. New parents introduce their child to relatives using the name. Relatives show photos to their coworkers using the baby's name. Each instance in which the name is associated with the individual is a new link on the semiotic chain. Anyone who can associate the individual with his name therefore forms a network. Membership in this network is defined by having once been part of a semiotic act that formed one of those links. A person who is not a member of this network will not be able to name the individual or will not understand who he is if the name is mentioned in conversation. Members of the network need not know each other, and they need not have been present at the baptismal event itself or even know that it took place. They simply have to have been present for at least one semiotic event in the chains radiating from it.

Institutions come about in a similar way through long historical chains of signs and interpretants. The Classic Maya royal court, for instance, can be traced back to a founding ancestor, who established hereditary authority at a particular site. This establishment itself resulted from individual acts, such as the arrival or first settlement at a new community, the adoption of particular titles, and the acquisition of emblems of office from other royal courts. As subsequent semiotic events unfolded, the royal court acquired status through its relationships of patronage and obligation with other community members and among other royal courts by military or marriage alliances. The royal court was of utmost importance in Classic Maya society. It regulated economic relationships as well as social entitlements. Because of the importance of institutions such as these, they often appear inviolable and timeless. Discourses surrounding the royal court, such as those of rulers and affiliated elites, upheld these characteristics partly because of their self-interest in doing so. But the court could be reconfigured by competing discourses about membership within particular lineages or obligations to other communities. Thus, the court could undergo rapid or violent change if internal conflict developed or if it was conquered by outside forces.

Because they are based on specific semiotic processes, institutions cannot endure beyond the historical moment in which their importance is interpretable and upheld. Thus, social institutions are in fact inherently fragile and subject to change, even while promoting their own timelessness, because they are shaped by actors through individual semiotic acts. For example, prior to the 1960s, the Roman Catholic Church was an immensely powerful institution in Quebec and was primarily responsible for the education and healthcare of francophone Quebecers. But a convergence of semiotic chains known as the Quiet Revolution caused rapid changes to political institutions in the 1960s and 1970s. These included political discourses leading to rise of the Quebec Liberal Party as well as the declarations of the Second Vatican Council. The Quiet Revolution saw sweeping reforms that led to the secularization of public services and the loss of political power by the Catholic Church.

Ideology and Ritual

Institutions often have an aura of inviolability or timelessness. This is due to metapragmatic behaviors and discourses that characterize the social status and entitlements of individuals involved in a particular institution. Such discourses, often referred to as "ideology," are authoritative; that is, they justify and reproduce models of social hegemony because of a variety of strategies that they employ (Agha 2007:73–77). One of these is a naturalizing strategy. These discourses present social institutions or specific features of those institutions as part of a wider system of signs such as the physical world, the cosmos, or the nature of society in general. For example, when Mississippi declared its secession from the United States in 1861, it argued, "the institution of slavery [is] the greatest material interest of the world. Its labor supplies the product which constitutes by far the largest and most important portions of commerce of the earth. These products are peculiar to the climate verging on the tropical regions, and by an imperious law of nature, none but the black race can bear exposure to the tropical sun. These products have become necessities of the world, and a blow at slavery is a blow at commerce and civilization" (State of Mississippi 1861). The success of such strategies is based upon the difficulty in recognizing that this model of the universe is also developed through semiotic processes and is thus historically contingent, not a timeless truth.

In addition to naturalizing discourses, another strategy presents institutions as linked to wider social projects deemed good. For example, political pundits justify military spending by reference to protecting American freedom. "Freedom" is widely acknowledged to be worth protecting because of historical semiotic chains linking it to national identity and particular entitlements of citizens. Like naturalizing discourses, this strategy works because most people have difficulty discerning other models of how "freedom" might be defined or protected.

Another strategy of speakers who produce authoritative discourses is appeal to tradition and timelessness. In order to do this, these signs must link past events, which are given an ahistorical, transcendental quality, to events in the here and now. Religious discourses and rituals are particularly effective in this regard, presenting models of the current social world as reproductions of timeless models. For example, J. B. Stanford, a California politician, wrote against women's suffrage that "woman is woman. She cannot unsex herself or change her sphere. Let her be content with her lot and perform those high duties intended for her by the Great Creator, and she will accomplish far more in governmental affairs than she can ever accomplish by mixing up in the dirty pool of politics. Keep the home pure and all will be well with the Republic.

Let not the sanctity of the home be invaded by every little politician that may be running up and down the highway for office" (Sanford 1911:1–2).

All of these strategies are effective because of their use of widespread discourses already in circulation in society. Thus, most ideologies are genuinely believed, among those whom they both benefit and disadvantage (Mann 1986:23). But in spite of the efficacy of these discursive strategies, they do not always yield success. As in the example of the Quiet Revolution noted earlier, if competing reflexive models arise within a society, even totalizing and naturalizing discourses can be overturned.

As many archaeologists have observed, ritual is an important element of institutional legitimacy and long-term endurance. Rituals usually uphold social models and formulate norms of conduct. For example, a coronation ceremony—by virtue of its iconic similarity to previous coronation ceremonies and its indexical linkages to a particular individual—officially turns someone into a king, similar to previous kings. It thereby models future conduct toward him and toward all other individuals who stand in relation to him as subjects, relatives, enemies, allies, etc. Thus, particular rituals like coronation ceremonies are important for understanding how social institutions work. But the task of defining what "ritual" means is especially difficult. Various scholars have grappled with this concept, some preferring to define ritual as specific to religious practices, others seeing ritual as an element in all social phenomena. Ethnographers working on rituals tend to focus on those deemed especially significant by informants and thus focus on named ceremonies. Others have pointed out that basic repetitive behavior such as stopping at red lights can be seen as ritualistic. But scholars tend to agree on some common features. For example, Tambiah (1985:128) lists the features of "formality (conventionality), stereotypy (rigidity), condensation (fusion) and redundancy (repetition)."

Bell (1992:69) criticizes this mode of analysis, arguing that it inevitably leaves out some activities or sets up multiple categories to account for them. She proposes that, instead of defining ritual according to a set of criteria into which certain actions either fall or do not, we instead look at their degree of ritualization. By ritualization, she means aspects of certain activities that set them apart as particularly important or special. Thus, ritualization is a strategy meant to "establish a privileged contrast" (Bell 1992:90). As an example, she notes a distinction between a normal meal and a Christian Eucharistic meal. The distinction is drawn by the elements of the meal, such as a larger family gathering, a certain periodicity, and insufficiency of the food for actual nourishment. She notes that other strategies could equally have set the event apart, such as too much food or happening only once in a person's lifetime. Which strategies are chosen depend on which elements of the activity would contrast most effectively with other events.

Ritual practitioners can bring about this contrast in a number of ways. Often these involve the commonly cited features of ritual such as repetition, both within the ritual itself and across different instances of ritual acts. A high degree of formality and theatricality also accomplishes this contrast. Some researchers, including scholars of the Classic Maya, particularly emphasize theatrical elements—also referred to as "performative" elements (Tambiah 1985)—such as bright colors, loud noises, and many spectators (Houston 2006; Inomata 2006a, 2006b; Inomata and Coben 2006; Kertzer 1988). They argue that these features are the primary source of political efficacy for ritual events. However, rituals can be equally effective without these elements. Participants in a ceremony, however small, can initiate semiotic chains that establish the significance of the ritual among a larger population. Thus, ritual efficacy is not solely reliant on theatricality.

Ritualization—the process of setting certain activities apart as unique from their surroundings—is an especially salient type of semiotic activity and is often employed to legitimize or strengthen social institutions alongside ideological discourses. For example, some rituals formulate models of social conduct as being timeless, making it difficult for the participant to separate them from the specific historical context in which they are performed (Agha 2007:73). Others frame institutions as essential for the proper functioning of society more broadly or the cosmos itself. These features serve to "naturalize" these models in the ways described earlier. As I will show in subsequent chapters, patron deity veneration ritual among the Classic Maya formulated political institutions as natural, eternal, and socially justifiable.

But while ritualization can be a force for conservatism and naturalization of existing institutions, it can also be a potent force in changing social models as well. New institutions can borrow old ritual patterns, thereby signifying legitimacy (Kertzer 1988:42). Thus, ritual acts can have a wide array of practical results.

THE ADOPTION OF SOCIAL NORMS AND SOCIAL MODELS

Social norms and social models become widespread in society through the processes that were first documented by Peirce and later elaborated by Silverstein: semiosis, which creates chains of signs and interpretants—often involving ideological discourses and ritual behaviors—and metapragmatic activity, which comments upon their indexical nature. The same processes are involved in socializing specific individuals to these norms and models. Examining these questions from the standpoint of individual socialization leads to additional conclusions about agency and power—two social phenomena of great interest to archaeologists.

Some theorists have taken a top-down approach to the socialization process. Marx, for example, saw all social relations as springing directly from the organization of production within society; he attributed social beliefs and values to the same materialist source. Marx argued that these particular ideas do not come about by accident or by some progressive evolution of thought, but from the mode of production by which a particular society is organized. Ideology, in this model, is the set of ideas used by the ruling class to maintain its dominance (Marx 1998). The implication of Marx's concept of ideology is that this class, the only class with the power to produce ideas, intentionally distorts its representations of the world so as to serve its own interests. This means not only that the dominated classes, by virtue of their lack of power, are incapable of challenging these ideas, but that the ruling class is somehow able to see a more objective truth than those it dominates.

Bourdieu (1972, 1991) draws similar conclusions. He too sees society as composed of competing class interests and seeks to understand how class domination occurs. He argues that certain behavioral and communicative standards are imposed by institutions of the state upon the set of dispositions of the individual (what he calls the "*habitus*"). He argues that this process of sedimentation occurs without passing through consciousness or language (Bourdieu 1991:51). Once it is formed, the *habitus* constrains the individual to act only in certain ways because of his or her inability to imagine other possibilities. Because large-scale institutions are the agents of the process of inscription upon the individual in Bourdieu's account, they have "structural power," and the individual appears to lack agency. Thus, Bourdieu reached a similar conclusion to Marx's: that people are generally ignorant about the reality of oppression or class dominance within society. Agents are shaped by their *habitus* to respond appropriately in certain situations, but they are unaware of what makes something appropriate or not.

Bourdieu's description of the sedimentation of habits on the individual has several drawbacks. First, Bourdieu's assertion that the *habitus* is transmitted without passing through language is contrary to both semiotic theory and observable evidence. As Agha (2007:230) notes, Bourdieu's notion "is a systematic distortion, not an accidental omission: it reflects an inadequate grasp of the reflexive properties of language itself." In fact, the metapragmatic function of language is responsible for social norms and models and for socializing individuals to their use. But the power of metapragmatic behaviors is difficult to recognize because of their often implicit nature. For example, they may include small acts of ridicule for an inappropriate choice of clothing. Such behaviors are both consciously performed and highly apparent in the moment of use but are difficult to describe or even acknowledge after the fact (Agha 2007:229; Silverstein 1976:49–50). This makes it difficult for informants to report them and difficult for anthropologists or social theorists to recognize them. Nevertheless, such implicit metapragmatic acts may have profound effects on the personal clothing choices and other behaviors (habits) of an individual.

The socialization process, contrary to the models presented by these top-down theorists, is not imposed all at once by social institutions but occurs as part of widespread semiotic chains and metapragmatic discourses. Understanding this process in a given society or for a given individual requires attention to the specific semiotic events involved. At any point in these semiotic chains, individuals can affirm or reject the social models and norms that are presented to them—as Peirce observed, there are many possible interpretants. On the one hand, the interpretant may simply repeat and transmit prior norms and models without comment, yielding the special case of social continuity in which Bourdieu is particularly interested. At other times, novel interpretants may occur, creating new possibilities for future signs social models.

Agency and Power

The ability of individuals to interpret signs and choose responses—interpretants—is often referred to as "agency." However, Agha (2007:230–32) notes that agency is not a single property of social action but a set of three overlapping phenomena. First, individuals have interpretive ability—the capacity to understand semiotic acts and respond appropriately (or inappropriately, as the case may be). This is the phenomenon that Giddens (1984:3) calls "reflexivity." While this ability may seem basic and universal, not everyone has it equally at all times. In certain situations individuals may find themselves completely out of their element, unable to interpret semiotic activity and respond to it in a meaningful way.

This differential capacity to interpret and respond to semiotic events is due to the fact that no individual, especially in a complex society, can command all of the semiotic repertoires in circulation in that society. Semiotic repertoires, or "registers," are sets of signs that stereotypically index certain types of persons (Agha 2007:80). For example, legalese and academese are linguistic repertoires that give indexical (pragmatic) information about someone's identity as a lawyer or a professor. These linguistic signs usually co-occur with nonlinguistic signs such as clothing and grooming choices, ways of carrying oneself, etc. Some semiotic registers like legalese and academese are highly valued in society, lending those who use them social legitimacy. Others, such as different types of slang, may be less valued but are no easier to understand for the uninitiated. For example, a criminal prosecutor, who has access to the highly valued legalese register, may rely on a criminal informant to interpret audio recordings of a drug sale. In the case of the Classic Maya, a commoner in the presence of the ruler may have found himself completely confused, unable to interpret high-status language, unable to respond intelligibly to questions, and unable to interpret the consequences of his answers. Such a lack of interpretive ability in this situation renders him, in one sense, without agency.

The ability of certain individuals to command highly valued registers is dependent on a host of other factors relating to their social history (Agha 2007). It is linked to institutions like those described above, such as royal courts, lineages, or inheritance practices. By virtue of their connections to these phenomena, both large-scale and small-scale, individuals acquire knowledge of necessary registers and communicative skills. For example, Classic Maya elites were raised within the context of the royal court, which disseminated norms of appropriate language, dress, and comportment. By using this high-status semiotic register, elites embodied stereotypic social personae that linked them to social entitlements and specialized knowledge.

Thus, access to highly valued registers—both linguistic and nonlinguistic—is often a precondition of social privileges. Individuals differ in their entitlements to act in the world or in their entitlement to propose that others act in a certain way. This relative freedom to act vis-à-vis others is a second major aspect of agency. Entitlements are social models that represent *norms*, rather than *rules*, of behavior. Thus, they do not form a set of rigid constraints limiting other actors except in very particular cases when they co-occur with extreme violence. Usually, however, there are ways of getting around constraints through semiotic manipulation or outright refusal (Silverstein 1976:215–16). Through such implicit manipulation, individuals choose their own course of action, even in the presence of those who have entitlements they lack (i.e., "have power over them"). An example is the story of Kim Davis, a county clerk in Kentucky who opposes same-sex marriage and refused to allow her name on marriage licenses and to leave her government post. Through appeals to freedom of religion, alliances with politicians, and outright refusal of a judge's orders, Davis forced a compromise in which her name was removed from marriage licenses, though she eventually allowed her deputies to issue them. Furthermore, Davis and her supporters effectively manipulated Pope Francis into an implicit endorsement of her actions during his 2015 visit to the United States. First, Davis and her husband were surreptitiously included in a meeting between the pope and several dozen individuals in Washington, DC. Davis then released the news of this meeting, in an exclusive interview with ABC, only after the pope had returned to Rome. Thus, using a variety of strategies, Davis and her supporters very effectively disobeyed or manipulated individuals with more social entitlements. The fact that such strategies may have negative outcomes for actors does not preclude them as possible options or prevent them from occurring. Naturally, such strategies are most successful when they are used by people who have a good command of the relevant registers (have agency in the first sense of the term).

Finally, a third aspect of agency is the reflexive grasp individuals have of their own freedom in the sense just described. Individuals may see themselves as entitled, yet find themselves normatively constrained in certain situations. As Weber (1978:932) notes, "status honor is normally expressed by the fact that above all else a specific style of life is expected.... Linked with this expectation are restrictions on social intercourse." On the other hand, individuals who intuitively feel constrained may find that in some situations they have a greater amount of normative freedom than they had supposed. Of course, their entitlements and freedoms, as well as their reflexive grasp of them, vary depending on the specific social situations in which they find themselves.

Human beings do not all have agency to the same degree at the same time. In fact, variation in the ability of individuals to reflexively interpret social actions and the freedom they have and attribute to themselves and others help to explain social asymmetries and power differentials. Though many scholars have explored power and agency, a semiotic approach to these concepts demonstrates that communication—often linguistic—lies at the heart of a person's ability to "carry out one's will despite resistance" (Weber 1978:53) or to "make a difference" in the world through "transformative capacity" (Giddens 1984:14–15). Foucault (1982:786) asserts that communication and power can be analytically separated: "the production and circulation of elements of meaning can have as their objective or as their consequence certain results in the realm of power; the latter are not simply an aspect of the former. *Whether or not they pass through systems of communication*, power relations have a specific nature" (emphasis added). In fact, a semiotic approach to communication and power shows that they are analytically inseparable.

SEMIOTIC ARCHAEOLOGY

Parmentier (1997:43–44) observes that there is a reflex within Western culture to view linguistic signs as meaningful, decontextual, and impermanent, while objects are practical, contextual, and permanent. Archaeological theorists, especially since postprocessualism, have debated the similarities and differences between objects and language and reflect this tendency (e.g., Hodder 1982a, 1982b, 1987, 1989; Shanks and Tilley 1987; Tilley 1991; Wylie 1982; Wynn 1993). Many view linguistic signs as specific, arbitrary, and referential, while physical objects are said to be ambiguous, motivated, and subconscious. Somewhat contradictorily, objects' durability allows them to retain meaning over time and to become more ambiguous, according to Hodder (1989:72–73). As discussed earlier, most of these arguments are based on the Saussurean model of the sign and do not grasp the importance of the pragmatic and metapragmatic functions of language (Preucel and Bauer 2001).

Recent efforts to explicate the role of material objects in social relationships fall under the umbrella term "materiality" (e.g., Maran and Stockhammer 2012; Miller 2005; Preucel 2010:5; Tilley 2007). While some archaeological approaches to materiality are explicitly based on Peircian semiotics (e.g., Baron 2014; Bauer 2013; Crossland 2014; Fogelin 2014; Houston 2006; Joyce 2012; Knappett 2005; Preucel 2010; Preucel and Bauer 2001; Pugh 2013; Watts 2008), others proceed with the study of ancient societies by largely sidestepping language altogether. For example, proponents of a new "symmetrical archaeology" argue that language has been overemphasized by previous archaeological theorists at the expense of material objects (Olsen 2003, 2010; Olsen et al. 2012; Shanks 2007; Webmoor 2007; Witmore 2007). Borrowing from Actor-Network Theory (Callon 1986; Callon and Latour 1981; Latour 2005; Law 1986), symmetrical archaeologists treat humans and objects as cyborgs—joint participants in social action. As such, objects have agency in the sense of participating in social relationships. (Needless to say, this definition of agency is very different from the one I have presented here.) The problem with such an approach is twofold: (1) it ignores the role of language (through metapragmatics) in shaping the social function of objects, and (2) it risks creating a simple equation between artifacts and people (Bauer 2013:3). For example, Webmoor (2007:571) argues that "San Martin orange ware is consistently found at Teotihuacan. . . . A symmetrical archaeology would treat Teotihuacanos and orange ware of this period as inextricable. For understanding prehistoric practice, is it helpful to distinguish the users of the ubiquitous ceramics from the ceramics themselves?" In fact, treating orange ware and Teotihuacanos (people) as indistinguishable is highly problematic. Instead, by analytically separating pots from their users and treating them as signs, it is possible to analyze norms of ceramic usage—and breaches of those norms—by reference to other signs such as their contents and their actual distribution (Herzfeld 1992).

Silverstein's (1976) insight, discussed earlier, was to note that both language and material objects have pragmatic meaning, making them analytically similar. Others (Agha 2007; Parmentier 1997:43) have also shown the importance of metapragmatic language in shaping the meaning of material objects themselves (as in the example of wallpaper, discussed earlier). However, because metapragmatic effects are often difficult to explicitly report after the fact (Silverstein 1976:49–50), they are usually left out of archaeological analyses of the function and meaning of material culture. Nevertheless, metapragmatic activity has far-reaching effects because of the chaining of signs and interpretants described by Peirce. This chaining, called semiosis, allows the normative meaning of material objects to be widely established in a society and allows for individuals within that society to be socialized to this meaning. In order to fully describe this process, cultural anthropologists must observe it in real time as it unfolds (Parmentier 1997:8). Unfortunately, this is not a luxury available to archaeologists. Not only is spoken language inaccessible but the vast majority of the material objects used in the past are also permanently gone. This makes archaeology not "the discipline of things" (Olsen 2003:89) but the discipline of radical evidential scarcity (Herzfeld 1992).

Lamenting the archaeological predicament, Parmentier (1997:49) observes, "absent other historical, contextual, or comparative information, there is no principled way to [delimit functional and symbolic parameters of objects] from the evidence provided *at* an archaeological site." In other words, without context, analogy, or written records, the meaning of objects remains opaque. Luckily, these are all methodological tools regularly used by archaeologists. Thus, adopting semiotic theory in archaeology does not require a new and unfamiliar set of methodologies.

Archaeological Context

Every archaeologist is familiar with the concept of archaeological context—the spatiotemporal relationship among artifacts and between artifacts and the landscape. This contextual information gives clues about the use and meaning of objects in the past, information that is lost when artifacts are removed from their context improperly. Archaeological projects regularly engage experts in multiple different artifact categories and analytical techniques so that the most contextual information can be squeezed from the archaeological record.

Some interpretive ("hermeneutic") approaches to archaeology posit that the archaeological record is composed of material signs that can be interpreted the way a reader reads a text (e.g., Hodder 1982a, 1989, 1992; Tilley 1991). But these approaches rely on the Saussurean rather than the Peircian model of the sign (Preucel and Bauer 2001). For example, Hodder (1982a:217) proposes a method he calls "contextual archaeology," which consists of cataloging which sets of binary oppositions are reflected in recovered artifacts, such as clean/dirty, male/female, and life/death. As discussed earlier, this process presupposes that artifacts carry meaning analogous to semantic meaning, which Silverstein demonstrated only applies to language. It misses the pragmatic (indexical) function of objects, which is where their meaning actually lies. It relies on the notion of "structure," a set of binary oppositions supposedly governing human behavior, rather than a set of social norms that may or may not be followed in a given situation.

The archaeological context is *not the same* as the semiotic context in which artifacts were originally used. This original semiotic context includes living human beings, linguistic signs, and other material objects that are often too perishable to survive to the present day. To read the archaeological record "as a text" is actually to analytically remove it from these other contextual elements. This critique can be leveled at a number of cultural phenomena interpreted as texts: "to turn something into a text is to seem to give it a decontextualized structure and meaning, that is, a form and meaning that are imaginable apart from the spatiotemporal and other frames in which they can be said to occur" (Silverstein and Urban 1996:1). All this means that the archaeological context alone is insufficient for semiotic archaeology. The missing elements of the semiotic context must be reconstructed somehow, either through comparative information (analogy), by using historical records, or both.

Analogy

Preucel (2010:261) observed that "ethnographic analogy ... remains the basis for all [archaeological] interpretation. All interpretation involves establishing and evaluating analogical cables or threads linking known and unknown cultural contexts." While I agree wholeheartedly, the use of ethnographic analogy has led to discomfort and protest on the part of some theorists due to the many social and cultural changes that have taken place between archaeological societies and modern ones (Wylie 1985). But if used carefully, ethnographic analogy is not problematic.

Archaeology is often seen as having an advantage over ethnography in that it has a much longer chronological scale of analysis. This is because, in the archaeological record, time scales become compressed so that archaeologists can see the precipitates of semiosis over hundreds or thousands of years within a single test unit. This time compression can be used as an analytical advantage. If a chronologically compressed archaeological record exhibits long-term continuity, it is reasonable to hypothesize that this continuity is the result of the relative stability of metapragmatic discourses that made up the relevant semiotic chains. In other words, long-term continuities in material culture probably indicate that these objects were used to signify similar things about their makers and users over long timeframes and that this stability was the result of similarly continuous metapragmatic discourses that defined and characterized the meaning of those objects. For example, if an archaeologist discovered that a particular room in a house had blue walls over many generations of use, he or she could reasonably conclude that those many generations had similar discourses about the indexical meaning of blue walls. Correspondingly, changes in the archaeological record might reflect changes in metapragmatic activity at some point in the past. Any society may exhibit continuities in some semiotic chains and discontinuities in others.

Archaeological analogy is a similar process: if the archaeologist observes continuities in linguistic and material signs between an ancient archaeological context and a recent and better-known semiotic context, it is reasonable to assume that the metapragmatic discourses that defined and characterized those signs have also remained relatively stable. This allows the archaeologist to take signs and interpretants from the ethnographic example and substitute them for missing sections of a semiotic context in the past. The long-term regularity of discourses is not the result of universal properties of the human mind but precisely because signs and interpretants are in fact strung together along long-term semiotic chains stretching over generations. This property allows signs to have social effects long after the moment in which they were created. Thus, analogy is a powerful tool, though it must be used with care.

This methodology relies on unbroken semiotic chains over the long term and thus is relevant only for direct historical analogies (also known as "specific" and "genetic" analogies). These analogies are used to generate interpretive hypotheses, which can be tested for consistency with the archaeological record (Binford 1967; Wylie 1985). Ideally, the analogous context should be a descendant community for whom semiotic chains are most likely to survive intact. In the absence of direct descendants, analogies to closely related communities can also be productive, since semiotic chain networks can radiate geographically as well as chronologically. However, the chances of success decrease as one moves farther away from the area of study (Hawkes 1954:161). Cross-cultural analogies to very distant, unrelated societies (also known as "unconnected," "general," and "formal" analogies) do not offer access to unbroken semiotic chains. These types of analogies may indeed be useful for answering some limited questions in archaeology (Asher 1961; Binford 1967; Clark 1951, 1953; Willey 1977; Wylie 1985).[1] However, for understanding social institutions, which are based on specific signs and interpretants linked across time and space, only direct analogies are useful.

Historical Records

Written texts provide an additional data set with which to reconstruct semiotic events in the past. Because they are linguistic artifacts, they differ from other material objects because they contain semantic meaning, a category unique to language (Silverstein 1976; Herzfeld 1992:67). This semantic meaning of written records is often easier to interpret than the contextual meaning of the archaeological record—even with the help of ethnographic analogy. It should be noted that the decipherment of the semantic meaning of texts also relies on an analogical process. Ancient scripts are intelligible by reference to surviving languages from the same areas (Coe 1999:44). In the case of Egyptian hieroglyphics it is Coptic, in the case of Linear B it is Greek, and in the case of Mayan hieroglyphics it is the modern family of Mayan languages. With the lack of an analogous language, ancient scripts remain unintelligible.

While the semantic meaning of texts often makes their interpretation seemingly straightforward, it is this overemphasis on semantics that has led to some of the intellectual debates between archaeologists and epigraphers of the ancient Maya. Those who point to the propagandistic nature of hieroglyphic inscriptions caution that texts might not represent the truth (e.g., Carrasco and Valencia 2013; Chase, Chase, and Cobos 2008; Marcus 1992; Ruz Lhuiller 1977). But the question of whether the decontextualized referential meaning of an inscription represents an actual state of affairs is a purely semantic question. And in evaluating ancient states of affairs the interpretation of linguistic artifacts is straightforward, since language alone conveys semantic meaning. In other words, while nonlinguistic archaeological materials cannot "lie," neither can they "tell the truth" because they lack semantic properties (Herzfeld 1992:67).[2] The trend in recent years has been to read hieroglyphic texts as true and to adjust interpretations of the archaeological record to accommodate this reading. Epigraphers and many archaeologists of the Maya remain unconcerned about the truth of hieroglyphic inscriptions because no text has ever been demonstrated to intentionally misrepresent actual states of affairs. For example, no two enemies ever claim victory in the same battle.

But it would be a mistake to ignore the "propagandistic" nature of Maya texts. This is a question of *pragmatic* meaning. Instead of simply asking what texts say and whether it is true, it is necessary to ask what texts accomplish socially. How do these linguistic signs formulate and characterize the social world? What is the role of rhetorical devices such as word choice, parallelism, and strategic omission? How do these devices contribute to broader ideological and ritual strategies? What metapragmatic discourses are contained in texts and how do these contribute to social entitlements and asymmetries? By using ancient inscriptions to answer these questions, archaeologists can gain unprecedented access to the semiotic chains of past societies. Those lucky enough to have historical data sets should therefore use them to their full potential.

Putting the Model to Work

A semiotic approach to archaeology, adopted from Peirce and his followers, has many advantages. It proposes a mechanism—metapragmatics—by which material objects take on meaning. With its study of semiosis—chains of signs and interpretants linking people across time and space—it demonstrates how social norms and models become widespread and is easily adapted to archaeology's long chronological scales. Finally, it advocates an experimental approach, in which the meaning of signs is empirically assessed through their interpretants, eschewing a model of culture that exists only in the mind. While the terminology of semiotics can be difficult to master, its insights can greatly enrich archaeological inquiry. The particular semiotic events described in this book and the effects they had on social relationships were unique to their historical context. But the mode of analysis I propose can be used by other investigators to gain new insights into the ancient societies they study.

NOTES

1. In addition to the drawbacks discussed here, general analogies can potentially lead to large circular arguments in which cross-cultural comparisons are used to demonstrate what was assumed from the outset: that different societies had similar practices or institutions.

2. "It has been said that the spade cannot lie, but it owes this merit in part to the fact that it cannot speak" (Grierson 1959:129).

3

This book focuses on patron deity veneration among the Classic Maya as an example of a semiotic approach to archaeology. While religious activities related to patron deities may seem like a highly circumscribed topic of inquiry, in fact, these activities had far-reaching pragmatic effects, especially within the political sphere. Through ritual acts and accompanying discourses of devotion toward patron deities, members of Classic Maya society created and disseminated social norms and status differentials. The role of physical objects such as effigies, temples, and offerings in this process was established through metapragmatic acts, which characterized the relationship between certain types of people and the realm of the supernatural. But before exploring the pragmatic and metapragmatic effects of patron deity veneration, I will begin by turning to the more basic question of what patron deities actually were. What terms did the Classic Maya use for these supernatural entities, and what did these terms mean from a purely semantic, referential standpoint? How were patron deities similar to and different from other types of supernatural entities venerated by the Classic Maya? What kinds of veneration practices actually occurred and how are they reflected in the archaeological record? After exploring these questions, I will turn again to their pragmatic effects in chapter 4.

Semantics

Defining Patron Deities

DOI: 10.5876/9781607325185.c003

WHAT WERE PATRON GODS?

Scholars have spent more than a century studying the nature of Maya gods and debating their similarities and differences compared with religious systems in other parts of the world. The observable parallels between Maya deities and those of other societies are themselves due to similarities in semiotic strategies employed in different times and places. As I discussed in chapter 2, a semiotic approach to Maya patron deities requires an exploration of those strategies rather than a reliance on psychological explanations for religious practices (Leone and Parmentier 2014). Schellhas (1904) pioneered early efforts to understand Maya gods within their own semiotic system by identifying deities in art and writing by their unique iconographic attributes. He assigned letters to the principal recognizable deities of the Postclassic Maya codices, many of which Mayanists still use today. Thompson (1950), Hellmuth (1987), and Taube (1992) all built off of Schellhas's work, recognizing connections between the iconography of the Classic and Postclassic periods in the Maya area as well as the deities of Central Mexico. More recently, Martin (2007) has demonstrated that these individual deity personalities were often fused together in Maya iconography so that the Maya could represent a greater variety of supernatural concepts. For example, he shows that "God N" of the Schellhas list was often fused with the "Principal Bird Deity" to create an entity that Schellhas labeled "God D."

This classificatory approach has been highly productive, allowing iconographers to identify important elements in religious artwork. However, other scholars have argued that it has a tendency to misrepresent Maya religion as a pantheon in the Greco-Roman sense (Baudez 2002; Marcus 1978, 1983a; Stuart 2005). They argue that, instead, pre-Columbian Mesoamericans represented deities as manifestations of a divine force that inhabits all things including humans, animals, plants, and objects (Houston and Stuart 1996:292; Stuart 2005:275; Townsend 1979:28). Maya art routinely shows objects that we might consider inanimate with faces and limbs, as if animated by such a force. And Martin's (2007) recognition that deities were frequently fused makes more sense if these deities were not individual characters but rather metaphors for natural phenomena that frequently occur together.

The Classic Maya Term for "God"

This debate over the nature of Maya gods boils down to the semantic referent of the word *k'uh*. This term appears frequently in the inscriptions of the Classic period as well as later periods. During the Colonial encounter, *k'uh* and its cognates in various Mayan languages were translated by Spanish friars as "god" (e.g., Martinez Hernandez 1929; De Ara 1986). In modern Mayan languages adding abstractive suffixes to cognate terms yields a variety of related concepts (Vogt 1969; Houston and Stuart 1996; Kaufman and Justeson 2003). The most often cited of these is the concept of *ch'ulel* in Zinacantan, Chiapas, as described by Vogt (1965, 1969). The Tzotzil term *ch'u* is a cognate of the Classic Maya *k'uh* and the suffix *-lel* is abstractive. Vogt translates *ch'ulel* as "inner soul." This interpretation lends support to the idea that *k'uh* is a divine force that inhabits all things (Houston and Stuart 1996:292) rather than an individual god.

However, there are problems with this interpretation. The *-lel* suffix that yields the abstract term *ch'ulel* in Zinacantan is attested in Classic Maya inscriptions (as in *ajawlel*, "lordship"/"reign"), but it never modifies the term *k'uh*. In fact, examples of the term *k'uh* in the Classic period all seem to refer to individual godly characters, not to a divine force (Zender and Guenter 2003; Houston 2004; Houston and Inomata 2009:198).

This is further borne out by a close examination of the glyph for *k'uh* and its iconographic origins (Figure 3.1a). The glyph was first deciphered by Ringle (1988). It consists of two elements. The first is a creature resembling a monkey (see Prager 2013). As a glyph, usually only the head of this creature is represented, but its full body is depicted frequently in the Postclassic codices (labeled "God C" by Schellhas) (Figure 3.1b). In these contexts, the monkey-like creature appears to stand in as a generic representation of any god (Taube 1992:30–31). Another example comes from a set of Classic period miniature temple models recovered from Copan (Figure 3.1c). A short text labels each model as *uwayibil k'uh* "the temple of the god." A depiction of the monkey-like creature adorns the front of each model—a generic deity sitting within his temple (Grube and Schele 1990).

The second part of the *k'uh* glyph is the "water group," a set of droplets above the head of the monkey-like creature or in front of his face (see Prager 2013). The "water group" often incorporates iconographic elements standing for greenness, yellowness, or spondylus shells (Figure 3.2a). Like the "God C" part of the *k'uh* glyph, the "water group" sometimes appears on its own in Maya art. At Yaxchilan and neighboring sites stelae depict rulers standing with arms spread, streams of droplets falling from their hands onto kneeling nobles or ritual objects (Stuart 1984b) (Figure 3.2b). Signs for greenness, yellowness, and spondylus shells adorn these droplet streams, just as they often do in the *k'uh* glyph. Stuart (1988, 2005) interprets these scenes as rulers transferring their divine essence (his interpretation of *k'uh*) onto

FIGURE 3.1. *The k'uh glyph: a. A typical example of the k'uh glyph, Palenque Temple of the Inscriptions, east panel (after Maudslay 1889b:plate 57). b. Example of codex "God C" (after facsimile of the Codex Tro-Cortesianus [Madrid Codex] 1967). c. Miniature temple recovered from Copan, on display at the Copan Sculpture Museum.*

subordinates and objects through the substance of their auto-sacrificial blood. Although the Yaxchilan monuments are stylistically unique in their depiction of this ritual, monuments across the Maya world display similar scenes of rulers dispensing liquid (Figure 3.2c). Such scenes, including Yaxchilan Stela 1, are frequently labeled with the caption *uchokow ch'aaj* "he scatters droplets" (Stuart 1995:228; Love 1987:11). Revealingly, these captions *do not* state that the rulers scatter *k'uh*.

The actual substance of these droplets is still open to debate, but it could include blood (Stuart 2005), water (Stone and Zender 2011:123), or tree resin incense (Hammond 1981; Love 1987; Stone and Zender 2011:69). In fact, in several examples of these scenes, including Figure 3.2c, rulers hold incense bags as well (Hammond 1981:78). The use of the signs for greenness, yellowness, and spondylus shells in the Yaxchilan images all mark this ritual liquid as precious (Stone and Zender 2011:69). Similar scenes appear in contemporary murals from the Central Mexican site of Teotihuacan (Figure 3.2d), where individuals holding incense bags release streams of liquid from their hands. Scrolls adorned with flowers and jades emanate from the streams, probably representing both preciousness and floral scent (Miller 1973:figs. 168–77, 183).

48   SEMANTICS: DEFINING PATRON DEITIES

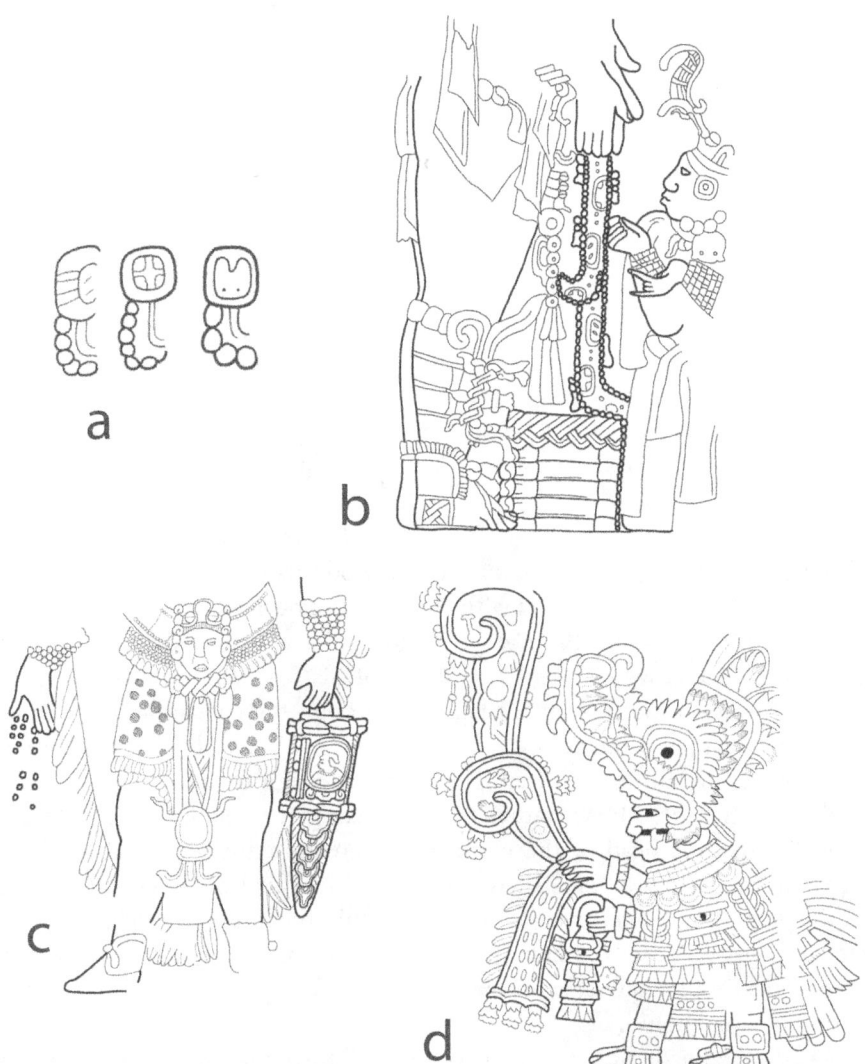

FIGURE 3.2. The "water group": a. Typical variations of the water group, Yaxchilan Lintels 16, 25, and 32 (after Maudslay 1889a:plates 84 and 89; Graham 1979:73). b. Yaxchilan Stela 1 showing "water group" motifs (after Maler 1903:plate LXIX). c. Lower section of Piedras Negras Stela 13; note the incense bag and scattered droplets. d. Figure from mural at Tepantitla, Teotihuacan; note the incense bag, stream of droplets, and scrolls of perfume (after Miller 1973:fig. 171a).

FIGURE 3.3. *The k'uh glyph rendered with the sign for "eat," Dos Caobas Stela 1 (after photo by Joel Skidmore)*

The "water group" of the *k'uh* sign is a condensed version of these depictions of ritual liquid, also often marked with signs of preciousness.

In sum, I understand the *k'uh* glyph to depict a generic deity with droplets suspended above his head or in front of his face. The intended referent, I believe, was a creature that is sustained through the consumption of ritual liquid rather than a divine force that inhabits all things. This interpretation is supported by an unusual example of the *k'uh* sign found on Dos Caobas Stela 1 (Figure 3.3). Here, rather than depicting the droplets of the "water group" above the head of the monkey-like creature, the glyph shows them above the sign for *we'* "eat." There can be no doubt that the intended reading of the glyph was *k'uhul*, given the context within the Yaxchilan emblem glyph (to be discussed shortly). I believe that the scribe creatively played on the idea of gods as droplet eaters, expressing the term *k'uh* by explicitly showing the eating of ritual liquid.

As I have already noted, the abstractive suffix *-lel* was never added to *k'uh* in Classic Maya inscriptions. The suffix *-ul*, however, was frequent. This suffix was used to turn nouns into adjectives, and thus "god-y" approximates a literal translation of *k'uhul*. By far the most common context in which this term appears is in emblem glyphs, or royal titles. The standard emblem glyph formula is *k'uhul [x] ajaw*, or "god-y [x] lord," where [x] refers to the name of a particular kingdom.[1] *K'uhul* usually appears in the titles of rulers of particularly large sites or sites that had subordinate allies or vassals. It also sometimes refers to important historical figures.[2] The adjective was not a necessary part of these titles, since it was sometimes omitted, perhaps to save space. Antagonists did not generally attribute the *k'uhul* adjective to their enemies, as if to deny them the honor (Houston and Inomata 2009:140).

Often Maya scholars translate emblem glyphs as "holy lord of [x]." I find this translation imprecise, since all Maya rulers—even those of small sites that did not carry the *k'uhul* adjective—had important religious duties, as I will discuss. Thus, the adjective more accurately refers to an exceptional influence over political affairs. I prefer to translate *k'uhul* as "godlike." Of course, calling a ruler "godlike" has pragmatic effects in the political sphere, which I will discuss in more detail in chapter 4.

The Dual Nature of Maya Gods

In Classic Maya texts the term *k'uh* refers to specific supernatural entities—gods—rather than a divine substance animating people and objects. These gods, however, were different in many ways from the gods of the Greco-Roman and Judeo-Christian traditions. The deities first recognized and lettered by Schellhas (1904) served as representations of natural forces such as wind, rain, sun, and agricultural fertility. The Classic Maya frequently depicted these gods on ceramic vessels, showing them in mythic narratives allegorically representing natural cycles such as the growth of maize or the waxing and waning of the moon. Rulers frequently impersonated these characters in costumed performance, linking political events to these wider mythical narratives (Houston and Stuart 1996; Nehammer Knub, Thun, and Helmke 2009). But in spite of their importance in Maya religion, these gods were distant from human social life. Unlike the Greek Apollo, the Maya Sun God did not normally intercede in the lives of people.

As a patron of a specific community, however, any god could shed this aloof character and became a member of the social world. Classic Maya texts about patron gods referred to them in very particular ways. The methodology used by Schellhas (1904) and his followers consisted of examining all the examples of a particular god in order to determine that god's attributes. A different pattern emerges when the geographical distribution of gods is taken into consideration. For example, the Sun God appeared frequently on painted ceramics. These scenes depict mythological narratives representing natural cycles such as the rising and setting of the sun. Most of the time, the Sun God was distant from human affairs. But at Palenque, where an aspect of the Sun God was a local patron deity, he was described differently. He was embodied by a physical effigy, which was fed, clothed, and housed in a special temple. He oversaw important political events such as accessions, and he was described as having a special friendship with the site's rulers.

Scholars have long recognized the existence of patron deities at particular sites (see Sachse 2004:9) but have not extensively documented or explored the phenomenon. For reasons not entirely clear, the inscriptions of Palenque were particularly detailed about the site's patron gods. Because Palenque played an important role in the history of the decipherment of Maya writing, Mayanists have sometimes taken the site to be representative of the Classic Maya in general. For instance, the three most prominent patron deities at Palenque, nicknamed GI, GII, and GIII (Berlin 1963), were believed to be not uniquely local patrons but gods associated with kingship and agricultural fertility more generally (Lounsbury 1985; Schele 1979). Other scholars (Stuart 2006a:160; Stuart, Houston, and Robertson 1999:II-57) later realized that the role played by Palenque's three main patrons was taken by other gods at Caracol and Tikal and that GI, GII, and GIII should thus be understood primarily as Palenque patrons. In conducting the present study, I identified patron deities in the inscriptions of more than thirty sites (see appendix). I believe that most if not all Classic Maya polities had patron gods, even when inscriptions recording their names have not survived.

The identity of nearly all of these patron gods can be traced back to an original general god of the kind that appears on ceramic mythical scenes. Sometimes patron gods had particular glyphic modifiers marking them as a unique aspect of this general deity. For example, all three of Palenque's principal patron gods had special names, two of which are still largely undeciphered. In other cases patron deities had the same names as the general gods from which they were derived. That the Classic Maya saw general and patron gods as the same kind of supernatural entity is indicated by this similarity of names and by the fact that they referred to both as *k'uh*.

The difference between a community's patron gods and all other gods was the special relationship it had with these patrons. This relationship involved the physical presence of patron gods in the form of effigies, the role played by these effigies in the social life of the community, and the ritual obligations of humans toward these effigies in return. Certain textual narratives indicate that these relationships were not timeless but rather initiated at important historical moments. For example, multiple texts at Palenque detailed the forging of this special relationship during the reign of the site's dynastic founder. Each of the three of Palenque's principal patron deities was said to "arrive" at Palenque, an event also described as a "birth" and "earth-touching" (Stuart 2006b). The same texts, in fact, described mythological events involving the patron god

GI before his descent from the heavens. For years, scholars were confused as to how GI could perform mythological actions before his own birth and concluded that there must actually be two different GIs (Lounsbury 1980:112). However, Stuart (2006a:173–74) has shown that these are actually just two forms of the same god—one prebirth and one postbirth. In other words, GI once existed solely as a general god but then "was born" or "touched the earth" as a patron god.

In addition to descending from the heavens, patron gods could be adopted from other polities, especially during war. As I will describe in chapter 4, this process involved a special ritual domestication, turning a foreign god into a benevolent patron. New patron deities frequently appeared in the historical records of different Classic Maya sites. But most of the time inscriptions did not comment upon the circumstances of their introduction. In general, once a god became a patron, it did not disappear from a site's pantheon but rather continued to be venerated even if new gods were later introduced. The result was the gradual accumulation of patron gods. Copan is a good example. Throughout its history, more and more patrons were added, accumulating into a list of at least seven principal patron gods (and numerous minor ones) by the end of the eighth century. Prager (2013:374) notes that Copan's last ruler, Yax Pasaj Chan Yopaat, specifically acknowledged his predecessors' role in introducing particular gods, depicting the site's patron deities alongside the ancient kings that introduced them. The same process appears to have been at work at La Corona, where rulers continued to venerate the deities introduced by their ancestors, in one case explicitly acknowledging the role of a previous ruler in the introduction of a patron deity. I will discuss this example further in chapter 5.

Patron Deity Sets and Categories

The processes of patron deity introduction and accumulation led to different god lists at different Maya sites. Often these lists overlapped somewhat, as different sites shared a patron deity or two. But when taken together, each site appears to have had a unique pantheon. And many sites also had different ways of categorizing the various patron gods that they venerated. One of the first patron deity categories that scholars recognized was labeled with what I call the Patron Deity Introductory Glyph (PDIG). This glyph appears at the beginning of god lists at Palenque and Caracol with some frequency, and three other examples can be found at Tikal and on the "Vase of the Seven Gods" (K2796) and "Vase of the Eleven Gods" (K7750). A Postclassic example

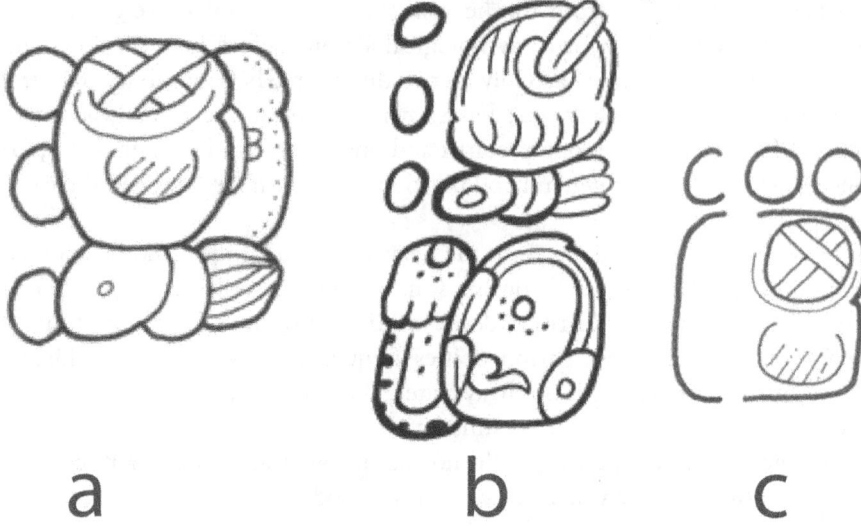

FIGURE 3.4. *Patron Deity Introductory Glyph: a. A typical example of the glyph, Palenque Temple of the Inscriptions, central panel (after photo by Linda Schele). b. The Patron Deity Introductory Glyph from the Vase of the Seven Gods, missing the crossed-band element (after photo by Justin Kerr). c. An example of the Patron Deity Introductory Glyph without the* –ti *phonetic complement, Caracol Stela 3 (after photos from archives of the University of Pennsylvania Museum of Archaeology and Anthropology).*

also appears in the Dresden Codex (see Prager 2013:582 for full list). Again, because of Palenque's prominence in the history of Maya epigraphy, this glyph has played an important role in the search for patron gods at other sites (Stuart 2006a:160; Stuart, Houston, and Robertson 1999:II-57). Its limited distribution, however, suggests that it was actually somewhat unusual.

The PDIG consists of three parts: the number three (*hux*), an undeciphered middle element, and the glyph for *k'uh* (Figure 3.4a). The reading of the PDIG hinges on the glyph's undeciphered middle portion, consisting of a sign that resembles the **lu** syllable with an infixed crossed-band element and the phonetic **ti** sign. Cuevas García and Bernal Romero (1999) propose that the crossed-band element should be read as phonetic **p'u**, rendering **p'u-lu-ti** for *p'uluut*, the Yucatec word for incense burner. They offer evidence for this interpretation in the form of Palenque's collection of elaborate incense burners, many of which were recovered near the temples of GI, GII, and GIII and which they believe depict these same gods. I find this interpretation unconvincing, however, for several reasons. First, *p'uluut* was probably not the word

TABLE 3.1. Terms analogous to *luut* in Mayan languages

Language and Term	Translation	Reference
Chontal: *lot*	*compañero* (friend/comrade)	Keller and Luciano 1997:150–51
Chol: *lut*	*gemelos* (twins)	Aulie and Aulie 1978:75
Tzotzil: *lot*	set together/objects standing together	Laughlin 1975:219
Proto-Mayan: **loot*	twins	Kaufman and Norman (1984:87, 125)

for incense burner at Classic Period Palenque, since its inscriptions do not record Yucatec but rather Classic Ch'olti'an (Houston, Robertson, and Stuart 2000). In fact, it is likely that the Eastern Ch'olan branch of languages, to which Classic Ch'olti'an belongs, did not even differentiate the glottalized /p'/ as a separate phoneme during the Classic Period, explaining the lack of deciphered phonetic **p'V** signs in the writing system (Wichmann 2006). A glyph for the cognate term *pul* "to burn" has already been identified in the hieroglyphic corpus, as has the syllabic **pu**. Neither sign is found in the PDIG. Finally, I disagree with the interpretation of Palenque's incense burners as depictions of GI, GII, and GIII, since their iconography was inconsistent with those gods.

A far more convincing reading of the PDIG is *hux luut k'uh*. The two ceramic examples and Postclassic codex example of the phrase all spell the middle portion phonetically as **lu-ti** (Figure 3.4b). The term *luut* probably referred to twins, friends, or sets (Table 3.1).

Kaufman and Norman (1984:125) propose that the Common Mayan form of this word was **loot* and that subsequent sound changes rendered the Proto-Cholan version **lut*. This reconstruction was made before epigraphers recognized the importance of disharmonic spellings in recording long or complex vowels in Classic Maya writing.[3] Houston, Robertson, and Stuart (2000:328) propose that this sound shift in fact turned the long vowel **oo* to the long vowel **uu*. For example, the Proto-Mayan **sootz'* ("bat") was rendered **su-tzi'** in Classic Maya writing, with the disharmonic spelling indicating a long vowel in *suutz'*. By the same logic, the Proto-Mayan **loot* ("twins") would be rendered **lu-ti** for *luut* in Classic Maya writing, consistent with the phonetic indicators of the PDIG. Unfortunately, neither Ch'olti' nor Ch'orti', the two Mayan languages most closely related to the Classic Mayan script, preserve this term, making it difficult to determine whether it existed during the Classic period.

To read the PDIG as *hux luut k'uh*, one must argue that the crossed-band element inside the **lu** sign either functions as a variant of the more typical **lu** sign or, alternatively, that it is a logogram reading **LUUT** somehow fused with the **lu** sign. The latter is probably the better explanation, given that in one example, the -**ti** suffix is totally absent, suggesting that it was not entirely necessary in order to read the middle part of the glyph as *luut* (Figure 3.4c).

The reading of the PDIG as *hux luut k'uh* was first proposed by Schele (1992:127–28). Those who accept this reading of the glyph typically interpret the *hux* ("three") part of the phrase as referring to three gods (Prager 2013:584). Because the PDIG was used frequently to introduce Palenque's patron gods and because Palenque's most important patrons were three in number, it is logical to assume that the *hux* in the glyph corresponded to the three gods listed after. This assumption has also led to the wider inference that patron deities primarily occurred as sets of three. As it turns out, both of these conclusions are incorrect. While many inscriptions did list patron gods as sets of three, they were often inconsistent. Take the patron gods of Calakmul, for example. Stela 58 named three gods, while Stela 54 named five. Cancuen Panel 1 named three Calakmul patron gods, but only two were the same as those listed on Stela 58. Other inscriptions mentioned only one Calakmul patron deity. At first glance, god lists appear to have been more formulaic at Palenque, since the typical triad of GI, GII, and GIII can be found eight times in its inscriptions. Twice, however, an additional three gods were added to the list. Once GII was paired with a different god, and on another occasion GI was listed with four other deities. The PDIG introduced deity lists at Palenque consisting of one, two, three, or six gods. And at Caracol the glyph introduced lists of three, four, and six gods. On the Vases of the Seven and Eleven Gods it appears to have referred to just one god in a list of many.[4] Thus, not only did Maya texts regularly list patron deities in groups other than triads but the "three" in the PDIG does not seem to have referred the actual number of gods that it introduced. In some hieroglyphic contexts *hux* had the extended meaning of "many" (Grube 1997:88). Given the lack of consistency in how many gods followed the PDIG, it may be best translated something like "the many-together god(s)" or "god(s) from a large set." Thus, the phrase is a quite literal description of patron deities, who were venerated in ever-accumulating pantheons.

Although the PDIG appears at a limited number of sites, patron deity groupings were common in Classic Maya inscriptions. Patron gods formed pairs more frequently than triads. The most popular of these appears to have been the Paddler Gods, a pair of deities who piloted the Maize God's canoe to the underworld in mythological scenes. I identified thirteen sites where these gods served as patron deities. Another popular choice was the pair Chanal K'uh and Kabal K'uh "Sky God(s)" and "Earth God(s)" (Stuart, Houston, and Robertson 1999:II-43), who appeared at three different sites as patrons. It is possible, however, that these terms referred not to individual gods but to a wider category of patron gods, some associated with the sky and others associated with the earth. Support for this comes from the inscriptions of Chichen Itza, where specific named deities were classified as "sky gods" (though not earth gods). Other descriptive terms for patron gods included *naah ho chan ajaw* "first five sky lord," referring to a mythological location in the sky (Freidel, Schele, and Parker 1993), and *ohlis k'uh* "heart god" (Stuart, Houston, and Robertson 1999:II-44), whose meaning is not entirely clear.

Although most contexts limited patron god lists to six or fewer, it is possible that these lists represented abbreviations of much larger sets. This is most apparent on Tikal Stela 31, where three different calendrical rituals were described, each with a god list more abbreviated than the last. Each list begins with the term *pik*, referring to the number 8,000 (Houston, Stuart, and Taube 2006:188), here probably representing the notion of "innumerable." The first list reads *pik chanal k'uh kabal k'uh* . . . ("innumerable sky gods, earth gods") followed by six other named deities. The second list reads *pik chanal k'uh kabal k'uh*, dropping the six additional names. The final list simply reads *pik k'uh* ("innumerable gods"). Another example comes from El Peru Stela 16, which refers to twenty-nine gods but names only three (Guenter n.d.:4). The abbreviation of god lists might explain why they were often inconsistent, even within the same site.

Patron Deities and Ancestors

In addition to gods, the Classic Maya venerated ancestors. McAnany (1995) describes this practice as "living with the ancestors," since it was exemplified by the common practice of burying deceased lineage members beneath household floors and continuing to interact with them after their death. This special mortuary treatment was reserved for the most important members of lineage groups, who thus entered the privileged category of ancestor. All lineages took part in this practice, from common farming families to royal households, whose ancestor veneration rituals were highly elaborated. McAnany argues that ancestor veneration allowed living lineage members to indexically link themselves to the mortal remains of important predecessors. This had the pragmatic effect of maintaining hereditary privileges such as land rights and social status. In the case of royal families, rulership itself would be one of these privileges maintained through indexical links to the dead. I will discuss the pragmatic effects of ancestor veneration at greater length in subsequent chapters.

Some scholars have surmised that Maya patron deities, and those of other Mesoamerican cultures, were in fact simply royal ancestors that were eventually deified by their descendants as part of the practice of ancestor veneration (Proskouriakoff 1978:116–17; Marcus 1983a; Marcus 1992; McAnany 1995:27; Wright 2011:232–33). Indeed, it can often be difficult to distinguish patron deities from ancestors in Maya inscriptions—both were listed on the monuments of particular sites; both were depicted emerging from ritual paraphernalia; and ancestors and deities could both be impersonated by rulers in ritual costumed performances. But in spite of these similarities, patron deities and ancestors were two separate categories of supernatural being with different veneration practices and different political implications. And, with careful reading, it is also possible to distinguish them in hieroglyphic texts.

To begin, the Classic Maya used different words to refer to ancestors and patron deities. While *k'uh* was the term for gods, *mam* was the word for ancestors. This explicit distinction can be used in many cases to differentiate supernatural characters in hieroglyphic texts. Other texts lacked such descriptive terms, but royal ancestors can be readily identified through historical linkages to their own monuments from when they were alive. In many cases these deceased ancestors were indeed depicted in the guise of gods—most often the Maize God, Sun God, and Moon Goddess in the case of female ancestors (Houston and Stuart 1996:297). But ancestors were not depicted with the attributes of their own site's patron gods,[5] further supporting the conclusion that patron gods and ancestors were understood to be separate entities. There are other important distinctions as well. For example, many inscriptions discussed the physical effigies of patron gods, while ancestor effigies were rarely mentioned, if at all.[6] Furthermore, patron gods were frequently described as actively participating in human social life, while ancestors remained distant, depicted as passively gazing down from on high.[7]

One potential source of confusion between patron deities and ancestors was the propensity for patron gods to be referred to as *ajaw*s "rulers." Different sites drew parallels between gods and rulers in different ways. In some cases, the word *ajaw* was an integral part of the god's name, as in the case of Yajaw Maan, a patron of Calakmul. In other cases gods were simply described using the term *ajaw*, as in *naah ho chan ajaw* "first five sky lord." At Palenque texts described the mythological accession of GI as ruler. At Copan the bench of Temple 21 depicted several patron gods seated on thrones, facing a line of Copan's human rulers seated the exact same way. Naranjo Altar 1 described ruler Aj Wosal as "in the line of" the Jaguar God of the Underworld, a phrase suggesting that this god was once a ruler. Notably, however, the Jaguar God was not given a numbered place in the dynastic count, as ancestors were in similar glyphic passages. The description and depiction of patron gods as rulers is a noteworthy parallel to the description of rulers as godlike (*k'uhul*) in emblem glyphs, as discussed above. What was the pragmatic function or functions of these tropes? This is an important question that I will return to in chapter 4.

Disambiguating Some Famous Supernatural Characters

By noting the important differences between deceased ancestors and patron gods and by recognizing that the Maya frequently used tropes describing or depicting their patron gods as rulers, it is possible to clarify the identities of three famous supernatural beings from the Classic Maya world. These include Naranjo's "Square Nosed Beastie," Palenque's [?] Ixim Muwaan Maat, and Tikal's Sak Hix Muut.

The "Square Nosed Beastie" (SNB) (see Martin 1996) has sometimes been called a patron deity of Naranjo (e.g., Martin and Grube 2008; Schele 1986; Tokovinine and Fialko 2007). However, this character is more accurately described as an ancestor, probably the founding ancestor of the Naranjo dynasty. The SNB was depicted on Stela 45 as a floating disembodied head gazing down from above. His attributes were fused with those of later known ancestors (Tokovinine and Fialko 2007). Patron deities were never depicted in this manner. Moreover, the SNB originated a dynastic count. In other words, later kings counted their reign numbers from his, much as President Obama is counted as forty-fourth in the line from George Washington. (The Jaguar God of the Underworld, in contrast, was not given a number in this dynastic count).

There are two sources of confusion for the SNB's identity. First, on Tikal Temple IV Lintel 2 his name was preceded by the *k'uh* glyph. However, it is most productively read as an abbreviated adjective *k'uhul* ("godlike"). Recall that important historical characters were sometimes described in this way. If the *k'uh* glyph were actually labeling the SNB as a god, it would be grammatically expected to appear after his name rather than before. The other source of confusion is that Naranjo monuments gave the dates of his accession as impossibly ancient (Mathews and Stuart in Martin 1996:226n6). Altar 1 dated his reign to 20,000 years prior, while Stela 1 dated it to nearly a million years in the past. This has been interpreted to mean that the SNB could not possibly have been an actual human being and must therefore have been divine in some way. However, hyperbolically ancient dates were not uncommon in

Classic Maya narratives. The fact that two Naranjo inscriptions gave two entirely different dates for SNB's accession suggests that chronologies could be manipulated. Indeed, such tropes are sometimes still used today in Maya descendant communities. Christenson (2001:68) describes a conversation with an informant in the Tz'utujil community of Santiago Atitlan about a recent community ancestor named Francisco Sojuel: "He told me that the entire altarpiece was two thousand years old. He then went on to tell me that his grandfather had known the *nawal* Francisco Sojuel, who was a great sculptor and helped carve the altarpiece. . . . I asked him when Francisco Sojuel had died and he replied 1907. Was the altarpiece, then, carved about that time? 'Just so, in 1907, two thousand years ago, when the Spaniards first came to Santiago Atitlan.'" In this example the accurate chronological placement of this ancestor is less important than the framing of his life within significant events in community history. Similarly, at Naranjo the lifetime of the founding ancestor was likely pushed back in time for pragmatic effect.

Palenque's inscriptions contained narratives of a similar individual named [?] Ixim Muwaan Mat ("[?] Maize Hawk Cormorant"). Previous scholars have also referred to him as "Lady Methuselah" (Lounsbury 1976) and the "Triad Progenitor" (Stuart 2006a). He has long been identified as a deity, mostly because his relationship to the site's patron gods was described in similar terms to that between fathers and sons. This led scholars to believe that he was the parent of GI, GII, and GIII (Lounsbury 1980). However, the phrase in question, *ubaah uch'ab yahk'abil*, linked rulers to patron gods in inscriptions at Caracol, La Corona, and El Peru. This suggests that [?] Ixim Muwaan Mat was actually a ruler. [?] Ixim Muwaan Mat's accession, dated to 2325 in the inscriptions, was called "the first," even though the god GI was described as having acceded as ruler even earlier. Here again is the same pattern seen in the Naranjo texts—although the patron god GI was described as a mythic ruler of the site, it was [?] Ixim Muwaan Mat who started the dynastic count in the hyperbolically distant past.

Unlike the SNB and [?] Ixim Muwaan Mat, the Tikal character called Sak Hix Muut has been misidentified as an ancestor when in fact he was a patron god. This deity, whose name means "White Feline Bird" (Martin and Grube 2000:50), was mentioned in several inscriptions from Tikal. The most extensive of these is the roof comb of the Temple of the Inscriptions, which was undoubtedly his temple (Jones 1977; Martin 2014, 2015; Stuart 2007a). This text described how Sak Hix Muut "oversaw" calendar rituals, one of the most common verbs attributed to patron gods but never to ancestors. El Encanto Stela 1 and Ixlu Altar 1, both satellites of Tikal, list Sak Hix Muut along with other patron gods. The El Encanto monument even explicitly describes him as a god (*k'uh*). The main source of confusion as to Sak Hix Muut's identity is the use of the full Tikal emblem glyph to describe him on the Temple of the Inscriptions. But given the widely attested and diverse ways in which the Maya compared their patron gods to rulers, it is not surprising that they would give this god royal titles.[8]

PATRON DEITY VENERATION PRACTICES

Religious rituals of various kinds were practiced by all different segments of Classic Maya society. For example, domestic rituals were frequent, and it is possible that commoners used the relative privacy of their homes to more freely shape the content of religious practice away from the watchful eyes of the elite (Gonlin 2007; Joyce and Weller 2007). However, participation in public ritual was also an important component of Maya religion and played a role in shaping power relations within many Mesoamerican groups (Beekman 2016; Joyce and Weller 2007:146–47; Joyce et al. 2016). Patron deity veneration involved a variety of public acts, usually sponsored by rulers but sometimes involving commoner participation as well. Most of these acts involved the physical effigies of patron deities—their construction, care, and maintenance. Classic period inscriptions included many references to these acts, which can be read semantically to establish an inventory of identifiable veneration practices. Some of these can also be detected in the archaeological record as well.

Building and Maintaining Deity Effigies

Physical effigies, as I have discussed, were one of the primary characteristics distinguishing patron deities from more aloof general gods. The term *winbaah*, meaning "effigy," appears in only two inscriptions—the jumbled stuccos of Palenque Temple XVIII and on Dos Pilas Stela 15 (Houston and Stuart 1996:302). But several inscriptions discussed patron deities as obviously physical beings that were constructed and maintained. The inscriptions of the Cross Group Temples at Palenque are an excellent example. These texts described events in Palenque mythology concerning the principal patron gods GI, GII, and GIII and the dedication of their temples in 692. About a year and a half before the temple dedication, according to the Tablet of the Foliated Cross, the gods were made (*patlaj*). Stuart (2006b) interprets this passage as the fashioning of ceramic effigies. The very next day, according to the Tablet of the Cross, a subordinate of the Palenque ruler performed a "conjuring" ritual. The same rite was described in inscriptions from many different sites, including Copan, La Corona, Naranjo, Piedras Negras, Tikal, and Yaxchilan. The verb *tzak*, usually translated "conjure," in fact means "to grab hold of" in the sense of hunting or capturing (Houston and Stuart 1996:300–301; Hull 2005:108; Kaufman and Justeson 2003:903; Stuart 2005:276). The glyph itself depicts a hand grasping a fish, conveying the sense of catching something slippery. This suggests that patron gods were considered materially evasive and needed to be ritually caught by the ruler or his immediate subordinates in order to enter the effigies created for them.

Various textual references and depictions demonstrate that patron deity effigies were frequently larger than human beings and were carried on large float-like palanquins (Martin 1996, 2000a). Calakmul Stela 89 described an event in 731 in which one such palanquin was carried (Schele and Grube 1994). But an earlier inscription from Tikal indicates that a similar palanquin, carrying the Calakmul patron god Yajaw Maan, had been captured decades earlier and brought back to Tikal (see chapter 4). Stela 89 thus described the construction of a replacement effigy, using the phrase *patlaj k'in ajaw* ("the sun lord was made"). "Sun lord" was probably a reference to this effigy, since the same title referred to a patron god on Naranjo Stela 32.

Finally, both the Naranjo Hieroglyphic Stairway and Caracol Stela 3 recounted an incident in which the Kaan dynasty ruler of Dzibanche gave a patron god to the ruler of Caracol. This deity had already been well established at Caracol for nearly a century and was mentioned in several earlier inscriptions. Thus, the incident was not the introduction of a new god cult but simply the gift of a new effigy, perhaps meant to replace one that was old or damaged.

Once constructed, these patron deity effigies were carefully maintained. Inscriptions at Copan, Naranjo, Piedras Negras, Tikal, and Tonina all state that patron deities were bathed (Stuart, Houston, and Robertson 1999:II-50). The tablets from the Temple of the Inscriptions at Palenque described multiple occasions throughout the history of the site in which rulers dressed effigies of patron gods, usually on major calendrical junctures. Clothing included headdresses, necklaces, and ear flares (Macri 1988:116; Stuart 2006a:166–67). Dos Pilas Stela 15 mentions the "adorning" (*nawaj*) of the effigy of the patron god of Seibal (Houston and Stuart 1996:302).

Patron deity effigies were also fed. Yaxchilan Lintel 35 described the capture of a noble from Calakmul who was eaten by two of Yaxchilan's patron gods (Houston, Stuart, and Taube 2006:123). Naranjo Stela 2 also described patron deities eating, this time on the occasion of a calendar ritual, although the items consumed were not specified. Monument 6 of Tortuguero is incomplete due to looting and erosion, but it was probably carved to commemorate the dedication of a temple for two patron gods. An incomplete passage in the text referred to pulque, an alcoholic beverage, and cacao, a chocolate drink, suggesting that the gods drank these offerings as part of the dedication ceremony (Gronemeyer and MacCleod 2010:45). Finally, the Temple of the Inscriptions at Palenque also referred to patron deities drinking, this time on the occasion of a visit by an assembly of foreign lords and gods. From these examples it seems likely that rituals in which gods ate and drank usually involved some kind of liquid. While the Naranjo example is ambiguous, the eating of a captured prisoner at Yaxchilan probably involved the unfortunate man's blood. This supports the interpretation of the *k'uh* glyph as a representation of a creature sustained through ritual liquid.

Given the rich textual references to patron deity effigies in Classic Maya inscriptions, it may come as a surprise that they are not found archaeologically. One probable Preclassic example comes from the site of El Portón, located in the Salama Valley of Baja Verapaz, Guatemala. It was recovered by Sharer and Sedat (1987:49–70) from Structure J7-4B. They identified six phases of construction on this building stretching back to the Middle Preclassic, many with evidence of ritual activity in the form of multiple caches and stone monuments. The penultimate phase of the building, J7-4B-2, was T-shaped and opened toward the west (Figure 3.5a). Ceramics from this phase indicate a date of ca. 1–200 CE. In the rear was a heavily burned adobe plinth about 5 centimeters high, into which was set a ceramic effigy 45.2 centimeters tall and 20.8 centimeters in diameter. It depicted a seated anthropomorphic individual wearing a necklace and flanked by wings depicting growing maize plants (Sharer and Sedat 1987:plates 3.25, 3.26). Its head had been removed in antiquity. Around the figure they recovered fragments of pyrite mirrors and a stone bead, perhaps once used to dress the effigy. From the subsequent Classic Period phase of construction (J7-4B-1), the authors recovered two larger-than-life ear flares and suggested that they may have originally belonged to a later deity effigy that was also similarly adorned.

The fact that this effigy was found without a head suggests that it had been ritually destroyed. Since the epigraphic evidence indicates that effigies were periodically renewed, it is possible that this ritual termination was simply a part of the renewal process. Another possibility is that it was destroyed intentionally as part of a hostile attack on this community. As I will discuss in chapter 4, the destruction of patron deities during warfare was highly significant. Furthermore, because of the religious importance of patron gods, it is unlikely that a fully functional effigy would ever have been left behind in the case of

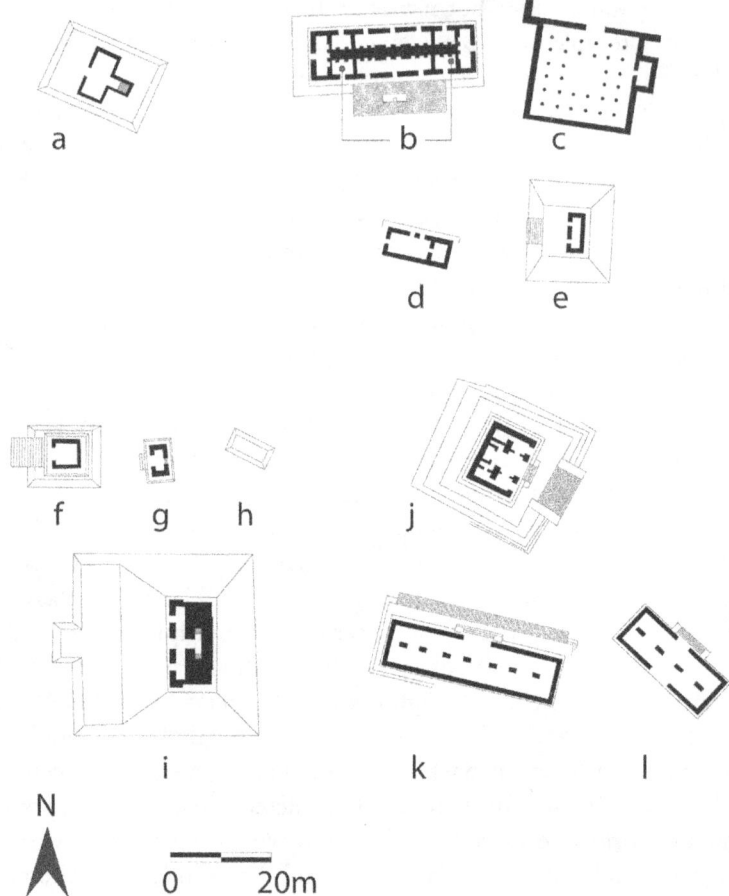

FIGURE 3.5. *Reconstructions of identifiable patron deity temples drawn at same scale and orientation: a. El Portón Structure J7-4B-2 (after Sharer and Sedat 1987:figs. 3.1, 3.13). b. Las Monjas complex at Chichen Itza, noting the positions of Rooms 17 and 19 (after Bolles 1977:38). c. Chichen Itza Temple of the Hieroglyphic Jambs (after Ruppert 1943:fig. 3). d. Chichen Itza Temple of the Four Lintels (after Ruppert 1952:fig. 109). e. Yula Structure 1 (after Anderson 1998:fig. 16). f. La Corona Structure 13R-3 (after Canuto 2006:fig. 1; see also chap. 5 in this volume). g. La Corona Structure 13R-5 (see chap. 5). h. Yaxchilan Temple 3 (after Graham and Von Euw 1977:7). i. Tikal Temple VI, Temple of the Inscriptions (after Berlin 1951:figs. 1 and 2). j. Palenque Temple of the Sun (after Barnhart 2001:fig. 2.3). k. Palenque Temple XIX (after Barnhart 2001:fig. 2.3). l. Palenque Temple XXI (after Barnhart 2001:fig. 2.3).*

community abandonment. Under such circumstances, the absence of intact patron deity effigies in the archaeological record is not surprising.

BUILDING TEMPLES

El Portón Structure J7-4B-2 can be tentatively identified as a patron deity temple based on the recovery of the ceramic effigy. But the lack of other similar artifacts makes this an unreliable way of identifying patron deity temples in general. Archaeologists use the term "temple" to refer to many different kinds of structures, including buildings whose precise function is unknown. In general, the term denotes a structure without obvious domestic or administrative functions, often set atop a high pyramidal platform. Many such structures were funerary in nature, with tombs of elite individuals found beneath their central axes. Funerary temples were most likely the loci of ancestor veneration rituals like those described by McAnany (1995). But many structures called "temples" by archaeologists did not have this obviously funerary function. Some of these were presumably meant to house patron deities.

The Classic Maya recorded a number of different words for patron deity temples in their inscriptions. The most common of these was *wayib*, meaning "place for sleeping" (Houston and Stuart 1989), suggesting that patron gods were believed to sleep between ritual activities. Inscriptions from Copan, La Corona, Palenque, Piedras Negras, Tikal, Yaxchilan, and the unidentified site of Sak Tz'i' all use this term to refer to structures associated with patron gods. Another term, which was used at Piedras Negras and Chichen Itza, was *otoot*, meaning "house" (Stuart 1987:33–38). This term was much more frequent in nonreligious contexts, where it referred to any kind of domestic structure, including royal residences. At Palenque and Tortuguero, inscriptions used the term *pibnaah* to refer to patron deity temples (Houston 1996; Stuart 1987:38–39). In modern Yucatec the word *pib* refers to both a pit oven and a sauna (Houston 1996), while Classic period inscriptions used *naah* to denote a structure of any kind. Thus, Houston reads *pibnaah* as "sweat bath" while Stuart (2006b) reads it as "underground house." Two other architectural terms were used at Palenque to refer to patron deity temples: these were *kun* "platform" (Stuart in Houston 1996:137) and *chak [?] naah* "red [?] structure" (Stuart 2006a:73).

Of the many temples that have been excavated by archaeologists, only a handful of them can currently be linked to patron deity veneration by associated hieroglyphic inscriptions. Four of these are located at Chichen Itza, all of which were labeled *otoot* "house." These include Rooms 17 and 19 of the second story of the Monjas Complex, the Temple of the Hieroglyphic

Jambs, the Temple of the Four Lintels, and Structure 1 from the nearby site of Yula. Of these, the Monjas Complex was the most extensively excavated for the purposes of architectural reconstruction (Bolles 1977). The second story consists of eight rooms: along the south (front) of the structure is a long room (Room 18), flanked by the smaller Rooms 17 and 19 (Figure 3.5b). The same arrangement is mirrored on the south side. Other small rooms can be found on the east and west sides (Bolles 1977:135–45). A series of inscribed lintels adorns the doorways on the front and sides of the structure, dating to 880 and naming human or patron deity owners of each of the rooms. All the rooms in this structure were called "houses" (*otoot*), but only Rooms 17 and 19 were said to have patron deity owners (Baron 2013:406–7; Boot 2005:325–32; Plank 2004). This suggests that the Las Monjas structure was a palace in which elite residents lived together with patron gods. Under these circumstances, one might expect the gods named on the lintels to be household gods, but in fact they included two Chichen Itza patron deities known from other hieroglyphic contexts. Thus, Rooms 17 and 19 appear to have served as private domestic shrines for community-wide deities. Interestingly, a later phase of construction necessitated the destruction of Room 18—owned by humans—to make way for a new staircase. Rooms 17 and 19 were carefully left intact on either side, however, perhaps because of their important religious function.

While the other examples of patron deity temples at Chichen Itza were not human residences, they were also referred to as "houses" (*otoot*). The Temple of the Hieroglyphic Jambs (Structure 6E3) was excavated by the Carnegie Institution of Washington (Ruppert 1943:233) and is found in a section of the site nicknamed "the market." The structure contains a partially roofed patio of approximately 18 × 18 meters with an entrance on the north side (Figure 3.5c). On the east of the patio is a small vaulted room measuring approximately 2.5 × 5 meters (Ruppert 1943:fig. 3). The north patio entrance is flanked by two inscribed jambs, which date the building to 832 and name the whole structure as the house of another deity, this one unique in the inscriptions of the site (Grube, Lacadena, and Martin 2003:65). The small vaulted room must have served as this god's shrine. Other structures of the same general layout, called "gallery-patio" structures, may have served a similar purpose to Structure 6E3, but none of them had accompanying hieroglyphic texts.

The Temple of the Four Lintels (Structure 7B4) is another "house" (*otoot*) of patron gods. Two of its inscribed lintels were first discovered by Thompson (in Morley 1925). Ricketson undertook excavations in 1925 under the auspices of the Carnegie project with the hope of finding more inscriptions. He records that the whole structure is 12.75 meters long from east to west and 5 meters wide from north to south (Ricketson 1925:267–68) (Figure 3.5d). Its interior is divided between a small eastern room (measuring 3.6 meters from north to south and 2.6 meters from east to west) and a larger western room about twice that size. The whole structure sits on a low platform measuring 21.6 meters long and 20 meters wide. Lintel 1 adorns a doorway separating the two interior rooms. Lintels 2 and 3 adorn north-facing front doorways, while Lintel 4 was found on a western doorway. Although Ricketson did not attempt a full excavation of the structure, he did recover eleven stone heads of unreported size. He notes that many of them had a "twisted doughnut" motif on their faces (Ricketson 1925:268), an iconographic feature today associated with the Jaguar God of the Underworld. He also reports the recovery of a coarse red bowl in the doorway between the two rooms. The inscriptions from Structure 7B4 date the building to 881. Two deities were named as owners of the temple on its lintels (Boot 2005:335–42; Plank 2004). One of these was a version of the Waterlily Serpent, also mentioned in other Chichen Itza inscriptions. The second was a god called Uchoch Yokpuy, who may have been captured from a different community, as I will discuss in chapter 4. It is possible that the eleven stone heads recovered by Ricketson somehow depict this deity.

Yula is a small secondary site outside of Chichen Itza proper. Yula Structure 1 is one of several structures located on the larger Platform B. It measures approximately 4 × 7 meters and rises to a height of approximately 4 meters (Anderson 1998:130–31). It faces to the west with nine stairs leading down to Platform B (Figure 3.5e). In front of this stairway was an uncarved altar. The superstructure consisted of a single vaulted room with two front-facing doorways (Anderson 1998:291, fig. 16). Each doorway contained an inscribed lintel dating to 874 and 878. Lintel 1 labeled the structure as a "house" (*otoot*), and Lintel 2 named two aspects of the Maya rain god: Yax Ha'al Chaak "First Rain Chaak" and Pomun Chaak "Rumbling Chaak" (Boot 2005:312–14).

Wayib, meaning "sleeping place" was a more widespread word to refer to patron deity temples, although it can be associated only with specific buildings at La Corona, Tikal, and Yaxchilan. At La Corona, Structures 13R-2, 13R-3, 13R-4, and 13R-5 were *wayib*s for patron gods. I will discuss these temples in much greater detail in chapter 5. Here I will simply note that each of these temples was built atop a pyramidal platform whose superstructure contained a single room (Figures 3.5f and 3.5g). One of these temples had a vaulted roof and a carved hieroglyphic bench, while the other three had perishable roofs and no recovered inscriptions.

Very little information is available about Yaxchilan Temple 3, where Lintel 10 was recovered (Figure 3.5h). This lintel was the site's last known carved monument and dates to 808. It referred to the structure as a *wayib* for several patron gods of the site. Maler (1903:119–20) describes the utter decay of the temple:

> I noticed certain ruins which were, however, so interwoven with a powerful network of roots that I was forced to give up all idea of making an excavation among them. Near the west side of the temple there must formerly have stood a little edifice, which may have been of masonry, but cannot have been roofed over with stone; the roof must have been made of some perishable material (beams and palm leaves). Only thus can the fact be explained that there was scarcely any other debris to be found on the spot, where I excavated the two half-buried lintels, for a broken-down stone roof always leaves a large heap of ruins.

This tiny and eroded Yaxchilan structure can be contrasted to Tikal Temple VI, also known as the Temple of the Inscriptions. Set on top of an 11-meter pyramidal platform, the temple's superstructure consists of two vaulted rooms (Figure 3.5i). The front room opens to the west and has three doorways rather than the usual one (Berlin 1951:35–37). It measures 14.97 meters wide and 1.82 meters deep. A single doorway provides access to a back room measuring 4.03 × 1.25 meters. On either side of this back room was a small bench. Above this level towered a 12-meter roof comb, bringing the structure's total height to 28 meters. It features an inscription with massive hieroglyphs—each 60 × 90 centimeters—the largest known in the Maya area (Berlin 1951:47; Martin 2014). This inscription indicates that Temple VI was constructed by Yihk'in Chan K'awiil, ruler of Tikal, in 735 for the patron deity Sak Hix Muut. This phase of construction was completed less than a year after the ruler's accession but was probably built on top of an earlier construction phase (Martin 2015).

Interestingly, Panel 12 of Piedras Negras discussed the dedication of a patron deity temple in 518 (Martin and Grube 2000:141). This temple was referred to both as a *wayib* and as an *otoot*, suggesting that the terms were actually interchangeable.

The only identifiable *pibnaah* structures for Maya patron deities are found at Palenque.[9] The Temples of the Cross, Foliated Cross, and Sun face into a single plaza and were built in a single construction phase (Damien Marken, personal communication 2011). Each temple was built atop a pyramidal platform modified from natural hill. The extensive hieroglyphic texts of the three temples composed a single narrative and indicated that they were all dedicated on the same day in 692 by the Palenque ruler K'inich Kan Bahlam. The texts primarily deal with the mythology of the three principal Palenque patrons, GI, GII, and GIII, each of whom owned one of the three temples. Each temple had its own proper name in these inscriptions, reflected in the iconography decorating the façades. Each had a small interior vaulted sanctuary measuring approximately 3 meters wide and 2 meters deep (Figure 3.5j). This small sanctuary was nested within a larger room, which was surrounded by two side rooms and a front room with three doorways. While the size of the temple rooms varied, the size of the smaller sanctuaries remained consistent across all three temples (Houston 1996:134). This was a unique architectural arrangement, and it is possible that the word *pibnaah* in fact referred to this interior shrine, either as a symbolic sweat bath (Houston 1996) or as an "underground structure," a shrine set within the metaphorical cave of the larger room (Stuart 2006b). The texts of the Temple of the Cross use the term *kun* "platform" to refer to the pyramidal base of the structures. After the initial construction of the temples, various offerings were cached within the structures, characterized as "humble" by their excavator (Fernández 1985:225). In addition, numerous effigy incense burners have also been recovered buried within the platforms of these temples (Cuevas García 2000; Sáenz 1956).

After the death of K'inich Kan Bahlam, subsequent rulers of Palenque continued to sponsor construction projects near these three Cross Group temples. Temples XIX and XXI were both dedicated during the reign of K'inich Ahkal Mo' Nahb. These temples also had extensive texts dealing with royal authority at Palenque and the mythical history of GI, GII, and GIII (Stuart 2006b). Temple XIX was dedicated in 734 for GI, while Temple XXI was dedicated in 736 for GII and GIII (Stuart 2006b; 2007b). Both temples are referred to using the phrase *chak [?] naah* "red [?] structure." The architectural forms were similar to one another, each with a single north-facing doorway and a single long room running from east to west (Figures 3.5k and 3.5l). The roofs were supported by a line of piers running along the central axis of the rooms (Straight 2007). Temple XIX measures approximately 33 × 7 meters with seven piers, while Temple XXI measures approximately 19 × 6 meters with four piers (Barnhart 2001:fig. 2.3). They both contain inscribed pedestals that were dedicated on the same date in 736.

Several inscriptions from Palenque refer back to an earlier patron deity temple that has not been identified. The Temple of the Inscriptions was itself a funerary temple for the deceased ruler K'inich Janahb Pakal. Dedicated by his son in 684, it contained a long hieroglyphic text that discussed the devotions of various Palenque rulers to the site's patron gods. One passage referred to the dedication of a platform (*kun*) for the god GI in 672. It is likely that this unidentified temple was ritually destroyed prior to the dedication of the Cross Group Temples twenty years later. A parallel passage on all three Cross Group Temples referred to the burning in 690 of a building variously called a *wayib* and a *chitin* ("oven"). While Stuart (2006b) interprets this to refer to the kilns fired to create ceramic deity effigies, I believe the use of the word *wayib* points to this event as the ritual destruction of the earlier temple.

These archaeological examples of patron deity temples show a wide diversity of size and architectural form, even when labeled with the same descriptive terms (Plank 2004). This demonstrates that the size of a particular temple did not reflect on the relative importance of the patron god it housed. Furthermore, individual patron deities sometimes had multiple temples within the same site. The terminology used in Maya texts to describe these structures suggests an analogy to domestic structures; *wayib*s and *otoot*s—apparently interchangeable terms—were places where gods lived and slept, much like their human counterparts. The terms *pibnaah* and *chak [?] naah*, both found at Palenque, may have referred to more specialized architectural forms, perhaps even places where the gods were believed to bathe in the case of *pibnaah*. *Kun*, on the other hand, referred to pyramidal platforms in general, whether the substructures of *wayib*s or *pibnaah*s.

Identifying Patron Deity Ritual

Under the present circumstances, it is impossible to isolate architectural characteristics that are exclusively indicative of patron deity temples. Hieroglyphic inscriptions remain the best way of distinguishing them from other architecture in the absence of deity effigies. But the feeding of patron gods—an activity mentioned in several inscriptions—has potential archaeological correlates. Three of the four textual references to feeding gods involved liquids of some kind, and the other reference was nonspecific. Furthermore, the *k'uh* glyph itself, I have argued, suggests an entity that was sustained by ritual liquid. Patron deity veneration ritual should therefore correlate with archaeological indicators of liquid production and consumption and possibly incense burners as well. Such items may not be present in the shrines of patron deities themselves, as these spaces would probably have been regularly cleaned. But areas immediately adjacent to patron deity temples may have seen the accumulation of ritual middens.

Of the identifiable patron deity temples at El Portón, Chichen Itza, Palenque, Tikal, and Yaxchilan, none was excavated with the intention of locating middens or ritual refuse. However, I made this an explicit goal of my excavation program at La Corona's patron deity temples (see chapter 5). In the end, this proved to be a fruitful avenue of inquiry, and I recovered the remains of patron deity feeding rituals from a time span of over a century.

SUMMARY

Careful analysis of Classic Maya inscriptions reveals that patron gods were a semantic category that was separate from both generalized deities and from deceased ancestors. These patrons were said to "touch the earth" in specific localities, where they were embodied by physical effigies. In order to inhabit these effigies, patron deities had to be ritually "caught" (*tzak*) by a ruler or ritual specialist and placed within the appropriate physical image. Effigies were carefully maintained by bathing, dressing, and feeding and were also periodically renewed, perhaps due to normal wear and tear or to intentional damage. They were housed within special shrines, known as "houses," "dormitories," and "sweat baths," that had a wide variety of architectural forms and sizes.

Each community had more than one patron god—often many—and these patron gods were introduced periodically over the course of the Classic Period. This process led to gradually accumulating pantheons, since old patron gods were not usually abandoned when new ones were introduced. Why was this the case? What purpose did El Peru have for twenty-nine gods, for example? Why did Late Classic Copan continue to see new god cults right up until its collapse? These questions can only be answered by turning to the pragmatic functions of patron deity veneration and associated discourses. These religious activities and linguistic acts were indexical—they signified something about participants through their contextual association with patron gods. What was this indexical significance? And how did individual acts such as feeding a god or building a temple contribute to the social asymmetries on which the Maya political system rested? To answer these questions, I will turn now to the pragmatics and metapragmatics of Classic Maya patron deity veneration.

NOTES

1. As mentioned in chapter 1, much scholarship has been conducted on the exact referent of this middle portion of emblem glyphs. Is it the name of the kingdom? the capital city? the ruling dynasty? the mythical place of origin of the city's inhabitants? The answer to all of these questions appears to be yes, sometimes. A full discussion is beyond the scope of this book.

2. Occasionally, lesser nobility were described as *k'uhul* as well. One example comes from Tonina, where a monument posthumously ascribed the *k'uhul* adjective to an important court official, probably a caretaker for the underage king. My suspicion is that rulers honored particular subordinates with this adjective, though only those who couldn't actually pose a challenge to their royal authority.

3. Phonetic Mayan hieroglyphs record syllables rather than single phonemes, as our letters do. These phonetic syllables were composed of a consonant followed by a vowel, such as the syllables **lu** and **ti** that I have been discussing here. But most Mayan words end in consonants, so the final syllable of the word usually drops its vowel when read aloud. This is why **lu-ti** is read *luut*. Synharmony is when the vowel recorded in the final syllable (the vowel that gets dropped) is the same as the internal vowel of the word. Disharmony is the opposite—when the dropped vowel is different from the internal vowel of the word. Thus, **lu-ti** is an example of disharmony. At first, epigraphers ignored synharmony and disharmony, thinking that it did not record phonetic information. Eventually, though, they realized that disharmonic spellings were indicating some kind of vowel complexity, such as a long vowel in the case of *luut* (Houston, Stuart, and Robertson 2004).

4. The PDIG on Stela 26 of Tikal is difficult to interpret. The text described the dedication of the stela and made reference to several ancestral rulers of the Tikal dynasty. The PDIG was preceded by a reference to what may have been a ritual grinding stone (Stuart 2014) and was followed by a list of characters, some of whom were probably ancestors rather than patron gods. Thus it is unclear how many gods were introduced by the glyph.

5. The only exception to this statement is the lid of K'inich Janahb Pakal's sarcophagus at Palenque, which depicts the deceased ruler rising out of the jaws of the underworld with the attributes of the Maize God and the Lightning God K'awiil. The ruler takes the pose of an infant, suggesting the name of GII, "Infant K'awiil" (Stone and Zender 2011:31). However, rather than morphing a king into a patron god, I believe this scene represents more universal themes in Maya art, specifically the rebirth of the Maize God as a new maize plant after the first lightning of the rainy season (Martin 2006). A similar scene appears on Copan Stela 11, with the deceased ruler dressed in the attributes of the Maize God and Lightning God standing over the open maw of the underworld.

6. David Stuart (2012a) has interpreted a glyph that appears at several sites as referring to ceramic effigy incense burners for both gods and ancestors. For various reasons, however, I prefer the more traditional interpretation of this glyph as a stone altar (Schele 1989:41). Archaeologists recovered a set of ceramic models of Copan rulers in the fill around the tomb of Ruler 12, but these did double-duty as incense burners and may not represent true effigy embodiments of deceased ancestors.

7. This may come as a surprise to some readers, since the active quality of ancestors has been asserted in some publications (e.g., Fitzsimmons 1998, 2002). But there are only four examples in Maya texts in which deceased ancestors supposedly took an active role, and all of them are problematic: (1) The Tablet of the 96 Glyphs at Palenque appears to make the long-deceased K'inich Janahb Pakal the subject of the verb *uchabjiiy* ("to make happen"). However, the syntax of the sentence and the presence of the currently untranslated verb *ukobow* make it similar to other glyphic passages that draw parallels between the past and the present (Helmke, Kettunen, and Guenter 2006:15–18). Thus the passage probably discusses events during the deceased ruler's own lifetime. (2) Fitzsimmons (1998) interprets Piedras Negras Stela 8 to refer to a dance by Ruler 2, the deceased father of K'inich Yo'nal Ahk II. However, a more detailed drawing by Stuart and Graham (2003:48) reveals that the dancer is in fact the son, not the father. (3) Although the Caracol ruler Yajawte' K'inich was no longer in power when he "saw" a ritual, as recorded on Stela 6, other glyphic passages suggest that he in fact abdicated the throne and was still alive during his son's early reign when the ritual took place (Martin and Grube 2000:90). (4) Quirigua Zoomorph G records the death of ruler K'ahk' Tiliw Chan Yopaat in July of 785 but then connects him to a monument dedication in October of the same year. But the king's recent death suggests that he may have commissioned the monument originally and died before it was finished (Stuart 2011).

8. Interestingly, Helmke and Nielsen (2013:144) identify a mural fragment from the Tetitla compound of Teotihuacan as another example of Sak Hix Muut's name glyph. This points to people of Tikal origin as residents of Tetitla.

9. Stela 6 of Tortuguero also mentioned a *pibnaah* dedicated to patron gods, but unfortunately the site has been largely destroyed by modern development, and it is unlikely that this structure will ever be identified.

4

Pragmatics

Using Patron Deities

In the last chapter I explored the semantic component of Classic Maya discourses about patron gods—what these beings actually were and how they were worshipped according to Classic Maya texts. I also described some of the archaeological correlates of patron deity veneration, such as patron deity temples and one lone example of a Preclassic effigy. Recall that Michael Silverstein (1976) demonstrated that the purely semantic function of signs is unique to language alone. Semantic content consists of descriptions of actual states of affairs that can be judged as true or false. Pragmatic function, on the other hand, refers to the indexical nature of signs—signs that produce action or understanding by means of a spatial or temporal co-occurrence with their objects. Wallpaper, for example, can signify the wealth, femininity, or age of a homeowner by physically co-occurring with her in a house. People assign these meanings to items like wallpaper through metapragmatics—discourses that comment upon the indexical significance of signs either explicitly or implicitly.

In this chapter I will turn to the pragmatics and metapragmatics of Classic Maya patron deities—how patron deity effigies and other ritual objects signified the power or status of those who venerated them and how these semiotic links were established through related discourses. Although a close reading of Classic period texts will be revealing, these questions cannot be fully answered without reconstructing part of their original semiotic context through ethnographic analogy.

DOI: 10.5876/9781607325185.c004

PATRON DEITIES IN INTERCOMMUNITY POLITICS

In the constantly shifting political world of the Classic Maya, communities frequently interacted with one another through hostile military engagements or friendly ritual gatherings. Within the context of these interactions, the Maya established "suprastate" hierarchies in which some communities became subordinate to political overlords, often paying tribute to them or rendering military service. Patron deities appear frequently in textual records relating to these intercommunity patron/client relationships, and they apparently served as indexical signs of political interests.

Patron Deities and Alliances

Cancuen Panel 1 described a local ruler's accession in 656 in a ceremony performed under the auspices of his political patron, the ruler of the Kaan polity at Calakmul (Guenter 2002). Using phrasing common in hieroglyphic texts, the panel expressed Cancuen's political subordination to the Calakmul ruler by crediting him for the accession ceremony using the verb *uchabjiiy*, roughly "he made it happen." The Cancuen panel gave extra details about the ceremony, however, stating that three of Calakmul's patron gods also witnessed the ceremony. The verb was *yichonal*, which, like the English verb "oversee," implied both vision and hierarchy (Houston and Stuart 1996:301).[1] The physical copresence of the patron gods with the Calakmul ruler at the accession ceremony was thus indexical of Calakmul's political and ritual power over its client.

Another accession ceremony sponsored by the Kaan dynasty, then based at Dzibanche, took place at Caracol in 619 (Martin 2009). Similar to the Cancuen example, the Caracol ruler underwent the ritual while the Kaan ruler "made it happen" (*uchabjiiy*). The text immediately continued to recount the arrival of a new patron deity effigy at Caracol in 622. As I discussed in chapter 3, this effigy was a gift of the ruler's political patron, the Kaan ruler, and was apparently a replacement for an old or damaged Caracol effigy. Here the indexical relationship between the Kaan ruler and his gift of a new effigy implied a sponsorship of Caracol's local religious cults. The discourse of the Caracol stela thus reinforced the relationship between political overlordship and patron deity veneration.

El Peru was also a political client of the Kaan lords periodically throughout its history. The principal patron god of El Peru was an aspect of Akan, a god of drunkenness. A carved stairway block from Calakmul mentioned this El Peru deity together with Calakmul's main patron god, Yajaw Maan (Martin 2008a). The deities were connected by the verb *bukuy*, although the larger context of the passage is now missing. This was a mediopassive construction—similar to

TABLE 4.1. Terms related to "gathering together" in some Mayan languages

Language and Term	Translation	Reference
Tzeldal: *bucuyon*	*juntarse* (gather together)	(De Ara 1986:252)
Yucatec: *bukul*	*juntarse mucha gente en algun lugar* (gather together many people in one place)	(Barrera Vásquez, Bastarrachea Manzano, and Sensores 1980:68)
Ch'orti': *b'ukb'a, b'ukwan*	*amontonar* (to pile up), *estar amontanado* (to be piled up)	(Hull 2005:13)

the more familiar passive construction in which the subject of the verb is its patient, but in which the agent was absent or deemphasized. In other words, mediopassive verbs are those that happened as if by themselves. The root *buhk* means "clothing" in several modern Mayan languages (Kaufman and Justeson 2003:1014), and it is possible that this phrase referred to the dressing of deity effigies, as discussed in chapter 3. However, given the mediopassive construction, I prefer to interpret the phrase as "the gods get gathered together" based on evidence from three languages (Table 4.1).

Given the known political alliance between El Peru and Calakmul, it is possible that the event described in this text was a gathering in which the relationship between the two communities was indexically signified by the meeting of the two patron gods.

A recently discovered stairway from El Palmar, Campeche, also implied friendly political relations. The text was commissioned by a noble from El Palmar who visited the distant polity of Copan in 726, probably as an emissary from the El Palmar or Calakmul court. There he met the Copan ruler at an event that also involved Chan Te' Ajaw, Bolon K'awiil, and K'uy Saak? Ajaw, three important Copan patron deities (Tsukamoto 2014:282–87). Although the nature and political context of this event are still somewhat obscure, the presence of these gods at this meeting indexically signified a supernatural sanction of the political relationship. The overall text of the El Palmar stairway celebrated its owner's lineage and highlighted his visit to the Copan kingdom, almost as if it were the pinnacle of his career as a diplomat. The fact that he chose to mention the Copan patron deities in this textual discourse indicated their central role in the political encounter and further reinforced their indexical significance in such events.

In the political ceremonies described in these four examples, the presence of patron gods was probably a ritualization technique, used to "establish a privileged contrast" (Bell 1992:90). The presence of patron gods at events in which political alliance or subordination was enacted formulates this social relationship as part of a wider cosmological scheme. Patron gods, indexically signifying particular rulers and communities, gave spiritual sanction to human dominance or subordination.

Patron Deities and War

Patron gods were not only involved in friendly social encounters. They appeared frequently in references to warfare. One interesting example can be found on inscriptions from Yaxha and Naranjo, a pair of warring communities. Both had similar patron gods: Yaxha's patron was an infant aspect of the Jaguar God of the Underworld, while Naranjo recognized two different versions of the Jaguar God as its patrons. But this similarity of religious devotion did not lead these two communities to identify with one another politically. On the contrary, Yaxha Stela 31 attributed a successful war against Naranjo to the baby Jaguar God's intervention using the familiar verb *uchabjiiy* "the god made it happen" (Martin and Grube 2000:82). On a different occasion, Naranjo Stela 35 described a victory over Yaxha as follows: *ch'ahkaj ubaah ti yotoot [Jaguar God] uk'uhil ma'ch'abil mahk'abil K'inich Lakamtuun Yaxa' ajaw*, meaning "the head of the Jaguar God is chopped in his house, he is the god of the defeated K'inich Lakamtuun, ruler of Yaxha" (Marc Zender, personal communication 2012). The stela also retold a myth, known elsewhere from a painted ceramic scene, in which a deity burned the baby Jaguar God alive. The front of Stela 35 depicted a reenactment of this myth, with the victorious ruler of Naranjo brandishing a torch over the unfortunate captured Yaxha ruler, forced to play his own patron god in the pageant (Martin and Grube 2000:82). The text thus used different semiotic strategies to signify Yaxha's political and ritual defeat: the iconic similarity between the costumed pageant participants and their supernatural models as well as the indexical linkages in the text between the ancient destruction of the infant jaguar and his recent destruction at the hands of the Naranjo ruler. These strategies produced an ideological discourse in which a historically particular state of political affairs was made to seem timeless and inevitable by creating semiotic links to a more widely circulating mythic narrative.

Naranjo and Yaxha were not unique in their use of patron gods in war. Several other texts described the destruction or capture of enemy deity effigies. Stelae from Dos Pilas and Aguateca—twin capitals of a single polity—both recorded an attack on the nearby city of Seibal that took place in 735. They also stated that on the day after the attack "the painted back of K'awiil was chopped" (*ch'ak utz'ibil paat K'awiil*). K'awiil was the name of the Maya lightning god, so it is likely that this was a reference to the destruction of a painted deity effigy. After the attack by the Dos Pilas polity, Seibal became its subordinate and eventually its co-capital as well. All of Seibal's inscriptions postdate this military conquest, and none of them mentioned this K'awiil effigy. They did describe a more prominent patron god, however, whom I will discuss shortly.

A more ambiguous war reference can be found on Quirigua Stela I. This retrospective account told the story of the victory of Quirigua's ruler K'ahk' Tiliw Chan Yopaat over his former overlord, the Copan ruler Waxaklajun Ubaah K'awiil. According to this text, six days prior to Quirigua's victory an event took place involving Copan's patron deities. The stela reads *jimaj ute'*, perhaps "their wood is toppled" (Kaufman and Justeson 2003:888) and *[?]-aj uk'ahk' unen* "their fire and mirror are [verb]ed." The owners of these items were Chan Te' Ajaw and K'uy Saak? Ajaw, two well-known patron deities of Copan who were also mentioned on the El Palmar stairway discussed above (Grube, Schele, and Fahsen 1991; Looper 1999:268). While difficult to interpret, the text thus appears to have linked the defeat of the Copan ruler to the downfall of his own patron gods (Houston and Stuart 1996:302).

A series of texts at Palenque described conflicts in 659, including the capture of the ruler of Santa Elena. Probably to confirm his new subordinate status, the Santa Elena ruler visited Palenque shortly after this defeat (Martin and Grube 2000:164–65). Several months later, other individuals also arrived at Palenque, including two patron gods, Yax Ha'al Chaak and Chan Ujol K'uh. At this gathering of lords and god effigies the Palenque patron deities were also given liquid to drink, as discussed in chapter 3. While it is unclear whether Yax Ha'al Chaak and Chan Ujol K'uh were the patrons of Santa Elena or one of Palenque's other conquests, the context of the passage indicates that foreign gods came to Palenque, perhaps even as prisoners, after Palenque's successful military campaign. Under such circumstances, the physical copresence of defeated ruler and defeated god would have framed Palenque's victory as a supernatural, as well as political, conquest.

A captured and subordinated god was featured in the inscriptions of the Temple of the Four Lintels at Chichen Itza as well. The lintels of this small building, dedicated in 881, recorded two deity owners. Yax Chich Kan, the local variant of the Water Lily Serpent god, was mentioned in several Chichen Itza inscriptions (Boot 2005:352). The other god, called Uchoch Yokpuy, was unique and was described as a "foreigner" (*nachil*) (Boot 2005:338). Sixteen days after the dedication of the temple a Chichen Itza noble carried out a series of rituals, including the announcement of a festival, the interment of an offering, the sprinkling of water or incense, and the presentation of a god

(Boot 2005:341–42). This description suggests that the foreign god was captured and brought home to Chichen Itza, where a series of rituals was performed to ritually accommodate him to his new home.

Similar rituals of deity "domestication" were recorded on wooden lintels at Tikal.[2] Lintel 3 from Temple I recorded the victory of the Tikal ruler Jasaw Chan K'awiil over Calakmul in 695. Having endured over a century of defeat and possibly economic distress thanks to Calakmul's conquests, Tikal appears to have experienced a reversal of fortune due to this victory. During the battle Jasaw Chan K'awiil managed to capture Calakmul's principal patron god, Yajaw Maan (Martin 2000a). Forty days later, on a day specifically timed for its calendrical significance, Jasaw Chan K'awiil carried the god atop his palanquin platform, conjured him, and built something for him in Tikal itself. The accompanying scene depicted the god—an enormous jaguar effigy with claws outstretched—towering over the palanquin and the triumphant Tikal ruler seated below (Figure 4.1). It is clear from the text that Jasaw Chan K'awiil, rather than destroying the captured god, took the opportunity to make the deity his own. This would have created new indexical linkages between a god formerly associated exclusively with Calakmul and its victorious rival Tikal. Like the destruction of defeated effigies, this domestication would have thus reframed Tikal's success as a supernatural one and Calakmul's defeat as the abandonment of its own spiritual protector. Calakmul did not allow this indexical reframing to go uncontested, however. As mentioned in chapter 3, a new palanquin and effigy for the god were constructed in 731, recorded on Calakmul Stela 89 (Schele and Grube 1994).

A second lintel in Tikal Temple I accompanied the first, representing other events on the same important date. It depicted another deity effigy on a palanquin, the war god Waxaklajun Ubaah Kaan (Figure 4.2). This serpent deity, whose name means "Eighteen Images of the Snake," was long venerated at Tikal but was originally of Teotihuacan origin. By the time the lintel was carved, this powerful Central Mexican city had already been abandoned, but it had previously been an important participant in the politics of the Maya area. To give historical context, in 378 a series of events were recorded in the inscriptions of Tikal and other nearby sites that have been interpreted as a military conquest by Teotihuacan: the reigning lord of Tikal met an early death and a new ruler was placed on the throne, son of "Spearthrower Owl," possibly the Teotihuacan king (Stuart 2000). This new Tikal ruler and his son both adopted explicit Teotihuacan imagery on their carved monuments as well as titles associated with the Central Mexican site. However, Spearthrower Owl died in 439, and within a few generations the Tikal dynasty stopped emphasizing foreign ethnic

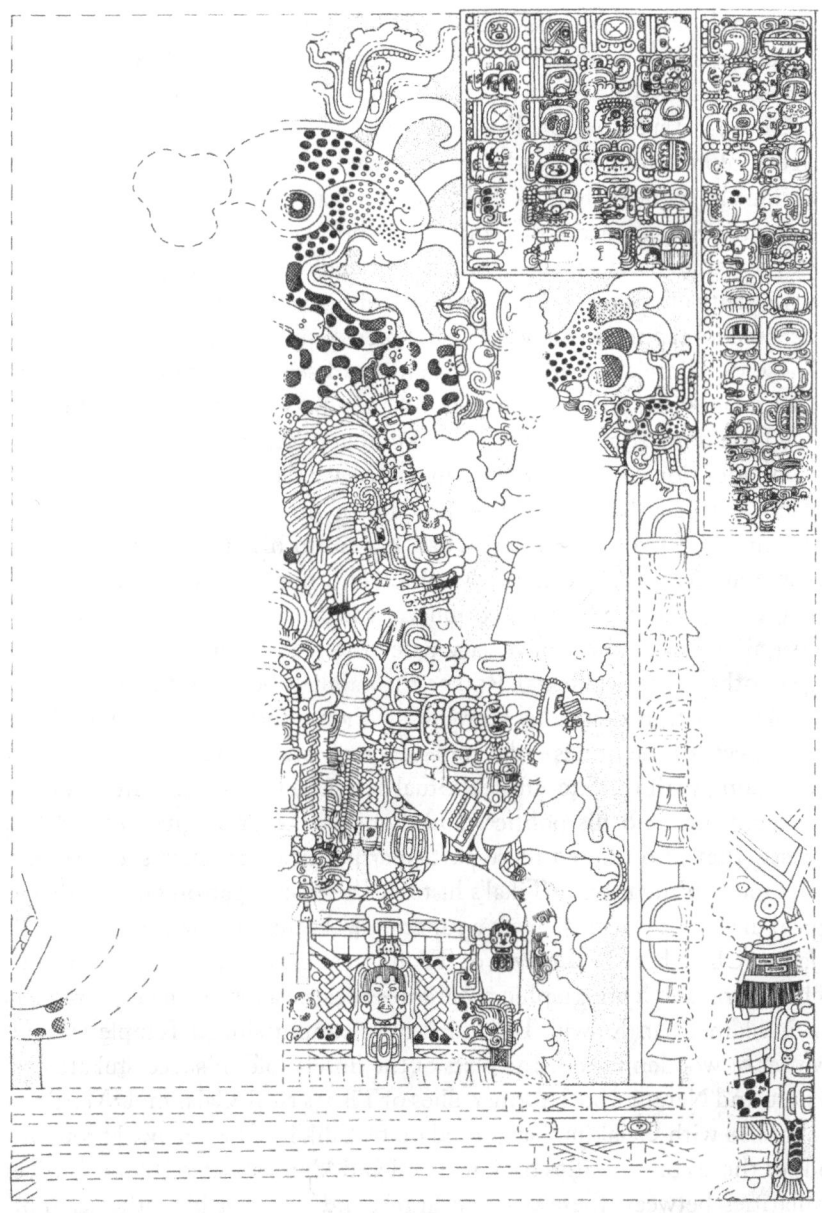

FIGURE 4.1. *Lintel 3 of Tikal Temple I, showing the victorious ruler Jasaw Chan K'awiil with the captured god Yajaw Maan of Calakmul. Drawing by William Coe (from Jones and Satterthwaite 1982:fig. 70). Courtesy of the University of Pennsylvania Museum of Archaeology and Anthropology.*

origins on their monuments. One of the lasting legacies of these events, however, was the veneration of the Teotihuacan serpentine war god, Waxaklajun Ubaah Kaan, who had arrived in 378 together with the Teotihuacan conquerors (Stuart 2000:493–94; Taube 2000). Thus, the lintel revived this ancient Teotihuacan imagery, representing the god as a bejeweled snake of Central Mexican style, towering above the seated Tikal king Jasaw Chan K'awiil. The ruler himself was shown dressed as a warrior of Teotihuacan (now an ancient memory) grasping a shield and atlatl darts. Notably, the date selected for this triumphal precession of the two deity effigies was the anniversary of Spearthrower Owl's death, exactly 13 *winikhaab*s (approximately 256 years) previously (Proskouriakoff 1993).[3]

These two lintels provide a rich example of semiotic chains linking events across generations. The iconic resemblance between the two lintel scenes framed the domestication of the Calakmul god Yajaw Maan as similar to the ancient adoption of the Teotihuacan god Waxaklajun Ubaah Kaan. Similarly, the iconic resemblance between the date of the triumph and the death of Spearthrower Owl linked Jasaw Chan K'awiil to his ancient predecessor and possible ancestor. The texts of the lintels did not explicitly state that Jasaw Chan K'awiil was the heir of Teotihuacan's legacy, nor did they explicitly state the significance of the anniversary date (the reader supplied it from knowledge of other historical texts). Rather, the parallels between the two rulers and the role of patron deities in sanctioning their conquests were entirely pragmatic effects of the lintels—the copresence of Jasaw Chan K'awiil in text and image along with warfare, effigies, ritual acts, and significant dates indexically connected him and his political ambitions to the prior greatness of Tikal's dynasty. They also framed these particular political maneuvers as a righteous or natural continuation of Tikal's history. The role of patron gods in this ideological discourse was to suggest a supernatural sanction for a resurgent Tikal.

Jasaw Chan K'awiil's revival of Tikal's past glory—an interpretant of his architectural and iconographic program—became a new sign employed by his son, Yihk'in Chan K'awiil. This Tikal ruler commissioned Temple IV and its own set of wooden lintels. The texts of the lintels told of successful attacks on El Peru and Naranjo, both former allies of Tikal's rival, Calakmul (Martin 1996, 2000a). As with Calakmul's captured deity, Yihk'in Chan K'awiil brought the gods of these communities back to Tikal and "domesticated" them. The iconic similarities between these wooden lintels and those of his father cannot be missed, nor can the indexical linkages between these newly domesticated foreign gods and Yihk'in Chan K'awiil's political ambition.

Though clearly carved as part of the same architectural program, the lintels described events years apart from one another, with the events on Lintel 3

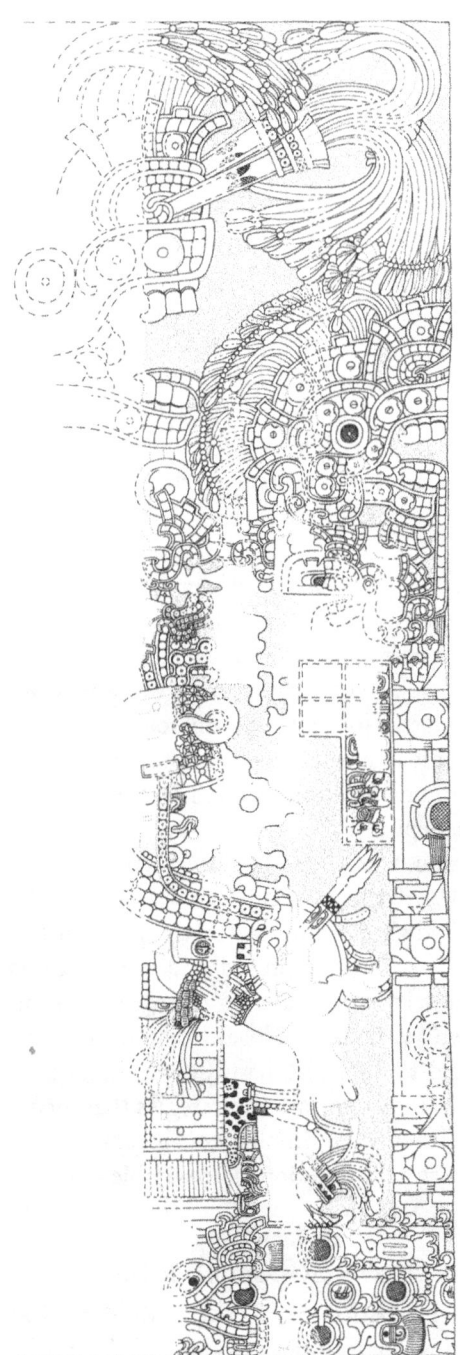

FIGURE 4.2. *Lintel 2 of Tikal Temple I, showing Jasaw Chan K'awiil with the Teotihuacan war god, Waxaklajun Ubaah Kaan. Drawing by William Coe (from Jones and Satterthwaite 1982:fig. 69). Courtesy of the University of Pennsylvania Museum of Archaeology and Anthropology.*

earlier than those of Lintel 2. Lintel 3 recorded a war in 743 against El Peru, a longtime ally of Tikal's rival, Calakmul. As a result, El Peru's main patron god, a version of Akan, was captured by Yihk'in Chan K'awiil (Martin 2000a). The next day, the captured god "completed his journey and arrived in Tikal." Following an unexplained three-year delay, Yihk'in Chan K'awiil impersonated Akan, now explicitly described as his own rather than the god of El Peru. The text also noted that the ruler was carried atop a palanquin, that he danced at the "Akan house," and that he built a temple called "Akan place" within the city of Tikal. The accompanying scene showed the ruler seated atop the palanquin. Its base was decorated with iconography popular at El Peru (Simon Martin, personal communication 2010) (Figure 4.3). However, the captured god Akan was not depicted, but rather an enormous arching feathered serpent. Though this god effigy was depicted in Maya style, it likely represented the Teotihuacan war serpent, Waxaklajun Ubaah Kaan. Perhaps the palanquin of the captured El Peru god Akan was repurposed to carry this snake deity after a new temple had been built to house him.

The other lintel in this set described events related Yihk'in Chan K'awiil's attack on Naranjo in 744, another ally of the Calakmul kingdom. This event took place less than a year after the war with El Peru and similarly resulted in success for Tikal. Naranjo's patron god, a jaguar/hummingbird deity, was also captured, along with his palanquin (Martin 1996). Unfortunately, sections of this text are now missing, but it is possible to read that after another three-year delay Yihk'in Chan K'awiil was carried in a triumphal march on the captured palanquin. The accompanying scene depicted this precession, showing the captured god towering over the victorious Tikal ruler (Figure 4.4).

The two lintels thus closely paralleled those of Yihk'in Chan K'awiil's father in Temple I. They both described the capture of foreign gods, just as Calakmul's patron deity Yajaw Maan had been captured and domesticated. They showed the Tikal ruler seated on deity effigy palanquins, one with a captured effigy, the other with Tikal's own Waxaklajun Ubaah Kaan. But in this case these signs were indexically linked to Yihk'in Chan K'awiil rather than his father. The lintels thus employed a variety of semiotic strategies that served to compare the Tikal king to his own father while simultaneously representing the defeat of El Peru and Naranjo as a ritually sanctioned, inevitable outcome.

THE RELATIONSHIP BETWEEN PATRON GODS AND RULERS

These various inscriptions indicate that patron deity effigies were manipulated by the Classic Maya nobility in order to indexically signify hostilities,

FIGURE 4.3. *Lintel 3 of Tikal Temple IV, showing ruler Yihk'in Chan K'awiil after his victory over El Peru. Drawing by William Coe (from Jones and Satterthwaite 1982:fig. 74). Courtesy of the University of Pennsylvania Museum of Archaeology and Anthropology.*

alliances, and hierarchies between different royal courts. But patron gods played a role in the internal politics of Maya communities as well.

In the previous chapter I detailed the types of actions that Classic Maya rulers performed in order to venerate patron gods. These included feeding gods, dressing and bathing them, and constructing temples to house their effigies. Like most Maya inscriptions, none of these texts made any reference to nonelite participation in these acts of veneration, although archaeological evidence at La Corona suggests that commoners did indeed participate (see chapter 5). This fact hints at the pragmatic function of these textual references—the framing of the ruler's relationship with patron gods as unique or exceptional. This was further reinforced through texts and images related to rulers' handling of patron deity effigies. For example, monuments at Palenque

FIGURE 4.4. *Lintel 2 of Tikal Temple IV, showing Yihk'in Chan K'awiil with a captured patron deity from Naranjo. Drawing by William Coe (from Jones and Satterthwaite 1982:fig. 73). Courtesy of the University of Pennsylvania Museum of Archaeology and Anthropology.*

and Xultun depicted rulers cradling patron deity effigies in their arms or holding them aloft. Naranjo Stela 6 showed the local Jaguar God emerging from the ruler's ceremonial regalia (Martin 2005a), and I have already discussed instances of giant effigy figures paraded on palanquins.

Textual narratives also emphasized the special relationship between ruler and patron god. The common possessive term *uk'uhil* "his god" employed the abstract suffix *-il*, signifying that rulers were intimately connected to their deities (Houston, Robertson, and Stuart 2001). Several texts also use kinship tropes to describe this unique relationship. Texts at Palenque and at the Tikal satellite El Encanto referred to patron gods as *ubaah ujuuntahn*, meaning roughly "the image of, the heart of [owner]." This phrase was much more common in parentage statements describing a mother's relationship with her child. Houston and Stuart (1996:294) argue that when referring to patron gods, it compares the ruler's care and protection of his deities to the care and protection of a mother for her child. Similarly, in texts from Caracol, Palenque, El Peru, and La Corona, deities were referred to as *ubaah uch'ab yahk'abil*. This phrase is more difficult to translate, meaning roughly "the image of, the penance of, the darkness of [owner]." The penance/darkness couplet can be broadly conceived as the ritual or procreative powers of the ruler (Stuart 2005:278).[4] The full phrase appears in parentage statements connecting fathers and sons, reflecting the generative role played by fathers in producing offspring. In the case of patron gods, the phrase suggests the importance of the ruler's ritual acts in generating or sustaining patron deities. Finally, the Temple of the Inscriptions at Palenque described the gods' emotional state, claiming that the king "satisfies the hearts of his gods" (*utimiw yohl uk'uhil*) with the gift of a new temple (Houston, Stuart, and Taube 2006:189).

Other texts also described the participation of patron gods in rulers' political acts. Various inscriptions noted that patron gods "oversaw" (*yichonal*) and "accompanied" rulers (*yitaaj*) at accession and heir-designation ceremonies and at rituals marking the ends of calendar periods such as incense scattering and monument dedication (Houston and Stuart 1996:301). Other contexts suggest an even more active role: Caracol Stela 3 and the Naranjo Hieroglyphic Stairway (originally a Caracol monument) both described the site's patron gods as ultimately responsible for (*uchabjiiy*) the accession of Ruler K'an II. Stela P of Copan also employed *uchabjiiy* to suggest that a pair of deities was responsible for the monument's dedication. These texts are thus examples of ideological discourses in which the ruler's authority was framed as consistent with supernatural will.

THE RELATIONSHIP BETWEEN PATRON GODS AND THE GREATER POPULACE

These rhetorical strategies commented upon the indexical linkages between patron gods and rulers—rulers dearly loved their gods, and gods' hearts were satisfied in return. Rulers took care of all of the gods' physical needs and in return received supernatural sanction for their accessions and calendar rites. But a large piece of this semiotic puzzle is still missing: rulers went to such great lengths to tie themselves to patron gods, presumably as a source of legitimacy among the populations they ruled. However, these textual references did not go into great detail about the overall benefits of patron gods themselves. Why should the populace care about the will of patron deities at all? What did their veneration achieve for the average Maya commoner? The answer to this question is only hinted at slightly in the epigraphic record from the Classic period. I will examine these hints and then turn to other sources of information.

Gods of a Place

Patron deities may have played a role in the community's sense of its own local or ethnic identity. On the benches of Temples 11 and 21a at Copan the site's patron deities were described as *koknoom Hux Wintik* ("the guardians of Copan") (Lacadena and Wichmann 2004:106). This is significant not only in that it expressed supernatural protection, but that the object of that protection was a toponym—a place itself and, by extension, all the people who lived there.

Another interesting example comes from the texts of Seibal and nearby sites (summarized in Figure 4.5). Seibal is located in the Petexbatun region of Guatemala, where the Pasion and Salinas Rivers flow into the Usumacinta. A number of communities in this area, including Seibal, Aguateca, La Amelia, Tamarandito, and Cancuen, all appear to have venerated a patron deity called "GI-K'awiil" (Houston and Stuart 1996:302).[5] Sometime in the mid-seventh century a new royal court was founded at Dos Pilas (O'Mansky and Dunning 2004). Its ruler was a part of the Tikal royal family and carried the Tikal royal title (Houston 1993; Houston et al. 1992). For the next 150 years the Petexbatun region was home to complex political machinations and increasing warfare. The veneration of GI-K'awiil, however, continued during this upheaval, especially at Seibal.

Importantly, the residents of Dos Pilas itself did not appear to have venerated GI-K'awiil. Instead, the Dos Pilas patron gods were probably imported from Tikal when the site was founded. According to Stela 8, the 698 accession of Dos Pilas ruler Itzamna K'awiil was overseen by four patron deities including the two "paddler gods," a deity whose name is undeciphered, and K'an Tuun Chaak ("Yellow Stone Chaak"). The same list also appears on Ixlu Altar 1, a Tikal satellite, suggesting a common Tikal origin of these deities (Schele and Freidel 1990:389–90). But although the Dos Pilas rulers did not apparently venerate GI-K'awiil, Dos Pilas Stela 15 acknowledged his

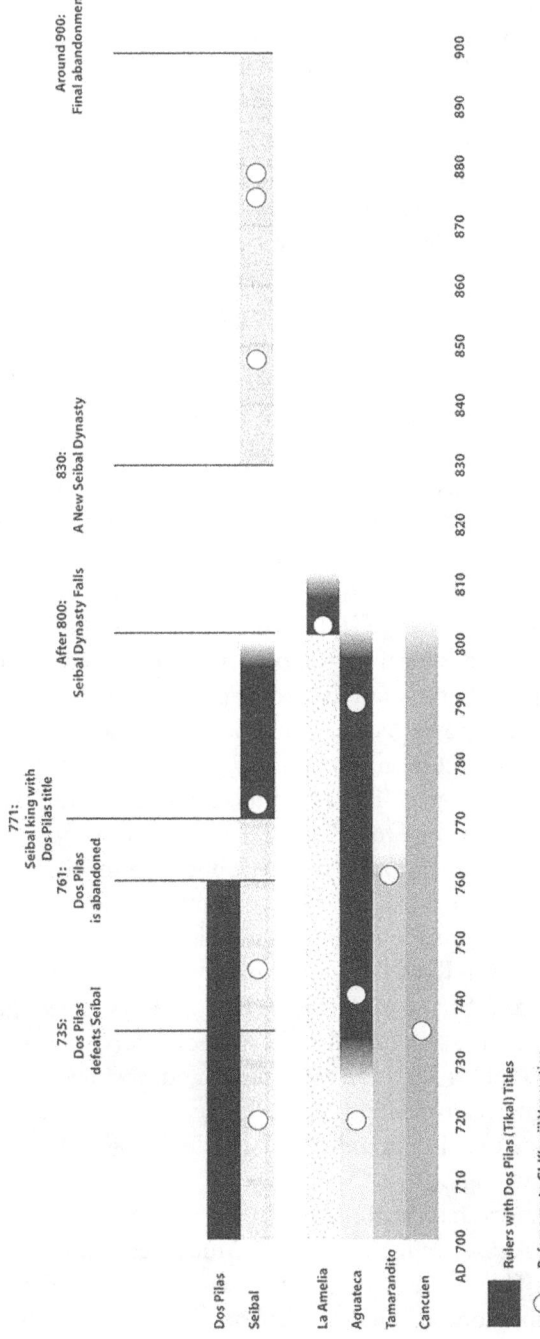

FIGURE 4.5. *Timeline showing references to the patron god GI–K'awiil and political changes in the Petexbatun region of Guatemala*

importance at other sites. Referring to a set of calendar rites performed in 721, the stela mentioned the "adorning" or "presentation" (*nawaj*) of the effigy of GI-K'awiil at Seibal (Houston and Stuart 1996:302) and the carving of a stela for GI-K'awiil at Aguateca.

The third ruler of Dos Pilas was married to a woman from Cancuen whose name included GI-K'awiil (Houston 1993:113). Although it is somewhat unusual for individuals in Maya inscriptions to be named for patron deities, this is not a unique case. It suggests that Cancuen also venerated GI-K'awiil, although no inscriptions from Cancuen itself can confirm this.

Not content to simply form political alliances with its neighbors, the Dos Pilas dynasty began a gradual takeover of the Petexbatun region. Aguateca became a twin capital rather than an independent kingdom (Houston 1993:116). In 735 the Dos Pilas ruler attacked Seibal, apparently destroying a deity effigy in the process (see above, "the painted back of K'awiil was chopped"). Thereafter, Seibal explicitly acknowledged the Dos Pilas dynasty as an overlord (Houston 1993:116). But after these political changes the veneration of GI-K'awiil at both Aguateca and Seibal continued on. In 741 K'awiil Chan K'inich, the fourth ruler of the Dos Pilas dynasty, performed a ritual scattering of droplets at Aguateca in the presence of GI-K'awiil. This indicates that the Dos Pilas ruler actually adopted the local patron of a site that he took over rather than introducing the gods that his family had imported from Tikal. In 746, a new ruler of Seibal came to power. Although he was an acknowledged client of the Dos Pilas dynasty, his accession ceremony was overseen by GI-K'awiil.

A hieroglyphic stairway at Tamarandito recorded events in 761 that had profound consequences for Dos Pilas and the whole region. K'awiil Chan K'inich was forced to flee, not to be mentioned again in later inscriptions (Martin and Grube 2000:63). Tamarandito itself was also attacked, although the identity of the aggressors in these two incidents remains unclear. Finally, the text mentioned GI-K'awiil, giving him credit for some sort of military victory (Houston and Stuart 1996:302; LeFort 1998:15). Although this text is ambiguous, I interpret it to mean that Tamarandito survived the turmoil with the help of the god. Dos Pilas, on the other hand, was hastily abandoned at this time, and Aguateca became the primary seat of the dynasty (O' Mansky and Dunning 2004:94). Tamarandito did not last long either and was abandoned within a few years.

By 771, the dynasty had begun to splinter, with petty kings ruling from Aguateca, Seibal, Aguas Calientes, and La Amelia, each claiming Tikal (Dos Pilas) royal titles (Houston 1993:119–21; Houston and Mathews 1985:18–24; Martin and Grube 2000:64–65). The splintered dynasty thus replaced the local rulers at each of these sites but continued to venerate GI-K'awiil. At Seibal, for example, the new king impersonated GI-K'awiil in 771. In 790 the Aguateca ruler performed a calendar ritual overseen by GI-K'awiil. At La Amelia the accession of the king in 802 was overseen by the god.

Not long after the start of the ninth century, royal authority collapsed in the Petexbatun region. The remnants of the Dos Pilas dynasty ceased to dedicate carved monuments. But in 830 a new dynasty, with different royal titles, established itself at Seibal (Schele in Martin and Grube 2000:227). The origin of these new rulers was the distant site of Ucanal (Schele and Mathews 1998:179). But they adopted the veneration of GI-K'awiil, just as earlier rulers had. In 849 the ruler impersonated the god, recorded on Stela 10 (Schele and Mathews 1998:185). In 874 Stela 3 also named GI-K'awiil, although the reference is hard to interpret. Stela 14, possibly dating to 879, was said to belong to GI-K'awiil. Not long after, royal authority disappeared again, and Seibal was abandoned.

This is a complex example, but it effectively demonstrates that the god GI-K'awiil was associated with a geographical location rather than with a particular ruling dynasty. By tracing the references to the deity at Seibal, for example, it is clear that his veneration continued unabated under rulers with three different dynastic origins (and three different emblem glyphs). While the Dos Pilas dynasty brought patron gods with it when it founded a new site, the move to new capitals necessitated the adoption of the local deity. Of course, none of these inscriptions mentions the common people who lived in this region. But the association between a god and a place on the landscape— as at Copan—suggests that GI-K'awiil belonged to all of the region's inhabitants rather than simply the royal family.

Gods' Protective Powers

Some Classic period hieroglyphic inscriptions suggest that gods were given credit for events that may have benefited the community as a whole. For example, a number of monuments placed patron gods at the center of calendrical period endings. The Mesoamerican calendar was extremely complex, and a full discussion is beyond the scope of this book. The Maya themselves emphasized the twenty-year cycle, called the *winikhaab* during the Classic Period and the *k'atun* in later times. Each of these twenty-year periods had a special set of prognostications and was marked with the dedication of stelae and altars. Copan Stela 7, referring to four local gods, recorded "they completed the calendar period" (*utzutzuw pik uchabjiiy* [gods]). Tikal Stela 3 used the same construction, "they completed the 13th year" (*utzutzuw huxlajun haab*). On Tikal

Stela 31 the word *tahnlam*, meaning "halfway through a twenty-year period," was given a verbal suffix, *-aj*, deriving it as an intransitive verb (Houston, Robertson, and Stuart 2000:325), and followed by a list of several patron gods. This can be roughly translated as "the gods halve the twenty-year period." All three of these examples imply that the gods themselves were responsible for the passage of time. Given the importance of these period endings within the cosmology of the Classic Maya, the gods' intercession in time's passage would doubtless have been seen as a benefit to society as a whole.

In addition, the aforementioned Yaxha Stela 31, and possibly the Tamarandito hieroglyphic stairway, explicitly credited the sites' patron deities with success in war (LeFort 1998:15; Martin and Grube 2000:82). References on the Tikal lintels to deity effigies carried into battle also suggest that gods were attributed a protective role in military hostilities (Martin 1996, 2000a). While wars ultimately served the political ambitions of the Maya elite, they would clearly have had a profound effect on commoners as well, who would have had to endure raids on their homes and crops as well as possible death or enslavement. Patron deities would have been well worth venerating if they were believed to confer such protection.

EVIDENCE FOR PATRON DEITIES IN LATER PERIODS

All of the hieroglyphic texts I have analyzed in this chapter had semantic content describing political and ritual events that in all likelihood actually took place. But beyond this semantic function, all of them contained pragmatic functions as well—they indexically linked the rulers and nobles who commissioned them to political relationships, military success, or status differentials. As I discussed in chapter 2, discourses that comment upon the indexical nature of signs are *metapragmatic*. And metapragmatic activity plays a key role in disseminating social norms and hierarchies. Written texts, as well as spoken discourses that must also have circulated during the Classic period, constantly shaped and reinforced the model that patron gods were linked with political communities and were cared for by rulers. The hieroglyphic texts I have examined are thus metapragmatic links on long semiotic chains that connected patron deity effigies, ritual offerings, and status differentials between human beings.

While the archaeological and epigraphic record affords only a partial reconstruction of these semiotic chains that operated during the Classic period, they may have continued to stretch across time and space to survive partially intact today. If so, ethnographic analogies can be used cautiously to reconstruct missing information. In the following pages I will trace patron deity veneration practices from the period of Spanish contact through the recent past using historical and ethnographic accounts. This information allows me to propose an answer to why Maya commoners may have found patron deity veneration important and why they were such a central component of ruler's claims to legitimacy.

Patron Deities at Contact

A number of written documents produced in the years immediately after the Spanish conquest give a rich account of patron deity veneration across Mesoamerica in the Postclassic period. In the Maya area the most useful of these is the famous Popol Vuh, or "Council Book," which contains the history of the K'iche' people of highland Guatemala (Christenson 2003). In the early eighteenth century a Catholic priest named Francisco Ximenez obtained the manuscript, which he transcribed and translated into Spanish. The original is now lost, and all that survives is the Ximenez transcription. Other highland documents also provide important supplemental information. The Título de Totonicapan (Carmack and Mondloch 1983) was written in the sixteenth century by a group of K'iche' leaders and was first translated into Spanish in 1834 by the priest Dioniso José Chonay. The Kaqchikels are a closely related ethnic group who also live in highland Guatemala. They recorded their account of history in the Annals of the Kaqchikels, also known as the Memorial de Sololá, between 1571 and 1604 (Otzoy 1999). In 1844 it was discovered in the archives of a convent and translated by abbot Charles Etienne Brasseur de Bourborg. Though all three documents were written after the conquest using the Spanish alphabet, they clearly reflect pre-Columbian beliefs and narrate a history stretching back to the first human beings.

The Popol Vuh is divided into two sections. The first of these is more famous and tells of the creation of the world and the heroic deeds of gods. But the second part of the book is more informative about patron deities. It begins with the creation of the first human beings. According to the story, the gods created the first four men out of maize dough, and three of them went on to found the ruling lineages of the K'iche's. These four men traveled to the primordial city of Tulan, where other nations were also present. At Tulan each of the nations received patron gods in the form of effigies. Each of the four K'iche' progenitors received a patron god. The most important of these was Tohil, given to the senior K'inche' lineage, founded by Balam Quitze. *Tohil* refers to obligation, debt, or tribute (Christenson 2003:211). The second god was called Auilix, meaning "you are cared for," and the third was Hakavitz and was possibly a fire god (Christenson 2003:211). The fourth god was called Nicacah, meaning "Middle Valley," and was given to Balam Acab, the only one of the four original K'iche' men who did not found a lineage and was not mentioned again (Christenson 2003:212).

The Annals of the Kaqchikels tell a similar story of gods at Tulan. According to this document, the Kaqchikels received a god named Chay Ab'äj, meaning "Obsidian Stone." They were later given three other gods as well: B'eleje' Toj ("Nine Storm"), Jun Tijax ("One Flint"), and K'axtok' ("Deceiver") (Otzoy 1999:157; Orellana 1981:159; Christenson 2003:97). Oddly, the Popol Vuh reports none of these gods but instead says that the Kaqchikels received a god called Chimalkan ("serpent that moves quietly") (Christenson 2003:231).

The gods who created the universe and the first people were clearly differentiated from patron gods in the Popol Vuh, although both categories were referred to using the term *k'ab'awil*. Recall that Classic period inscriptions implied a connection between general gods and patron gods, since they were both referred to as *k'uh*. In Classic period inscriptions gods that started out as general deities "touched the earth" to become patrons of particular communities. In the Popol Vuh a messenger from the creator gods admonished the first K'iche' men, "Tohil is your god (*k'ab'awil*). He is your provider. He is also a substitute and remembrance of your Framer and Shaper [creator gods]" (Christenson 2003:215). These documents also emphasized the physical nature of the patron deity effigies as opposed to the nonphysical nature of the creator gods. Before they received their patron gods, the Popol Vuh states, "[The first people] did not yet call upon wood or stone. They remembered the word of the Framer and the Shaper..." (Christenson 2003:206). The Título de Totonicapan mentioned that the god Hakavitz was made of precious stones (Carmack and Mondloch 1983:177). Stone effigies were also implied by the names of the Kaqchikels' gods, and Chay Ab'äj was at one point called "the wood and the stone" (Otzoy 1999:156). Occasionally, however, these deities appeared in other forms: the K'iche' patron gods appeared as young men (Christenson 2003:240), while the god K'axtok' possessed a man in order to tell the Kaqchikels not to pay tribute to the Spaniards (Otzoy 1999:187). There is no evidence in the Classic period for patron gods appearing as men, but god impersonation may be the Classic period equivalent of deity possession.

Just as in the Classic period, patron deities among these Guatemalan highland groups played an important role in interethnic relationships. Immediately after leaving Tulan, the K'iche' and other nations suffered from cold since the first sunrise had not yet occurred. Tohil gave fire to the K'iche' so they could survive. Other nations came to beg the K'iche' to share this fire, but Tohil refused to give it unless they would pledge to embrace him. This turned out to be a clever trick in which the nations inadvertently pledged to give up their hearts in sacrifice to Tohil, a prediction of the future political dominance of the K'iche' nation. Only the Kaqchikel nation did not fall for the trick and simply stole the fire instead. This narrative emphasized their deceit while providing an explanation for the inability of the K'iche' to conquer them. Similar to the accounts from Classic period inscriptions, patron deity effigies among these highland groups were targets for attacking armies. In the Popol Vuh enemy nations plotted to capture Tohil: "This Tohil, he is a god. We also shall worship him. But we shall capture him" (Christenson 2003:248). According to the Annals of the Kaqchikels, they were successful in capturing Tohil after a battle (Otzoy 1999:178). And similar to Classic period accounts, a passage in the Título de Totonicapan also describes a friendly, diplomatic gathering of lords and their patron gods (Carmack and Mondloch 1983:195–96).

Postclassic highland rulers performed the same services to patron gods as those recorded in Classic period inscriptions. When the K'iche' founded their capital at Cumarcah, they built temples for the three patron gods. They also made offerings to feed the deities, such as the extracted hearts of captured enemies and autosacrificial blood from rulers themselves: "You shall carry out your responsibilities by first piercing your ears. You shall prick your elbows. This shall be your petition, your way of giving thanks before the face of the god" (Christenson 2003:219). Other offerings included animal blood, pine resin incense, flowers, and corn. Similar offerings were also described in the Título de Totonicapan and Annals of the Kaqchikels (Carmack and Mondloch 1983:191; Otzoy 1999:155, 168). The latter document admonishes the Kaqchikels that they must "carry, feed, and eat with" their gods (Otzoy 1999:156). This suggests a similar set of obligations reflected in Classic period inscriptions, whereby gods were handled and fed. It also suggests the additional requirement to participate in commensal feasts with patron deities. In addition to feasting, periodic fasting and sexual abstinence by K'iche rulers and ritual specialists were also emphasized in the Popol Vuh as a necessary aspect of patron deity veneration. Finally, a passage from the Título de Totonicapan describes a ceremony in which Tohil's effigy was dressed, just as Palenque's gods were dressed in the panels from the Temple of the Inscriptions: "the son of the ruler was the first to load the hand of Tohil with jades, metals, mirrors and offerings all around, and a loin cloth wound around his hips" (my translation is based on Carmack and Mondloch 1983:196; Christenson 1993).

The Guatemalan highlands are not the only source of information about Contact-era patron deities. Other historical records indicate that similar practices took place across the Maya area and in Mesoamerica more broadly. For example, the Paxbolon-Moldonado Papers were written in the early seventeenth century to record the merits of Don Pablo Paxbolon, Maya governor of Tixchel on the Yucatan Peninsula. The document recounted the conversion of the Acalan Chontal by Fray Diego de Béjar: "He wanted everyone to come and display his idols. Having heard what the father told them, they began to bring out their idols, first the idol of the ruler, which bears the name of Cukulchan, also the devil of Tadzunun, and those of Tachabte, Atapan, and Taçacto, and the other idols. . . . The idols hidden in their secret places by the Indians, such as Ykchua, for so this idol was called, another called Tabay, another called Ixchel, another called Cabtanilcabtan, and many other places of idols were sought out in all the pueblos" (Scholes and Roys 1968:395).

In this passage each of the four quarters of the city of Itzamkanac had its own patron god: Tadzunun had Ykchua, Tachabte had Tabay, Atapan had Ixchel, and Taçacto had Cabtanilcabtan. The principal patron god of the whole city was Cukulchan and was associated with the ruler himself. Of these five gods, Ykchua, Ixchel, and Cukulchan are all recognizable names of general gods who were common across the Yucatan and were apparently adopted as local patrons.

Similar references to patron deities can also be found in Spanish accounts of the Itza Maya of Lake Petén Itza in what is now northern Guatemala. This independent kingdom survived the Spanish conquest until 1697, when it was finally brought under the administration of Yucatan. Various Spaniards visited Noh Peten, the island capital of the Itza, and described a large number of temples. The Franciscan missionary Avendaño went to the island in 1696 and reported "nine very large buildings, made in the form of churches of this province [Yucatan]" (Means 1917:18). Villaguitierre, who compiled the history of the conquest of the Itza in 1701 from various firsthand accounts, reports that General Ursua and his men found twenty-one temples when they invaded Noh Peten the following year (Villagutierre Soto-Mayor 1983:313). Among these was one principal temple while all the others "were common to all the people. . . . In none of these sanctuaries did they perform the cruel sacrifice of taking out live hearts, nor anything of this kind, except in the main sanctuary or temple" (Villagutierre Soto-Mayor 1983:316). Jones (1998:73) reports that the conquering Spaniards referred to the nine tallest of these sanctuaries as "*adoratorios.*" These may have corresponded to the nine mentioned by Avendaño. He argues that these nine temples corresponded to the eight administrative districts of the Itza kingdom, with an extra principal temple corresponding to the capital. If so, this would be a similar organization to that described at Itzamkanac, in which political/administrative districts each had its own deity.

The Spanish visitors also described the deities venerated by the Itza. The most famous of these was an effigy of a horse called Tziminchak (Thunder Tapir),[6] which was destroyed by the Franciscan missionary Fuensalida when he visited the capital in 1618. The effigy is supposed to have represented a horse left behind by Cortes when he passed through the Petén in 1525 (Villagutierre Soto-Mayor 1983:72–73). The later missionary Avendaño claims to have seen "a box suspended, in which we saw indistinctly (although hastily) a bone of the leg or thigh, very large in size, which appeared to be that of a horse (Means 1917:136). When Ursua conquered the Itza in 1697, in the main temple of Noh Peten he found "a half decayed shin bone; below it was a small bag, three handbreadths long, and in it were small pieces of bone, also decayed. . . . Among other things, when they asked a very old Indian woman who had been captured the day the Petén was taken what the shin bone and the other fragments were, she replied it was the tezmín [tapir] of the great captain . . . they were the bones of a horse that had been entrusted by a king who passed by there a long time ago" (Villagutierre Soto-Mayor 1983:314). The fact that three separate Spaniards who visited the Itza capital specifically mentioned this veneration of Cortes's horse indicates the total fascination that they had both for this foreign religious practice and for Cortes's legacy. However, given the lack of actual information about the horse's veneration and the unusual circumstances under which it came to be worshipped, I hesitate to put it in the category of a patron god.

Other deities, however, are more easily classified as patron gods. According to Villagutierre Soto-Mayor (1983:302–3), "they had two other idols which they adored as gods of battle: one they called Pakoc, and the other, Hexchunchan. They carried them when they went to fight the Chinamitas, their mortal frontier enemies, and when they were going into battle they burned copal [incense] and when they performed some valiant action their idols, whom they consulted, gave them answers, and in the mitotes or dances they spoke to them and danced with them." This description matches documents from the Guatemalan highlands, in which patron gods were also carried to war, and Classic period accounts of similar practices.[7]

The veneration of patron deities was not unique to the Maya area, and Contact-era accounts of similar religious practices can be found across Mesoamerican ethnic groups. Although there are some notable differences between the religious practices of different Mesoamerican peoples, this broader region was united by constant contact and economic exchange. Because of these far-flung social relationships, Mesoamerican peoples shared a common semiotic network, in which discourses about gods and politics could have radiated over great distances and in multiple directions. For this reason, data from Postclassic non-Maya groups can also be useful for reconstructing the Classic Maya semiotic context.

Among the Mixtecs and Zapotecs of Oaxaca, for example, numerous Spanish chroniclers reported the presence of stone and wooden effigies of deities, to whom they offered sacrificial blood and animal sacrifices (Lind 2015; Spores 1983:344).[8] One Zapotec chronicler noted, "all of the natives of these communities worshipped the devil in the form of a statue made of wood and stoned which they called deities . . . each pueblo had a deity as its patron which it revered above all the rest" (quoted in Spores 1983:344). Whitecotton (1977:159) notes that the Zapotec town of Teocuicuilco held a feast in honor of its patron every 260 days, in which the people of the town brought quails, feathers, and precious stones to give to the god's priests. The priests then performed autosacrificial rites for the god and supplicated on behalf of the community for health and agricultural fertility.

The *Relación de Michoacán*, which tells the history of the Tarascan Empire, relates that villages throughout the region had specific gods, which were carried into battle on the backs of priests (Craine and Reindorp 1970:23, 28, 104). The patron of the ruling ethnic group, Curicaueri, was also brought into battle on a dais made of branches (24). The veneration of Curicaueri involved covering him in blankets to keep him warm, feeding him soup, dressing him, and burning fires in his temples (104).

Accounts of patron deity veneration among the Aztecs are especially informative.[9] The Spanish friar Duran (1971:128) noted, "in pagan times each of the cities, towns, and villages of New Spain had its own god worshipped by the natives. And though the gods were revered by all, adored, and their feasts celebrated, each town had a special one who served as patron of the place, honored with greater ceremonies and sacrifices." Of these, the most famous was Huitzilopochtli ("Hummingbird on the Left"), patron of the Mexica of Tenochtitlan. Details of the veneration of this god appeared in numerous historical accounts from the Colonial period by both Spanish and Native authors. The story of the acquisition of Huitzilopochtli by the Mexica was similar to the account in the Popol Vuh. Like the K'iche', the Mexica were said to have migrated from their original homeland carrying the god effigy with them. When they arrived in Central Mexico, they came into conflict with other Aztec groups who were already there, each with its own gods. Huitzilopochtli guided the Mexica, commanding them to migrate until they reached the site where they founded Tenochtitlan.

In addition to this principal god, the Mexica also carried deities that would eventually represent the various administrative quarters of Tenochtitlan (Chimalpahin 1997). According to (Duran 1994:46), "Huitzilopochtli commanded them to distribute the gods among them and that each barrio choose a special place where the deities might be revered. Thus each neighborhood was divided into many small sections according to the number of idols it possessed." This organization is thus similar to that observed at Itzamkanac and at the Itza capital.

The Mexica venerated Huitzilopochtli in ways similar to those observed among the Maya. They frequently offered human blood, either in the form of sacrificed captives or with the blood of autosacrifice. According to Duran (1994:357), the emperor Ahuitzotl ritually dressed Huitzilopochtli. Temple building was also an important aspect of his veneration—when they reached Tenochtitlan, this was the Mexica's first task (46).

Aztec patron gods also played a role in relationships with other communities, just as with the Classic and Postclassic Maya examples. The Aztec glyph for conquest was a temple with a collapsed roof with flames shooting out (Nicholson 1971:409–10). Just as recorded in the Maya inscriptions of Tikal, the Mexica captured the gods of their enemies, bringing them back to Tenochtitlan and housing them in a prison-temple, where they were maintained in ritual exile (Sahagún 1969a:234). Relationships with pacified nations were indexed by veneration rituals for Huitzilopochtli. Nobles from subordinate communities paid their respects to the deity, offering him feathers, weapons, jewelry, animal skins, and autosacrificial blood (Duran 1994:158). Duran described an incident in which a war between Chalco and the Mexica was reframed as a fight between patron gods. Chalco, attempting to buy some time during the war, told the Mexica they had an announcement: "O brothers, know that five days from now we shall celebrate the festival of our god Camaxtli and we wish to celebrate with the blood of Aztecs so that our god will be more honored and glorified. Therefore, we ask that on that our god's day you come into the field, in this very place, to join us in battle, because we wish to solemnize our feast with your flesh" (138). Sadly for the Chalcas, they lost the subsequent battle, for which the Mexica taunted them: "O little girls, do not ask for another truce because we shall not grant it to you.... On this spot you will find out who the Aztecs are, and we shall see who celebrates the feast of their god, the Chalcas or the Aztecs! Let us see how you fulfill the oath you have sworn to your god!" (140).

In summary, the historical evidence from Postclassic Mesoamerica indicates that Maya, Zapotec, Tarascan, and Aztec ethnic groups practiced patron deity veneration quite similar to that of the Classic Maya. All of these groups had gods that they associated with particular places and political units, including whole communities as well as individual neighborhoods or administrative districts. These patron gods took the form of physical effigies made of wood or stone. They also had similar veneration practices for these gods such as feeding and dressing them, carrying them, and building temples for them. Also similar was the role patron deities had in indexing friendly and hostile relationships between communities, especially in war.

The Colonial Encounter

Upon their arrival, Spanish missionaries observed the similarities between patron deity veneration and that of patron saint veneration in their native country. For example, Duran (1971:128) noted, "each town had a special [god] who served as patron of the place. The same situation exists today, for, though the people solemnize the feasts of all the saints, the feast of the town and its patron is carried out with the utmost solemnity. So in ancient times on the feasts of the idols each village had its own idol as patron. On this day extremely elaborate festivities and expenditures were common."

The veneration of patron saints in Spanish communities in fact departed from the canonical Catholic doctrine that missionary friars espoused. The theology of the universal Catholic Church was based on sacraments, liturgy, and an official holiday calendar. Spanish folk Catholicism was based on sacred places on the landscape, images, relics, patron saints, and a holiday calendar that was sometimes at odds with the official one (Christian 1981). Patron saints themselves came in several different varieties. Some were inhabitants of the local community, believed to have led saintly lives, whose remains became objects of devotion after their deaths. Others were cults centered on the Virgin Mary, with a local aspect tied to landscape features such as springs or trees (Christian 1981:125). Finally, if Mary's protection proved insufficient to protect the town, other patron saints were introduced to deal with specific problems such as natural disasters or illness. Often the coincidence of such a disaster with a particular saint's day in the Catholic calendar was taken as a clear sign that the saint should be chosen as patron.

Once a Spanish town chose a patron saint, the whole community took on responsibility for his or her devotion in the form of a vow (Christian 1981). These vows included the obligation to build a chapel, carve the saint's image, and especially to observe the saint's feast day. This last obligation required fasting the day before the saint's day, not working on the appointed day, holding a precession to the chapel, and hosting a feast in which all members of the community, including the poor, could eat commensally with the saint. Small agricultural communities in sixteenth-century Spain could lose only a certain number of workdays per year, especially during the harvest season, before they reduced their yields. This meant that towns often came into conflict with the Universal Church, which considered universal holidays more important than local devotions (Christian 1981:174–75).

Parishioners in rural Spain compared their patron saints to the familiar hierarchy of the Spanish royal bureaucracy (Christian 1981:56). Communities were frequently involved in administrative disputes over lands, taxes, and obligations to the nobility. These cases were argued by hired attorneys in far-off courts using communal funds and town debts. Similarly, the term *abogado*, meaning "advocate" or "lawyer," was applied to patron saints, and villages paid them for their intercession before God in the form of debts for future masses and workdays. In return, saints did not merely placate a wrathful God but confronted unnamed adversaries to obtain his favor. Christian (1981:56) sees in these beliefs an analogy to the "monarch who rewards and punishes after multiple intrigues and influences of favorites."

Friars, trained in doctrines of the Universal Church, would express reluctant tolerance for such local beliefs of the Spanish countryside, sometimes wondering if they had a whiff of paganism. On the other hand, these same friars often spoke with pride about the local shrines in towns where they themselves grew up (Christian 1981:20). Missionizing friars brought the same attitude to New Spain, where they attempted to indoctrinate indigenous communities to the beliefs of the Catholic Church, while simultaneously bringing a fondness for their childhood devotions and, in some cases, a tolerance for local beliefs. Once friars began to found churches in Mesoamerica, they insisted that each church should have a patron saint (*abogado*) and set about introducing them (Lockhart 1992:244). In some cases, friars intentionally chose saints with similarities to local patron gods and, in other cases, assigned them purely based on personal whims (Farriss 1984:310; Lockhart 1992:244). These new cults directly competed with patron deity veneration at the community level (Farriss 1984:300).

Nutini (1976) provides four examples of this process in Tlaxcala, Central Mexico. Prior to the conquest, Tezcatlipoca was the patron god of Tianguismanalco and was replaced by San Juan. Nutini notes iconography on the church altar related to this ancient deity. Similarly, Santa Ana replaced the goddess Toci in the town of Chiautempan, since they were both grandmothers of major deities. San Bernardino replaced Camaxtli, the patron god of the whole Tlaxcalan polity. Finally, the Virgin of Ocoltán replaced Xochiquetzalli, the wife of Camaxtli. Xochiquetzalli was a goddess associated with arts and flowers and was said to appear to supplicants in a burning pine tree. Iconography depicted her in a blue shirt and white skirt. The cult of the Virgin of Ocoltán began in 1541 when an indigenous man, Juan Diego Bernardino, reported the appearance of the Virgin Mary within a burning pine tree, dressed in a blue blouse and white skirt. She told him to build her sanctuary atop the ruins of the Xochiquetzalli shrine. The cult spread so rapidly that local friars felt obligated to confirm the miracle. Friar Hojacastro's account concludes that the event was providential because the Virgin chose to appear to Juan Diego in a form that the indigenous population could understand. He expressed some doubts that it was actually the Virgin that appeared, rather than the pre-Columbian goddess herself, but reasoned that it didn't really matter, since everything would eventually become clear to the pilgrims who came to the new chapel. While the Virgin of Ocoltán thus has obvious pre-Columbian features, Nutini (1976) argues that she is in fact a new supernatural entity created from a fusion of two belief systems.

Some readers will recognize a similarity between the story of the Virgin of Ocoltán and that of the Virgin of Guadalupe, the patroness of the modern Mexican nation. The Virgin of Guadalupe appeared to another indigenous man named Juan Diego in 1531 at a site called Tepeyacac outside of Mexico City. Her image was imprinted on his cloak and is now considered a holy relic. The chronicler Sahagún (1969b:352) claimed that Tepeyacac was the site of an ancient shrine to a pre-Columbian goddess and that the cult of the Virgin was therefore pagan in origin. While some scholars (Burkhart 1993; Poole 1994) have expressed skepticism for Sahagún's claim, Lopez Lujan and Noguez (2011) describe two large pre-Columbian rock carvings on the adjacent hill of Zacahuitzco featuring depictions of pre-Columbian female deities, demonstrating the ritual importance of the location in pre-Columbian times. But while the Virgin of Guadalupe thus has an association with a pre-Columbian goddess, features of Juan Diego's story are clearly Spanish in origin. A recurring narrative in local Spanish religion was the appearance of the Virgin in the landscape outside of town to a marginalized member of the community such as a poor child. When this witness reports the miracle, authorities do not initially believe him. Eventually, the witness is vindicated and glorified, and the story serves as a morality tale about belief in God's miracles (Christian 1981:81). Juan Diego's story followed this familiar pattern: a young, marginalized indigenous man saw the Virgin, but he was not believed by the local clergy until he could produce her image on his cloak. Thus, pre-Columbian and Spanish beliefs and narratives were melded to create the Virgin of Guadalupe, a new entity.

Once patron saints had been assigned, indigenous Mesoamerican towns often developed mythologies explaining how the saint was chosen or pushing it into the pre-Columbian past. Watanabe (1990:135) gives an example from the town of Santiago Chimaltenango, Guatemala:

> They tell of when the first Chimaltecos found Santiago in the mountains.... After building the church that still stands in the center of town, these ancestral Chimaltecos fetched Santiago to his new home. The next morning he was gone. Searchers eventually found him back where they had first encountered him and once more returned him to the church. Again he fled to his old place but this time when they tried to carry him back to town, Santiago made himself so heavy that no one could lift him. Exasperated, the ancestors beat him with whips to get him into the church, leaving gouges on his back that can still be seen today. Santiago has dutifully abided in the church ever since.

Watanabe refers to the beating of Santiago as the "domestication" of the saint. But it is possible to apply the term more broadly to many ritual practices, which established indexical links between a foreign saint's image and an indigenous town, as well as such mythical narratives themselves, which metapragmatically characterize the origin of this indexical linkage. Once this domestication process occurred, patron saints took over the role of pre-Columbian patron deities.

The Veneration of Patron Saints

As I noted in chapter 3, Classic Maya patron gods can be distinguished from venerated ancestors by the terms used to refer them, their physical nature in the form of effigies, and in their active influence on the world. And while Classic Maya patron gods were of the same substance as more general, universal gods, they were unique to particular communities, forming special relationships with them. Similar supernatural categories can be distinguished among modern Maya groups of the Guatemalan highlands, as observed by John Watanabe (1990).[10] The Christian belief in saints as real historical figures that have been favored by God has disappeared, and saints are seen as purely supernatural entities. They can be distinguished from ancestors, who were once living people and founders of the communities and their traditions. Ancestors were the original owners of family lands, and offerings are made to them in order to maintain claim to these plots. Patron saints, however, were not founders but were introduced and domesticated by them. As (Watanabe 1990:140–41) explained, "Maya saint and ancestor persist as distinct images of community.... Neither figure, however, can now do without the other: alone, each contradicts itself—the stranger-saint who precipitates community, the life-giving ancestor whose now lifeless bones lie in the cemetery . . . . Mythically, ancestors appear to antedate the coming of the saints, yet only when the saints arrive are towns founded, churches built, and orderly social life established." This narrative is strikingly similar to that preserved in the inscriptions of Palenque, in which the city's patron gods "touched the earth" with the help of the dynastic founder.

Watanabe (1990) recognizes a third supernatural category in Santiago Chimaltenango, the Earth Lords. These entities live in the mountains surrounding the community. They are believed to possess great wealth, which they can grant to people, but are amoral and intractable, sometimes stealing souls. As such, they are often represented with characteristics similar to Ladino plantation owners. This reflects the racial politics of Guatemala in which Ladinos have access to wealth but live by different moral and cultural values than the indigenous population. Similar entities exist in other highland communities as well—represented as Ladinos, believed to control wealth, associated with mountains, and feared for their amoral nature. They are variously referred to as "mountain owners" (Siegel 1941; Watanabe 1990, 1992), Satan (Warren 1978), Judas (Bunzel 1959; Warren 1978; Watanabe 1992), and Maximon (Christenson 2001; Reina 1966; Watanabe 1992). In some towns these entities serve a similar role as the patron saints, while in other cases they are separate from the community. I believe Earth Lords to be similar to certain kinds of Classic Maya general deities—largely aloof unless brought into a patron-client relationship with a particular town.

Ritual practices of patron deity veneration recorded in early periods of Maya history have survived to the present day. Maya communities today see their saint effigies not as mere representations of supernatural figures but as their actual physical manifestations. This is apparent in the fact that many towns have more than one effigy of the same Catholic saint but consider them to be separate entities (Christenson 2001; Watanabe 1992; Wisdom 1940). For example, Santiago Chimaltenango has two images of Santiago (Saint James). The patron of the town is Santiago *Patrón*, while a smaller image, Santiago *Chiquito*, is prayed to separately. In his study of the Chorti Maya, Wisdom (1940:413) noted that all the saints with the same names from different towns were considered brothers, but not the same individuals.

Just as in earlier periods, the veneration of modern patron saints largely involves the care and maintenance of their effigies. This includes dressing the saint and making sure its clothes are clean and in good repair (Cancian 1965:34; Christenson 2001:92; Reina 1966:105, 145; Vogt 1993:118; Wisdom

1940:417), making sure the saint's home, the church, is cleaned and maintained (Cancian 1965:34–35; Oakes 1951:60; Reina 1966:102; Siebers 1999:53; Watanabe 1992:109), and keeping the altars of the saints well supplied with fragrant flowers, candles, and incense (Bunzel 1959:166; Cancian 1965:34; Oakes 1951:60; Reina 1966:102; Siebers 1999:53; Valladares 1957:148; Vogt 1993:18; Watanabe 1992:124; Wisdom 1940:376, 281).

Another important aspect of patron saint veneration is feeding and food sharing. In the case of the patron saint fiesta—which is set according to the Catholic, rather than pre-Columbian, calendar—all members of the human community are invited to participate in public feasting. This involves the consumption of huge amounts of alcohol and food (Bunzel 1959:254; Cancian 1965:38; Redfield and Villa Rojas 1962:150–56; Siebers 1999:64, 66; Siegel 1941:72; Watanabe 1992:124; Wisdom 1940:385, 387, 449–50). But patron saint fiestas also involve a more private kind of feast. Here only ritual specialists who organized the town fiesta are invited to participate along with their guests (Brintnall 1979:98; Bunzel 1959:166–68, 194–95; Cancian 1965:38, 41; Christenson 2009; La Farge 1994:116; Redfield and Villa Rojas 1962:154–55; Reina 1966:138; Siebers 1999:54; Watanabe 1992:124; Wisdom 1940:375). Both public and private feasts are carried out, usually multiple times, during any given fiesta.

Saints themselves are also fed during these public fiestas. Offerings can take the form of solid foods such as tortillas but often include liquids such as water, rum, stew, maize gruel, chocolate, or coffee (Reina 1966:115; Sullivan 1989:96; Watanabe 1992:76; Wisdom 1940:387). In addition, informants often state that saints "eat" candles and incense, as if they were food (Bunzel 1959:166; Reina 1966:120; Vogt 1993:1). As mentioned above, the idea of commensality with a saint was present in local Catholicism in sixteenth-century Spain (Christian 1981:59), so it is possible that the idea of saint feeding was partially imported during the conquest. On the other hand, offerings of food and drink are reminiscent of the Classic Maya *k'uh* glyph, depicting a god sustained by ritual liquid. They are also consistent with pre-Columbian narratives describing the feeding of blood, chocolate, and pulque to patron gods.

In addition to ritual feasting, some modern Maya ritual specialists engage in fasting. This can involve brief periods in which only corn is eaten (Wisdom 1940:435) or the practitioner abstains from meat, salt, and spices (La Farge 1994:114). It can also include longer periods of sexual abstinence up to a year (Oakes 1951:60; Wisdom 1940:376, 435). These requirements of fasting and feasting parallel patron deity veneration from earlier periods of Maya history.

Using Ethnographic Information to Interpret the Classic Period

The many similarities between patron deity veneration among the Classic Maya and that of later Mesoamerica indicate that the semiotic chains linking deity effigies, ritual offerings, and status hierarchies probably remained largely intact. This means that these documents can be used to reconstruct pieces of the wider semiotic context of patron deity veneration that are no longer available for the Classic period. Specifically, how did the indexical linkages between rulers and patron gods contribute to a ruler's social entitlements? How was patron deity veneration connected to the lives of ordinary people?

It is clear from historical and ethnographic documents that there was a close association between patron deities and ethnic or local identity during the Postclassic, Colonial, and modern periods. In the Popol Vuh, for example, the veneration of Tohil was tied to K'iche' ethnicity. This text was written by and for the Nima K'iche's, the dominant group of ruling lineages. Other K'iche' groups included the Tamub and the Ilocab. Although these groups were politically separate from one another, they all received Tohil as a god at the mythical Tulan, joining them in a single ethnic identity: "thus was the naming of the three K'iche's. But in this they freed themselves because it was the same god's name, Tohil K'iche', for all of them. It was Tohil for the Tamub as well as for the Ilocab. There was only one name for the god among them. Therefore, the three groups of K'iche's were not divided" (Christenson 2003:213). Similarly, the Mexica ethnic identity in Central Mexico was tied to the worship of Huitzilopochtli. Chimalpahin (1997:73) described this relationship: "[Huitzilopochtli] said to them: now no longer is your name Azteca: you are now Mixitin. There they also applied feathers to their ears when they took their name as Mixitin. Hence they are now called Mexica."[11] In another account a second group of Azteca broke off when the sister of Huitzilopochtli, the goddess Malinalxochitl, was abandoned during the migration. Those who stayed with her founded the town of Malinalco in her name, and she became their patron (Duran 1994:25).

In modern Maya highland communities, patron saints are dressed in the local clothing of their hometowns and prayed to in the local language rather than in Spanish (Watanabe 1990, 1992). In this region, where both language and dress differ substantially from town to town, these are both strong markers of local identity. The strong indexical linkages between supernatural patrons and local identity would explain the propensity for the Classic Maya to carry their gods to war with them, as well as bringing them along on more friendly visits. Indeed, such friendly visits still take place today, in which saints from indigenous communities are brought to visit one another and pay proper respects on fiesta days (Cancian 1965:39; Redfield and Villa Rojas 1962:153; Siegel 1941:72; Vogt 1993:101; Watanabe 1992:114).

Closely related to this idea of common identity between patron and community is the expectation of supernatural protection. I have already discussed the Classic Maya discourse of patron deity assistance in war and calendrical rites. Documents from later periods indicate further protective powers. The Popol Vuh, for example, records a lengthy prayer in which the ruler and noblemen pray to the patron gods as well as the general creator gods:

> May there be no fault, confinement, shame, or misfortune. May no deceiver come behind them or before them. May they not fall or be wounded. May they not be dishonored or condemned. May they not fall below the road or above the road. May they not be stricken or have impediments placed behind them or before them. May you place them on green roads and on green pathways. May they not be blamed or confined. Do no hide yourselves from them or curse them. May their existence be favored, so that they may be providers and sustainers to you, to your mouths and to your faces .... (Christenson 2003:289–90)[12]

Modern saints are also believed to provide the town with general protection and well-being. An interesting anecdote is related by Thompson (1960:25). In 1883 some residents from San Luis, Petén, crossed into British Honduras and founded the town of San Antonio. But after a year of bad luck, they found San Antonio to be an inadequate patron saint. They determined to kidnap Saint Luis, whom they had left behind in the original town. They successfully carried out the raid, capturing all the saints from their former hometown, thus conferring their divine powers on the new town of San Antonio. In more recent times townspeople in Santiago Chimaltenango, Guatemala, say that the saint protected the community from the worst atrocities of the Guatemalan civil war, while immediate neighbors suffered worse under the army occupation (Watanabe 1990:134). In Chinautla saints appear as visions to ritual specialists to predict the weather (Reina 1966:115). Individuals can seek the help of the patron saint against specific misfortunes (Redfield and Villa Rojas 1962:108), but the saint can also punish the town if veneration is inadequate (Reina 1966:18).

Under such circumstances, the role of the ritual specialist is especially important. Although individual community members both participate in saint-feeding rituals and can supplicate the patron saint on their own, it is the task of the ritual specialist to ensure that, as a whole, the town carries out its ritual obligations. In modern times this ritual role is often assigned to community leaders by means of a rotating *cargo* system, a *cofradía* system, or some combination of the two. The word *cargo* means "charge" or "burden" and is often referred to in Maya communities using an indigenous term with a similar meaning (Bunzel 1959:165; Redfield and Villa Rojas 1962:156–57). In this system responsibilities toward patron saints are broken down into different levels, starting with the daily maintenance of church and effigies and ending with planning and hosting the fiesta and ritual meals (Cancian 1965; Oakes 1951; Redfield and Villa Rojas 1962:157; Siebers 1999; Warren 1978; Watanabe 1992). Each year new cargo holders are appointed to the different levels. Since higher-level cargos are more expensive, more ritually important, and fewer in number, they are associated with greater social prestige. The *cofradía* system operates in much the same way as the cargo system. *Cofradías* are religious brotherhoods founded for the care of a particular saint (Hill 1986; Reina 1966; Siebers 1999:55). Many communities have several *cofradías*, each responsible for a different saint image or fiesta. Each *cofradía* usually owns a house where the saint's image and ritual paraphernalia are kept. Like the cargo system, each *cofradía* has different levels of participation. Thus, the two systems are similar except that the *cofradía* is organized around the shared property of the house.

In the 1960s and 1970s several scholars proposed that this rotating system was a highly conservative relic of a pre-Columbian version (Carrasco 1961; Coe 1965; Price 1974; Rathje 1970). More recent scholarship sees the rise of the cargo system as a response to changing circumstances under Colonial rule and the modern economy (Chance and Taylor 1985; Farriss 1984:349; Rus and Wasserstrom 1980). Evidence from the Classic period and from Postclassic documents like the Popol Vuh indicates that ritual specialists came exclusively from the ranks of the hereditary nobility and that the ruler himself was ultimately responsible for patron deity veneration. Remnants of this original system may be found in some communities where hereditary specialists assist cargo holders (Oakes 1951; Reina 1966; Vogt 1973). Both cargo holders and hereditary specialists command great authority in the community beyond religious matters. These include regulating the behavior of youth, schoolteachers, and mayors. Thus, the "burden" of ritual office is rewarded through political authority.

In the discourse of the Popol Vuh, the ruling K'iche's explicitly framed their political authority as a just reward for their ritual efforts on behalf of the people. The text emphasized the arduous burden of this responsibility:

> ... they fasted for long periods of time, and sacrificed before the faces of their gods. And this was their method for fasting: for nine score days they would fast, and for nine they would sacrifice and burn offerings. Then for thirteen

score days they would observe and fast and for thirteen they would sacrifice and burn offerings before the face of Tohil, as well as before the faces of the other gods. They would eat only zapotes, matasanos, and jocotes. They would not eat food made from maize.... Neither would they sleep with their women. They would merely provide for each other, fasting in the houses of the gods. Each day they would merely worship, merely burn offerings, and merely offer sacrifices. They were there in the darkness and at dawn, weeping in their hearts and in their bowels, pleading for the light and the lives of their vassals and servants. (Christenson 2003:288)

The text contrasts this noble comportment to the more suspect political authority derived from conquest alone: "They did not achieve their lordship, their glory, or their sovereignty by deception or theft. They did not merely crush the canyons and the citadels of the small nations and the great nations" (Christenson 2003:291). These protestations indicate either the K'iche' disapproval of other rulers who made war their sole focus or, more likely, an attempt by the K'iche's to frame their own conquests as part of a greater spiritual enterprise.[13] Finally, the text describes the just rewards of ritual service: "Great was the price that the nations gave in return. They sent jade and precious metal, the size of four fingers across and even the size of a fist across with the thumb extended. They sent precious gems and glittering stones. They sent as well cotinga feathers, oriole feathers, and the feathers of red birds.... Many groups of the nations came with their tribute for the K'iche's" (Christenson 2003:291).

The Popol Vuh thus frames tribute payments as a reciprocal reward for the K'iche' ruler's supplication of the gods. In exchange for this arduous burden, the ruler was entitled to be sustained by the wealth of the people he governed. From this argument (in the Peircian sense), it is not a difficult leap to the discourse of overall similarity between the ruler and the patron god himself. Such a claim was made by the Aztecs, as recorded by Duran (1994:313):

You [Aztec emperor Ahuitzotl] will carry the same burden as does the god Huitzilopochtli, which is to provide and maintain this world order, that is, to provide the sustenance, the food and drink for your people. Eyes from the four directions are fixed upon you. You have now been given a sword and a shield that you may risk your life for your country. You have been charged with the responsibility for the mountains, the hills, the plains, caves, cliffs, rivers, and seas, pools and springs, rocks and trees. Everything has been commended to you and you must take care and see that these do not fall apart.

Here political power is described in the same terms as supernatural power, and the similarities between ruler and god are made explicit. Both must provide for their people, take charge of the landscape, and defend the nation in war. Implicit in this comparison is the reward owed to ruler and god: just as the patron deity is sustained through human efforts to house, bathe, feed, and clothe him, the ruler is entitled to be sustained by the people through tribute in the form of labor for architectural projects, sumptuary goods, and foodstuffs.

These discourses from the Postclassic and more recent periods are critical for understanding the role of patron deity veneration in social relationships back in the Classic period. I have already noted how Classic Maya rulers claimed an exclusive, personal relationship with patron gods through kinship tropes and affective phrasing. I have also shown the close links between Classic Maya patron gods, the landscape, and the people who inhabited it. Finally, I have discussed how certain hieroglyphic texts give credit to gods for events such as war and calendrical junctures that would benefit the whole community. Ethnographic materials from later periods indicate that patron gods were also believed to confer protection from shame, misfortune, dishonor, disease, and other forms of adversity. And they also indicate that the exclusive relationship between ruler and god justified political authority and tribute demands. These semiotic links help explain the importance of patron deity veneration in Classic Maya political discourse.

PATRON DEITIES AND CLASSIC MAYA POLITICAL AUTHORITY

The observed similarities between patron deity veneration in the Classic period and in later periods strongly suggest that these practices and discourses have survived largely intact over the centuries. These include the feeding, dressing, and care of effigies in which gods or saints are believed to physically reside, which indexically signifies the practitioner's devotion for the deity. They also include narratives in which the overall well-being of the community is dependent upon the deity's intercession. In these later periods, in which ethnographic information is more readily accessible, it is also possible to observe the metapragmatic discourses linking patron gods to political authority. For example, gods and saints are both implicitly and explicitly linked to ethnic identity, such that the veneration of a particular god indexically signifies membership within a particular community. Furthermore, political leaders are said to be particularly devoted to the deities, such that social status is enacted through exclusive ritual performance. Finally, ideological discourses frame the ruler's authority and tribute demands as a just reward for these devotions or even naturalize the ruler's position through his similarities to the patron god. It is safe to infer that similar metapragmatic discourses existed during the Classic period, given the observed similarities in patron deity veneration over time.

This interpretation helps to explain a hieroglyphic text at Yaxchilan. Step 3 of Hieroglyphic Stairway 3 describes the accession ceremony of a ruler in 681. An important aspect of these ceremonies was the presentation of a headband made of bark paper that served as a symbol of royal authority among many Mesoamerican groups. Maya texts indicate that these headbands had proper names, which varied from site to site. In this text the headband was called Bolon Tzak K'ahk' Chaak. *Bolon Tzak* refers to "many conjurings," a ritual discussed in chapter 3 in which the slippery essence of a god was made manifest as an effigy or as a vision. One of Yaxchilan's principal patron gods was Aj K'ahk' O' Chaak, meaning "He of Fire [Raptor Bird] Rain God," here abbreviated to K'ahk' Chaak ("Fire Rain God"). Thus, the name of the royal headband referred to multiple ritual manifestations of the site's supernatural patron and indicated that the office of kingship was intimately tied to this ritual obligation.

The Aztec comparison between the emperor and patron god Huitzilopochtli also echoes the Classic Maya comparison between gods and rulers. As I discussed in chapter 3, the adjective *k'uhul* "godlike" was used frequently to describe Classic Maya rulers and nobles of exceptional political influence. Gods themselves were also depicted as rulers, given royal titles, and even described as being within dynastic lines of particular sites. The discursive effect is to blur the line between the social role of the ruler and the patron god, suggesting similar obligations toward followers as well as similar entitlements in return. This ideological discourse thus justifies the ruler's tribute demands and his governing authority in light of his close association with, and similarities to, protective supernatural patrons.

The protective powers of these gods, if they were sincerely believed in by the Classic Maya, would provide obvious advantages to the whole community. This would have made their proper veneration a matter of necessity. Thus, arguments claiming the ruler's special relationship with gods and his just rewards for ritual service may have been highly effective at creating and upholding social asymmetries. Indeed, from the ruler's perspective, patron deity veneration and associated discourses of royal authority would have been especially important at historical junctures in which his authority was challenged by competing models of social relationships. For example, defeat in war or poor agricultural yields, shifting political alliances, or power struggles between noble families would all have generated alternative arguments about authority and reciprocal obligations between community members.

For example, an alternative discourse that is clearly observable throughout the Classic period and later is that of social privilege through ancestor veneration. As discussed in chapter 3, special mortuary treatment of particular lineage members, their burial beneath the floors of residences, and offerings made to them by descendants all indexically linked lineage members to the rights of previous generations, especially social status and land rights. McAnany (1995) argues that this system gave the descendants of a site's first settlers an advantage over later arrivals, and these first families may have gone on to found royal lineages. However, while Classic Maya rulers practiced ancestor veneration as a means of maintaining links to the authority of royal predecessors, kingship itself was a competing social model claimed to supersede ancestor-based authority. In other words, the ruler claimed social privileges not because his ancestors had possessed them, but because his social role entitled him to authority over the wealth and lands of other community members. Nonrulers may have continued to venerate their ancestors, but according to this argument, the ruler's claims were superior to all others'. These two competing models existed together during the Classic period, seeing different success rates at different sites. McAnany (1995:150) suggests that some emerging rulers may have actively attacked ancestor veneration among competing lineages as a means of promoting their own model of authority. For example, this may have included the destruction of ancestor shrines or the appropriation of lineage resources. I propose that another strategy would have been the increased promotion of rituals and narratives of patron deity veneration. This would have allowed struggling rulers to make ideological claims about the merits of the royal authority or allowed new rulers to establish legitimacy through claims of ritual success with patron gods.

The renewed promotion of patron deity veneration during times of political change or crisis may explain the observed accumulation of patron gods at Classic Maya sites, as discussed in chapter 3. While Classic Maya communities generally venerated traditional deities for generations, new gods were also frequently added to local pantheons. Though hieroglyphic inscriptions do not explicitly comment upon the reasons for the introduction of new gods, it may have been part of an overall strategy of increased patron deity devotions introduced by rulers whose authority was fragile. In chapter 5 I will demonstrate how this process worked at the Classic Maya site of La Corona, Guatemala. The exceptional historical record at this site, along with the archaeological record, demonstrate a prolonged conflict between at least two noble lineages, which appealed to competing social models of ancestor veneration and patron deity devotions over the generations.

The discourses preserved in Classic Maya hieroglyphic inscriptions, the material objects and ritual acts that they recorded, and the enduring repetition of those acts and discourses over thousands of years demonstrate the importance of patron deity veneration in creating and upholding social models that justified power differentials and status asymmetries. This example illustrates that social institutions like kingship are created and maintained one semiotic event at a time, not automatically generated through collective will or imposed in large chunks from above. Chapter 5 will demonstrate how rapidly these institutions can change when competing social models circulate.

NOTES

1. I favor the interpretation proposed by Zender (2007; Stone and Zender 2011:15) that the glyph *yichonal* recorded the root *ichon*, meaning "front/presence." He notes that the usual phonetic spelling of the glyph was sometimes replaced by a logographic version depicting a torso with an arm and hand held elegantly in the typical pose of a seated ruler. Stuart (1997:10), on the other hand, interprets the glyph as related to the Yucatec root *iknal*, meaning "in the company of." He also proposes a slightly different interpretation of the torso logogram, though one that still signifies a person "who sanctioned, oversaw, or attended to the ritual concerned" (Stuart 2006a:42). Thus, while the two epigraphers propose slightly different readings of these glyphic signs, they reach similar overall interpretations.

2. I borrow the term "domestication" from John Watanabe's (1990) account of modern-day patron saints in the town of Santiago Chimaltenango, Guatemala. See further discussion below.

3. A *winikhaab* (a.k.a. *k'atun*) is a period of approximately twenty years and was ritually important for Maya time-keeping practices from Preclassic all the way to Colonial times. The number 13 was also ritually significant within the calendar.

4. Texts that described captive rulers often referred to them as *ma'ch'ab mahk'abil* "without penance, without darkness," suggesting that capture rendered the ruler a powerless, pathetic figure.

5. GI-K'awiil is a partial nickname. The GI part of the name (pronounced gee-one) refers to a god with solar attributes found in iconography at sites across the Maya area. This god was first identified at Palenque, where a particular aspect is one of the principal patron gods of the site. His actual name resists decipherment, so the GI nickname has stuck. K'awiil, however, is an accurate reading of the name of the Classic Maya lightning god. The patron god found in the Petexbatun region is a unique combination of these two deities.

6. A tapir is a large herbivorous mammal native to Central America. Since the Itza had never seen a horse before the arrival of Cortes in their territory, this was the word they used.

7. Villagutierre Soto-Mayor (1983:302) describes another deity as well, called Hobo. He claims that the effigy of this god was a hollow metal statue in which sacrificial victims were slowly roasted. This description is so uncharacteristic of Maya religious practices that it strains my credulity.

8. It seems that in some instances Spanish chroniclers confused Zapotec royal ancestors for patron gods (see Whitecotton 1977:157–59n115). However, Marcus (1983b:348) probably goes too far when she argues that nearly all of the Zapotec patron gods were simply deified ancestors (see Lind 2015:30–33). She bases this argument on the fact that the names of these gods incorporate the terms *coqui* and *xonaxi* (male and female ruler) and calendrical day names. However, if Maya practices are any indication, the use of the term "lord" in god names did not mean that they were originally ancestors. Furthermore, Aztec gods were frequently named for the calendar, as in the case of Macuil Xochitl ("Five Flower"), and gods from all over Mesoamerica were frequently associated with specific dates in the ritual calendar.

9. I follow Smith (2012) in using the term "Aztec" to refer to any of the Nahuatl-speaking groups of Postclassic Central Mexico that traced their origins to the mythical Aztlan. I use "Mexica" to refer specifically to the founders of Tenochtitlan, the eventual rulers of the Triple Alliance (a.k.a. Aztec Empire). When directly quoting, however, I have preserved the terminology of the source material.

10. The Lacandon Maya of the Usumacinta River region are often imagined as direct cultural inheritors of the Classic Maya cultural tradition. Palka (2005) shows that their origins can in fact be traced to the early nineteenth century. During this time the jungles of the Usumacinta were remote and largely inaccessible to Colonial powers. The modern Lacandon (not to be confused with the Ch'olti'-speaking Lacandon documented by the Spaniards of the sixteenth through eighteenth centuries) speak a dialect of Yucatec and probably emerged as a discrete group from the intermixing of various Colonial period indigenous groups of southern Yucatan, northern Guatemala, and eastern Chiapas (Palka 2005:69–82). Many scholars have documented Lacandon religious practices, which in many ways resemble aspects of pre-Columbian patron deity veneration that I am describing in this book. Although Lacandon religious practices are changing, traditionally they worshipped a number of gods, including creator deities and deities representing natural forces. These gods were believed to periodically descend into physical form as effigy pots and incense burners that were decorated with their likenesses and animated by the addition of a stone representing a heart or other organ (Davis 1978; McGee 2002). The Lacandon gave offerings to these gods in the form of food, drink, incense, and rubber figurines decorated with red annatto dye,

representing blood. While the belief that creator gods can descend into physical effigies that require sustenance is clearly analogous to Classic Maya patron deities, these effigies do not belong to particular communities or political units (Palka 2005:247–67).

11. "Azteca" here refers to all people who trace their origins to the mythical Aztlan. In this account the Mexica become a unique subset of the Azteca.

12. The "they" and "them" in this prayer are elsewhere referred to as all the K'iche' people as well as the conquered nations.

13. As Preucel (2013:n.p.) observed, the fact that the K'iche' leaders needed to state that their sovereignty was *not* based on violence suggests that "some rulers behaved in less than honorable ways."

5

Patron Deity Introduction at La Corona, Guatemala

La Corona, a medium-sized Classic Maya site in northwestern Guatemala, illustrates the importance of discourses and practices related to patron deity veneration in political life. Split by factional rivalries, members of the La Corona community promoted competing models of social entitlement based on ancestral rights and relationships to protective gods. This history is revealed through the site's numerous hieroglyphic texts as well as a careful consideration of its archaeological record.

While factional competition has long been recognized as an important element of Classic Maya politics, Lucero (2007) proposes that it can be directly observed in the construction of temples at Maya sites. She suggests that different political groups such as noble families may have constructed different temples and that commoners could then choose which religious institution to support by choosing which temple to attend. Based on a preliminary study of the temples of Yalbac, Belize, she hypothesizes that the different plazas of the site contained temples from different sponsors. For example, the temples in Plaza 2 were built by the royal family, while the temples in Plaza 3 were built by non-rulers. This proposal is based on factors such as construction technique and quality of stone and fill, on the assumption that rulers would have had greater access to labor and materials and could thus construct superior temples.

While Lucero's study is laudable for its attention to factional strife, my observations of La Corona's

DOI: 10.5876/9781607325185.c005

construction history paint a different picture. Temple construction varied by plaza at La Corona as well, but this was likely related to the different uses of the plazas and temples. As I discussed in chapter 3, the English word "temple" is a catchall category that actually encompasses many different types of ritual structures. And, as I will demonstrate, those functions could even change over time. Furthermore, at La Corona I observed remarkably shoddy construction on a set of temples built by a ruler. This was a product of the speed with which they were constructed, not of reduced access to wealth and labor.

Lucero proposes that commoners at Yalbac had freedom of choice between different religious institutions and political factions. This scenario is thus somewhat analogous to modern American society, in which a number of religious denominations compete for followers and the resources they bring. The question of commoners' religious agency is particularly difficult to answer archaeologically. As discussed in chapter 2, agency is a complex phenomenon composed of one's awareness of social entitlements and their limits, one's freedom to act and bypass social constraints, and one's own reflexive awareness of that freedom in different social situations. It may be a mistake to see Classic Maya religion as an open marketplace of ideas; yet it would also be erroneous to assume that all commoners obediently followed the religious dictates of the ruler. The fact that rulers actively promoted ideological discourses about their special relationship with patron gods suggests that their followers may have needed convincing. As I will discuss below, archaeological evidence at La Corona shows that common people did participate in ruler-sponsored patron deity veneration.

INTRODUCING LA CORONA

A Brief History of Investigations

The looting of Classic Maya sites has been an increasing problem over the last century, and La Corona is no exception. During the 1960s a set of hieroglyphic texts appeared on the art market in the United States and Europe that shared common attributes such as small size, a unique and exquisite style, and the mention of a few specific names. Peter Mathews (1979) noticed the similarities among these looted stone monuments and proposed that they came from a common source site, which he called "Site Q." Mathews created a catalog of Site Q monuments, many of which are now known to have come from La Corona (Mathews 1998; Schuster 1997).

The search for Site Q was particularly urgent in the 1980s and 1990s because epigraphers initially misunderstood some of the content of the Site

Q inscriptions. These texts frequently discussed the Kaan (Snake) emblem glyph, title of the rulers of Calakmul. As I have noted, Calakmul was a particularly influential polity and commanded an extensive network of allies and subordinates. But before the mid-1990s the location of the Kaan polity was also hotly debated. Calakmul itself has poor limestone, and its monuments are not well preserved. Many scholars logically concluded that Site Q, with such fine monuments and frequent references to the Kaan emblem glyph, must also be the seat of the polity (Chase and Chase 1998:21; Martin 1993; Schuster 1997). Eventually, however, with additional research it became clear that Calakmul was in fact the location of the Kaan polity during the Late Classic period (Marcus 1973; Martin 1993; Martin and Grube 1994; Stuart and Houston 1994), while the Kaan court was located at Dzibanche in the Early Classic (Martin 2005b; Velásquez García 2004). It was also clear that the Site Q monuments didn't come from Calakmul itself but from one of its many subordinates (Martin and Grube 2000:110; Schele and Grube 1994:109). Nonetheless, the search for Site Q continued, as it promised to be a site with an exceptionally rich historical record.

The earliest documented discovery of La Corona came in the late 1980s, when chicle tappers working in northwestern Guatemala found the site and called it "Lo Veremos" after a camp they had established nearby. In 1989 German archaeologists visited the site and noted large structures, carved monuments, and numerous deep looters' trenches (Grube, Haase, and Sattler 1990). At El Peru, a site to the south of La Corona, remote sensing had revealed linear features possibly representing a road leading north. In 1996 Tom Sever and Dan Lee of NASA and Jim Nations of Conservation International visited La Corona to see if they could find evidence for this possible road (Barrientos and Canuto 2009). Upon noting the presence of carved monuments, they asked for the assistance of epigraphers. Ian Graham and David Stuart visited La Corona the following year (Graham 1997) and made the first map of the site. Observing five small temples that resembled the peaks of a tiara, they named the site "La Corona," meaning "the crown." (These five temples include the four that I describe in this chapter. They are now commonly referred to as "Coronitas.") Stuart made drawings of the monuments on site and noted important similarities to Mathews's Site Q catalog. For instance, La Corona Stela 1 referred to the works of Chak Ak', a ruler also mentioned on the Site Q monuments. La Corona Altar 1 also recorded the place-name Sak Nikte', which was the local toponym mentioned in various Site Q texts. In addition, he noted several references to the Kaan polity (Stuart in Schuster 1997:44), another common feature of Site Q monuments. However, while Stuart believed La Corona to be Site Q, Graham pointed out that the monuments in Mathews's Site Q catalog were all much smaller than those they found at the site and were carved in a different style.

Other archaeologists also doubted the identification of La Corona as Site Q (e.g., Hansen in Schuster 1997:43). To confirm his hypothesis, David Stuart asked Chris Hayward of the University of Manchester to analyze the limestone of one of the Site Q monuments for comparison with a sample of La Corona limestone (Stuart 2001). Their chemical composition proved to be similar, but other scholars believed that Site Q could simply be another site in the same geological region or perhaps a series of different sites (e.g., Martin 2001:183).

In 2005 the El Peru-Waka' archaeological project, directed by David Freidel and Héctor Escobedo, sent a team to La Corona to investigate its possible identification as Site Q (Canuto et al. 2006). During this trip Marcello Canuto found a carved panel (Panel 1) still *in situ* in one of the five "Coronitas" temples (I will discuss the contents of these panels later in this chapter). In a near perfect state of preservation, this panel not only listed characters known from the Site Q corpus and political interactions with Calakmul (Guenter 2005), it was also stylistically consistent with the Site Q monuments down to its small size. This confirmed Stuart's assertion that La Corona was Site Q. The El Peru project sent a second expedition to La Corona in 2006, in which Canuto carried out excavations in the structure where he found the panels (Canuto 2006).

In 2008 the La Corona Regional Archaeology Project was formed as a separate entity from the El Peru project and began work at the site under the direction of Marcello Canuto and Tomás Barrientos. That was also the year I began work at La Corona, and I carried out excavations for five field seasons until 2012. The project continues today, and each season recovers important new archaeological and historical material.

The Site of La Corona

Like most Classic Maya sites, La Corona is composed of several architectural groups containing monumental architecture such as temples, palaces, and elite residences. Surrounding these is a large area of more dispersed commoner households. La Corona is built around the edges of seasonal lakes known locally as *civales*. These would have provided the inhabitants of the site with drinking water, and they were also home to useful wildlife such as fish and waterfowl. Two architectural groups at La Corona made up most of its monumental architecture. The Main Group, on the west of the site center, contained

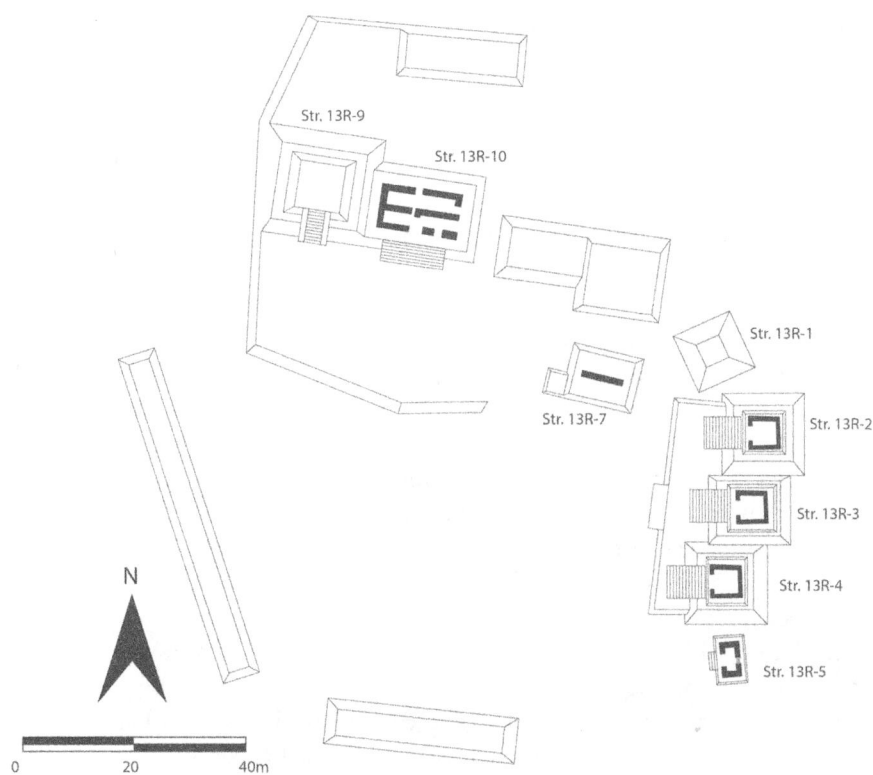

FIGURE 5.1. *Map of the Coronitas group (after Damien Marken in Canuto et al. 2006:fig. 4)*

a high palace acropolis, home of the site's rulers. It also contained two large pyramidal platforms, which were probably religious in nature, and two range structures, which were possibly used for administrative functions. The other group, known as the "Coronitas" group, is more important for this chapter (Figure 5.1). Along the eastern side of the plaza are the five small temple pyramids for which the site is named (Structures 13R-1 through 13R-5). A series of other buildings make up the north side of the group. One of these (13R-10) is an elite residence set on top of an elevated patio platform with a hieroglyphic staircase adorning its front. Along the western edge of this elite residence is another pyramidal platform (13R-9). Between Structures 13R-1 and 13R-10 in the northeast corner of the group are three smaller structures. 13R-7 may have been another elite residence. The west and south sides of the Coronitas group are defined by low range structures that separated the plaza from a *cival*. These have not yet been excavated at the time of this writing.

Excavations on the Coronitas Temples

I conducted excavations on Structures 13R-2, 13R-3, 13R-4, and 13R-5 over five field seasons. All four of these buildings had been extensively looted, some of them with multiple trenches. While most of this looting can be tentatively dated to the 1960s, when the Site Q monuments emerged, Structure 13R-5 saw subsequent looting in 2005 after Canuto recovered the panels from within it. These looters' trenches were exceptionally deep—most of those that I documented went down to bedrock, and some of them probably started out as tunnels that eventually collapsed. In many cases this created dangerous structural instability, which I had to consider when planning excavations. Dangers aside, this looting created other frustrations. Primary contexts were destroyed, especially tombs. Stratigraphic relationships were confused or erased. And huge piles of back dirt were left in inconvenient locations. In spite of these challenges, I obtained valuable information about construction histories and ritual practices on these buildings through a combination of extensive surface exposure as well as pitting, trenching, and tunneling.

In brief, I identified six overall stages in the construction history of the four temples (Table 5.1). Structures 13R-2, 13R-3, and 13R-4 had similar construction phases, while Structure 13R-5 was a bit different. The earliest of these stages was the initial construction of Structure 13R-5, probably completed during the fourth century. This building contained a burial, and I refer to it as the "K'inich Stage," after the probable occupant of that tomb.

The next three stages all consisted of construction on Structures 13R-2, 13R-3, and 13R-4. The "Mam Stage" (*mam* meaning "ancestor" in reference to its antiquity) dated to around the early to mid-sixth century. It consisted of a set of platforms and other architectural features whose stratigraphic relationship to one another is still largely unclear. The following stage consisted of the sequential construction of three pyramidal platforms to form what is now 13R-2, 13R-3, and 13R-4 over the course of the late sixth century. I call this stage the "Muk Stage" (*muk* meaning "burial") after the tombs discovered in 13R-2 and 13R-4. In the mid-seventh century the "K'uh Stage" was completed. This was a new façade that united these three sequential platforms into a single architectural program.

Construction continued on Structure 13R-5 in the mid-seventh century. I call this the "Ub Stage" after a god named on the panel found in this building. It included a new platform and superstructure. Finally, the last stage of construction is called the "Unen Stage" (*unen* meaning "baby") since it was the latest constructed. It consisted of a number of minor modifications to all four of the structures under investigation.

TABLE 5.1. Construction on the Coronitas temples

Architectural Stage (ceramic dates)	Structure 13R-2	Structure 13R-3	Structure 13R-4	Structure 13R-5
Unen (eighth and ninth centuries)	Platform connected to stairway	Platform connected to stairway; stucco decoration	New back terrace wall; low foundation wall	Low foundation wall behind structure
Ub (mid-seventh century)				New platform and superstructure
K'uh (mid-seventh century)	New façade on front	New façade on front	New façade on front	
Muk (late sixth century)	Burial 6; pyramidal platform	Pyramidal platform	Burial 2; pyramidal platform	
Mam (mid-sixth century)	Terraced platform	Wall features	Terraced platform	
K'inich (fourth century)				Burial 1; low platform

The contents of Panel 1 are especially important for the interpretation of the construction histories of all four temples. Carved in 677, it commemorates the completion of a *wayib* ("sleeping place") for a god named [?] Winik Ub (Guenter 2005). The panel also gave a retrospective account that the previous ruler had constructed three other *wayib* temples for three other gods in the year 658. As I will discuss, it is highly likely that the *wayib* completed in 677 was the Ub Stage of Structure 13R-5, the structure where the panel was found. It is also likely that the three earlier temples completed in 658 correspond to the K'uh Stage of the adjacent 13R-2, 13R-3, and 13R-4.

RECONSTRUCTING THE HISTORY OF CORONITAS

For this rest of this chapter, I will weave together the archaeological evidence from these four temples with historical data for the whole site following a rough chronological order (Table 5.2).[1] Some of the historical events from the early history of La Corona are known only from later monuments that give retrospective accounts. Thus, when I read these texts for historical information about earlier periods, I am approaching them from a semantic standpoint—whether their content is true or false and how it is reflected in the archaeological record. But when examining these texts within the era in which

TABLE 5.2. Important historical dates in La Corona texts

Date	Event	Monument	Monument Dedicated by
3805 BCE	A person came to La Corona from the Six Nothing Place	Panel 1	K'inich [?] Yook
314 CE	Tahn K'inich came to La Corona	Panel 1	K'inich [?] Yook
520	Lady Naah Ek', wife of Vulture, arrived at La Corona	Panel 6	Yajawte' K'inich
544	Calendar ritual by Vulture / Chak Tok Ich'aak	Stela 1	Chak Ak'
615	Birth of Chakaw Nahb Chan	Panel 3	?
625	Accession of Sak Maas	Panel 2	K'inich [?] Yook
635	Ballgame between Yuknoom Ch'een and Sak Maas	Elements 33, 34, and 35	Sak Maas; Chak Ak'
635	The Kaan Dynasty moved to Calakmul	Element 33	Chak Ak'
637	Sak Maas conjured Ikiiy	Stairway A	K'inich [?] Yook
655	K'uk' Ajaw acceded as ruler	Panel 2	K'inich [?] Yook
656	Sak Maas died with the edge of a stone	Panel 2	K'inich [?] Yook
658	K'uk' Ajaw died with the edge of a stone; Chakaw Nahb Chan acceded as ruler	Panel 2	K'inich [?] Yook
658	Dedication of three patron deity temples	Panel 1	K'inich [?] Yook
664	K'inich [?] Yook traveled to Calakmul	Panel 2	K'inich [?] Yook
667	Death of Chakaw Nahb Chan and his wife; return of K'inich [?] Yook	Panel 2	K'inich [?] Yook
667	First accession ceremony of K'inich [?] Yook	Panel 2	K'inich [?] Yook
673	K'inich [?] Yook went to Calakmul again	Panel 2	K'inich [?] Yook
675	Second accession ceremony of K'inich [?] Yook	Panel 1	K'inich [?] Yook
677	Dedication of temple for [?] Winik Ub god	Panel 1	K'inich [?] Yook

continued on next page

TABLE 5.2—*continued*

Date	Event	Monument	Monument Dedicated by
678	K'inich [?] Yook conjured Ikiiy	Stairway A	K'inich [?] Yook
679	K'inich [?] Yook's wife arrived from Calakmul	Panel 6	Yajawte' K'inich
680–681	K'inich [?] Yook danced for a calendar ritual	Stairway A	K'inich [?] Yook
683	K'inich [?] Yook gave pulque	Stairway A	K'inich [?] Yook
689	Accession of Chak Ak'	Stela 1, Element 56	Chak Ak'
721	Yajawte' K'inich's wife arrived from Calakmul	Panel 6	Yajawte' K'inich
746	Calendar rite by Yajawte' K'inich	La Cariba Altar 1	Yajawte' K'inich
791	Wife of new La Corona ruler arrived from Tikal	Altar 4	late La Corona ruler
797	Death of woman from Tikal	Altar 4	late La Corona ruler
805	Calendar ritual (last recorded date at the site)	Altar 4	late La Corona ruler

they were created, their pragmatic meaning comes to the forefront—what was the purpose of these texts and how did they use historical information to make arguments about political institutions and social entitlements? This is especially true with respect to Panel 1, recovered in Structure 13R-5. While its semantic content is pertinent to the construction phases of Coronitas, its pragmatic content is highly revealing about the ideological discourses of the seventh-century ruler K'inich [?] Yook.

The reader will notice the importance of La Corona's relationship with Calakmul throughout the site's history. Investigating this close relationship has been one of the primary goals of the La Corona Regional Archaeology Project, and research has revealed that La Corona was of essential strategic importance within Calakmul's network of allies (Canuto and Barrientos 2011, 2013). To secure this alliance, three rulers of the Calakmul polity sent daughters to La Corona to wed its local rulers and to tie the royal families together as perpetual in-laws (Martin 2008b). The rulers who married these women belonged to a powerful La Corona lineage, which commissioned most of the site's monuments. The epigraphic record thus heavily favors them and their exploits. I refer to them as the "Six Nothing" lineage, since they used this mythical place-name

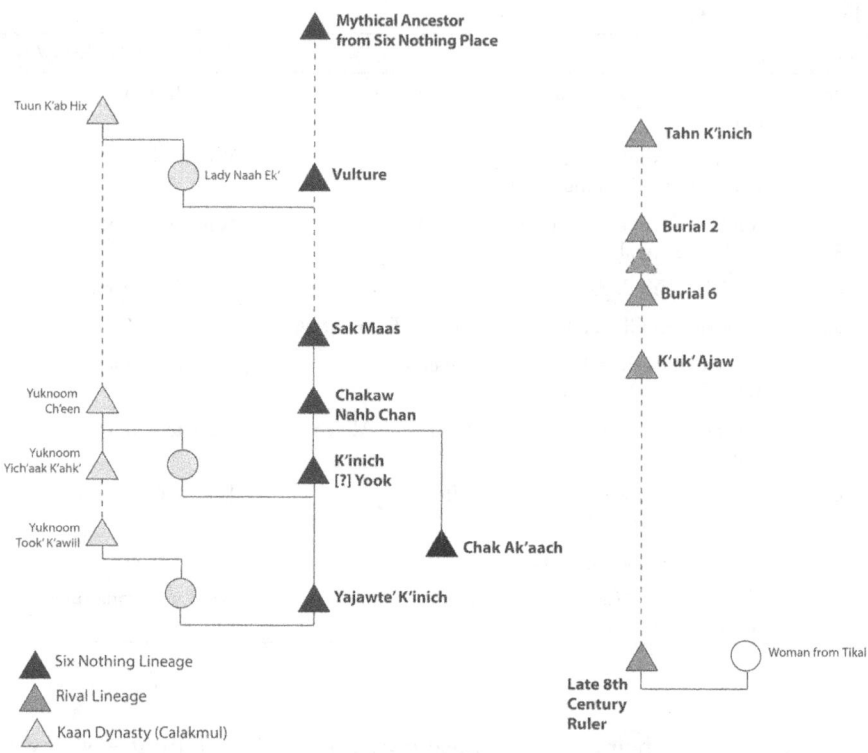

FIGURE 5.2. *Lineages of La Corona rulers. Solid lines indicate historically attested genealogical relationships; dashed lines represent reconstructed relationships.*

as a title in three different inscriptions. But beneath the surface of their historical narrative is a set of antagonists. The Six Nothing family did not rule La Corona for its entire history. In fact, there are periods about which their monuments were completely silent. Instead, it appears that at least two elite families competed with one another for rulership of La Corona: the Six Nothing lineage, supported by Calakmul, and a second, more self-reliant line of rulers (Figure 5.2). The ritual practices and historical narratives of these two families indicate that they used competing social models to justify their claims.

LA CORONA'S EARLY HISTORY

The earliest historical figure recorded in the known inscriptions of La Corona was an individual said to have come to La Corona in 314 CE (Guenter 2005). The only reference to this person was recorded on Panel 1, recovered

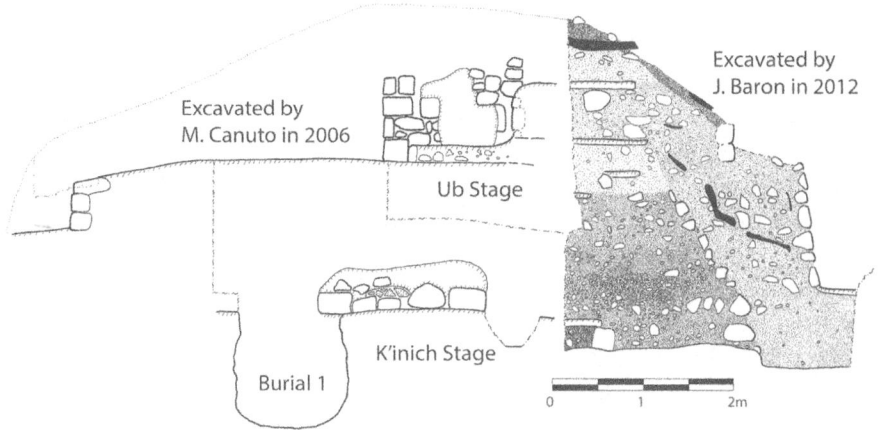

FIGURE 5.3. *North profile of Structure 13R-5 showing stages of construction and Burial 1*

by Marcello Canuto in Coronitas Structure 13R-5 (Canuto et al. 2006). The name of this individual is a matter of some debate, reading either "Alaan Tahn K'inich" or "Tahn K'inich Lajua'."[2] *K'inich* means "radiant" and refers to the name of Classic Maya Sun God, K'inich Ajaw. The term was used frequently in the names of Maya rulers, and its presence in this historical reference suggests that this early individual had an elevated status, at least in the eyes of subsequent generations.

One of the earliest datable archaeological contexts at La Corona is the first construction phase of Structure 13R-5, which I call the K'inich Stage (Figure 5.3). In fact, it is likely that this construction phase represents the funerary temple of the Tahn K'inich historical figure. Canuto (2006) first excavated this phase, identifying a low platform approximately 30 centimeters high. Into the bedrock below the platform the early inhabitants of La Corona had carved out an L-shaped burial chamber, which was sealed with a plaster floor. Such bedrock tombs required a good deal of labor to construct and thus indicate an elevated status on the part of the occupant. This tomb (La Corona Burial 1) was looted, but Canuto's excavations recovered pieces of jade and shell. Both exotic wealth items, these materials would have been more accessible to Maya elites than commoners. Canuto also recovered human bone fragments, which were analyzed by Erin Patterson (2011). She identified them as belonging to a young or middle-aged adult of undetermined sex. One of the recovered teeth had a circular cut for an inlay, a common indexical marker of status among Classic Maya elites. The bones had been treated with red pigment prior to burial, suggesting a reverential treatment by those who prepared the tomb. All of the features of La Corona Burial 1 thus suggest a person of elevated status.

After the tomb had been sealed, the platform and a masonry superstructure were built above, though only a few courses of wall have been preserved (Canuto 2006). Fill from these architectural features contained ceramics consistent with a construction date in the fourth century.[3] Another feature of the tomb strongly suggests that it contained the remains of the historical Tahn K'inich individual. Panel 1, which recorded the date on which this person came to La Corona, was set into the later phase of the same building in 677. And though the position in which the panel was set put it slightly off center from its own contemporary architecture, it was located above the central axis of the earlier Burial 1 (Canuto 2006). This indexical relationship strongly suggests that the text referred to the burial of Tahn K'inich below.[4]

Furthermore, the early date of this historical reference and corresponding dates of La Corona's earliest known architecture suggest that the site was in fact first settled around this time. Tahn K'inich may have been one of the site's earliest settlers. His royal name, combined with the indicators of high status found in his tomb, suggests that his status as first settler may have given him authority over other contemporary settlers, as proposed by McAnany (1995). And other archaeological contexts indicate that he conferred his royal status upon his descendants. However, both the archaeological record and the rhetoric of Panel 1, which I will discuss in the following pages, indicate that Tahn K'inich was not a member of the Six Nothing family. Instead, he appears to have founded a rival lineage.

THE SIXTH CENTURY: TWO HOUSEHOLDS

The sixth century saw two major stages of construction on Coronitas temples 13R-2, 13R-3, and 13R-4. The Mam Stage was probably constructed in the mid-sixth century, while the Muk Stage was built over the course of the latter decades of the century.

The Mam Stage

This period of construction history produced what is the earliest documented architecture of these temple platforms, although it is likely that even earlier remains are still hidden below. I found the remains of terraced platforms beneath Structures 13R-2 and 13R-4, each rising to at least 3 meters high

FIGURE 5.4. *South profile of Structure 13R-2 showing stages of construction and Burial 6*

(Figure 5.4). Structural instability of 13R-3 prevented deeper explorations of that platform, but all three structures appear to have shared a common front terrace. I located a terrace floor corresponding to this phase and a series of unusual curved wall features built on top of it. The relationship between these various Mam Stage architectural features could not be established stratigraphically, so their overall chronology and relationship is tentative.

The function of the Mam Stage platforms cannot be established with certainty. The instability of the structures precluded me from tunneling in search of burials, but it is very likely that they were funerary shrines. This conclusion

Mam Stage Midden	Vases	Bowls	Jars	Plates	unknown	Total
count	0	36	16	64	424	540
% of total	0.0	6.7	3.0	11.9	78.5	100.0
% of known	0.0	31.0	13.8	55.2		

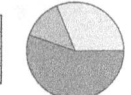

K'uh Stage Midden	Vases	Bowls	Jars	Plates	unknown	Total
count	13	32	11	10	211	277
% of total	4.7	11.6	4.0	3.6	76.2	100.0
% of known	19.7	48.5	16.7	15.2		

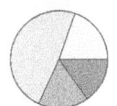

Unen Stage Midden	Fine Gray Bowls	(Other) Bowls	Jars	Plates	Unknown	Total
count	5	21	5	3	126	160
% of total	3.1	13.1	3.1	1.9	78.8	100.0
% of known	14.7	61.8	14.7	8.8		

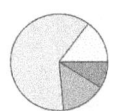

Front Terraces	Fine Gray Bowls	(Other) Bowls	Jars	Plates	Unknown	Total
count	1	18	62	5	192	278
% of total	0.4	6.5	22.3	1.8	69.1	100.0
% of known	1.2	20.9	72.1	5.8		

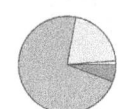

FIGURE 5.5. *Vessel forms recovered from three middens and on the shared front terrace of Structures 13R-2, 13R-3, and 13R-4*

is based on their overall context within what is a apparently a multigenerational necropolis. As I will discuss shortly, the Muk Stage platforms that were built over the Mam Stage were very obviously funerary in nature, as was the adjacent K'inich Stage platform discussed above.

A lack of recovered ceramics made dating the Mam Stage features challenging. The only context that yielded sufficient datable material was a small midden discovered behind the Mam Stage platform under Structure 13R-2. This platform had been constructed directly on top of bedrock, and refuse had accumulated against this back terrace in a layer that was less than a meter thick. Diagnostic sherds are consistent with a date around the mid- to late sixth century. Of the 116 vessel forms that were also identifiable, 31 percent were bowls, 14 percent were jars, and 55 percent were plates (see Figure 5.5). This indicates that activities on the Mam Stage platform emphasized solid foods served on plates, a marked contrast to the activities of later phases on the Coronitas temples (Baron and Parris 2013).

The Muk Stage

The Muk Stage represents a substantial modification to Structures 13R-2, 13R-3, and 13R-4, giving them the largest proportion of their total volume. Stratigraphic relationships between the platforms were much clearer in this stage, allowing me to reconstruct the sequence in which they were built.

The earliest of the Muk Stage platforms was Structure 13R-4, the southernmost of the three. First the platform's builders cut into the previous Mam Stage rear terraces and carved out La Corona Burial 2 into the bedrock below. This was a rectangular burial chamber, measuring 2.8 meters in length and 1 meter in width, with its long axis oriented east-west. Each of the chamber's long walls was lined with masonry. The top of the tomb was completely destroyed by looters, making it impossible to tell how the chamber had been roofed. In spite of the devastating looting, I was able to recover several ceramics, a single small prismatic blade of obsidian, and some human bone. Among the ceramics was a nearly complete hemispherical bowl with a rim diameter of 30 centimeters and sherds from black thin-walled bowls. These ceramics were quite similar to those recovered from the better-preserved Burial 6, which I will describe shortly. They point to a date in the mid- to late sixth century. Erin Patterson (2011) analyzed the human remains and concluded that they belonged to an adult, possibly of middle age, of undetermined sex. As with Burial 1, she observed red pigment on the cranium and some other bones. After completing and sealing the tomb, the builders put down a layer of leveling fill and constructed a new platform approximately 5 meters high on a natural hill. Burial 2 formed its new central axis, displacing the center of the structure backward to the east. Excavations along the back of this platform revealed that the finished façade consisted of two terraces with apron molding.

The Muk phase of Structure 13R-4 stood on its own for some time before the construction of its neighbor. During this period of use, approximately 30 centimeters of refuse accumulated along its base, which became the new surface on which the adjacent Muk phase of Structure 13R-3 was built.[5] The central axis of Structure 13R-3 appears to have been set back (eastward) several meters from that of Structure 13R-4, as indicated by the rear terrace walls (Figure 5.6). Like its neighbor, Structure 13R-3 also had two terraces but rose approximately 2 meters higher. This structure was seriously destabilized by a large looters' trench (or collapsed tunnel) on the back. Because of this structural instability, I did not attempt to locate a tomb under the platform, nor were sufficient ceramics recovered to date the fill of the structure.

Structure 13R-2 was the last of the Muk Stage platforms to be constructed, as revealed by the stratigraphic relationships of the back terraces. The base of Structure 13R-2 was built on a surface approximately 50 centimeters higher than that of 13R-3, this time covered in a layer of plaster. Its central axis was also set back (eastward) by several meters from that its neighbor.

A deep excavation into the center of Structure 13R-2 revealed that the Muk Stage of the platform, like that of 13R-4, had been built over a rock-cut tomb

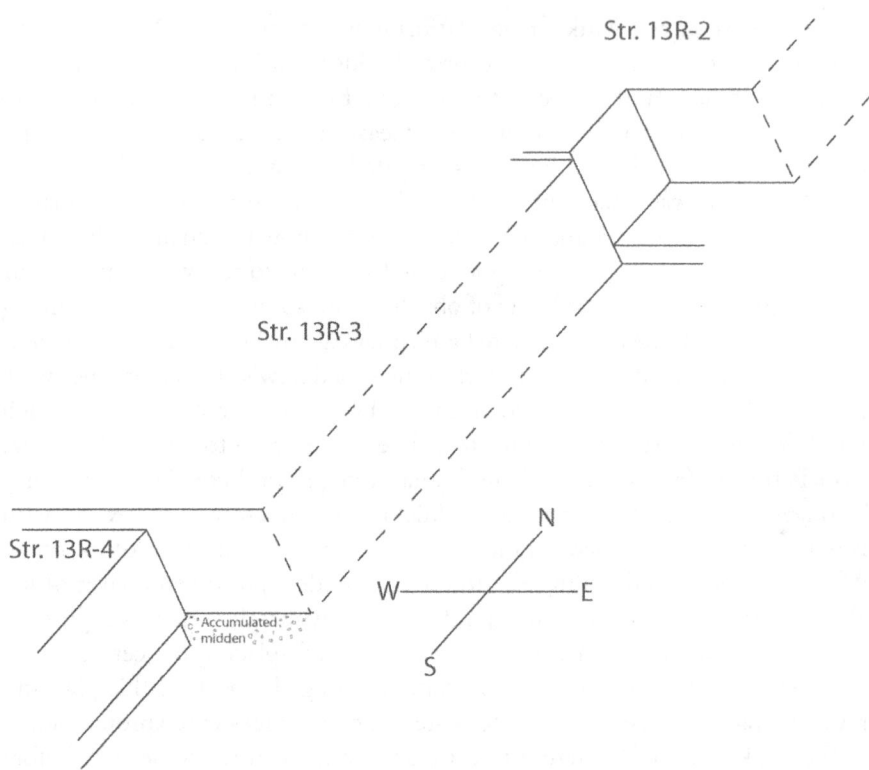

FIGURE 5.6. *Schematic representation of the Muk Stage back terraces of Structures 13R-2, 13R-3, and 13R-4 (not to scale)*

(La Corona Burial 6). This chamber was similar in construction to that of Burial 2, with a rectangular shape oriented east-west and measuring 2.75 × 1.5 meters at its base. The walls of the chamber were about 1.3 meters high, above which was cut a shelf on the north, south, and east sides. This shelf originally held a wooden roof, of which today only remains an organic black powder. The tomb was finished in masonry and plaster, giving it a smoothed appearance.

Burial 6 was not looted, but very nearly so. A deep looters' trench had scraped the top of it, causing water seepage and giving access to burrowing rats. The collapse of the wooden roof had also sent large fill stones tumbling into the burial. As a result, the context was badly damaged but was partially reconstructible.

I recovered human remains from throughout the tomb context. While animals had moved and jumbled them, cranial bones and teeth were concentrated toward the east while feet bones were concentrated toward the west. Erin

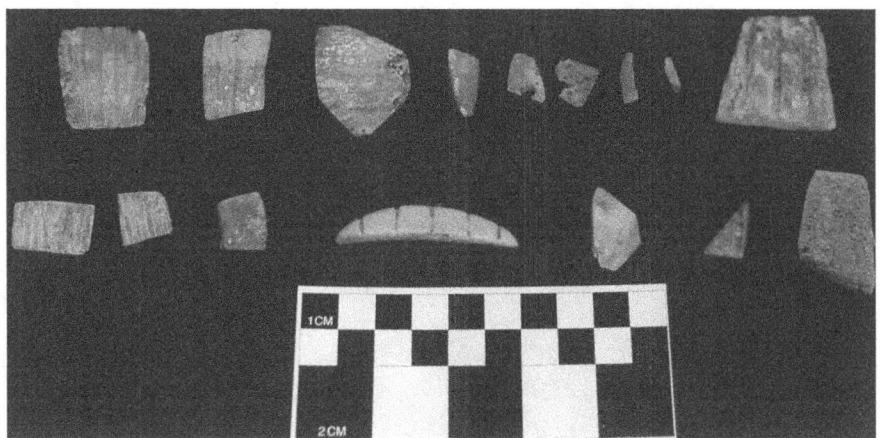

FIGURE 5.7. *Marine shell recovered from Burial 6*

Patterson's (2012) analysis of the bones revealed that they belonged to an adult of middle or old age. Sex was uncertain, though the large size of the teeth may point toward a male. Both central upper incisors were modified with a notch, and the bones, like those of the other burials, had been treated with red pigment.

The tomb occupant was buried with a number of grave goods. I recovered sixteen small fragments of marine shell, nearly all of them concentrated around the cranial area (Figure 5.7). One of these was white and carved to resemble a set of teeth. Simon Martin (personal communication 2011) suggested that this might represent a decayed headdress. I also recovered seven small ceramic beads in this area, possibly part of the same assemblage. Two tiny fragments of calcified textile were also recovered.

The occupant was buried with a considerable collection of faunal remains, analyzed by Diana Fridberg. She identified the bones of a turtle and a small crocodile at the feet of the individual. In addition, the tomb was scattered with hundreds of fragments of freshwater shells, both bivalves and gastropods. The Classic Maya commonly buried their rulers with shells, reflecting religious beliefs about a watery underworld. However, such shells are usually marine in origin. These appear to have been collected locally from the *civales* of La Corona, as with the turtle and crocodile (Baron, Fridberg, and Canuto 2011).

I recovered eight ceramic vessels that had originally been placed in the tomb (Figure 5.8, bottom right). These consisted of a set of three nearly identical glossy black bowls, another slightly larger glossy black bowl, a set of two dull black bowls, and a set of two red bowls. While they lacked polychrome

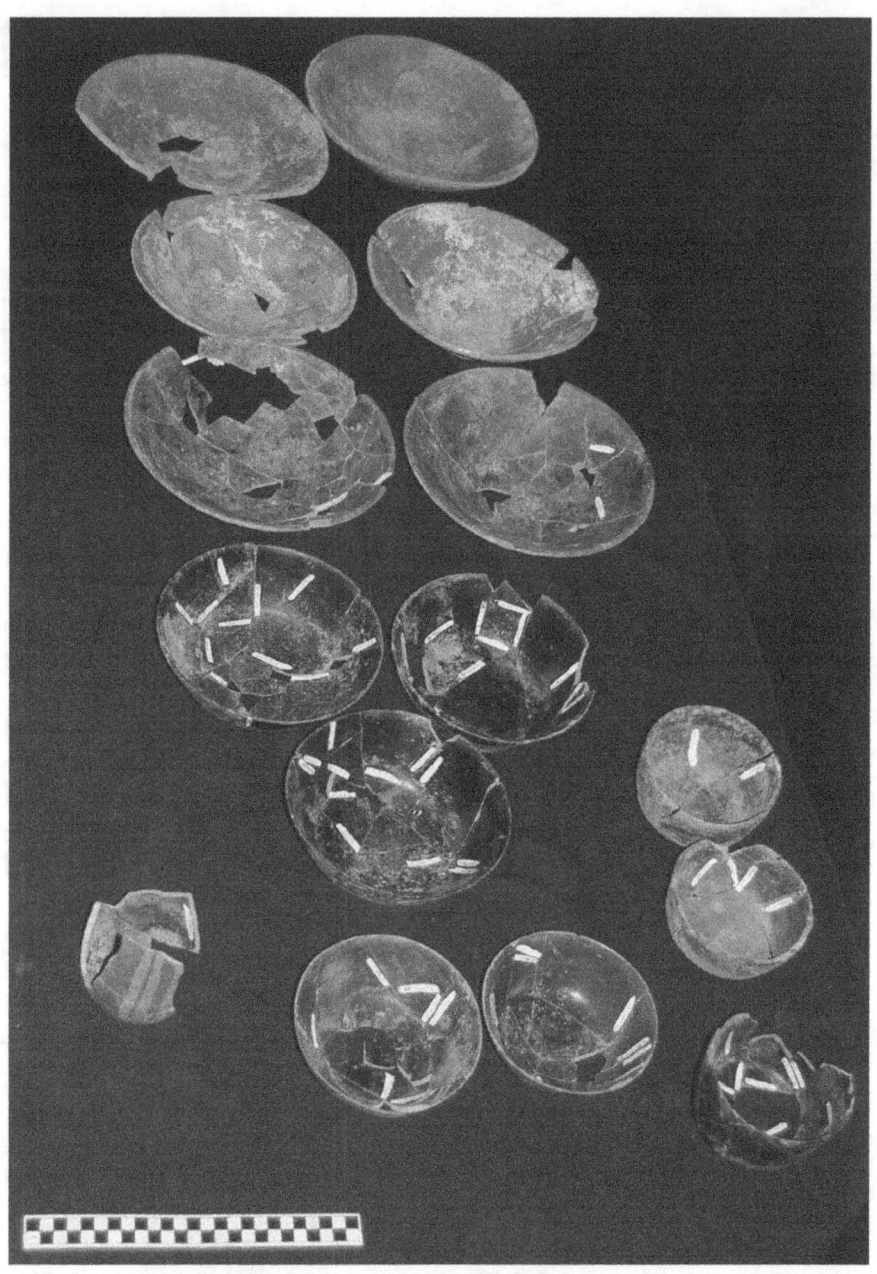

FIGURE 5.8. *Ceramics recovered from Burial 6. Vessels placed in the tomb itself are shown at the bottom right; vessels placed above the tomb are shown at the top and bottom left.*

FIGURE 5.9. *Impression of a woven mat left on the fill above Burial 6*

decoration, these ceramics were of high quality with delicate thin walls. Two soil samples from the tomb, analyzed by Clarissa Cagnato (personal communication 2012), indicated that these ceramics originally held maize, beans, and possibly fruit.

After the tomb was filled and covered with a wooden roof, a woven mat, indexical of Classic Maya rulership, was placed on top of it. Although this mat had decayed, it left an imprint in the wet fill above, which can still be seen (Figure 5.9). An additional set of ceramics was placed on top of this mat. These included five hemispherical bowls and one flat-bottomed bowl, each between 23 and 28 centimeters in diameter (Figure 5.8, top). I also recovered about half of a small cylinder vase painted with red and orange vertical stripes (Figure 5.8, bottom left). It is possible that additional offerings were also left above the tomb, but structural instability prevented us from exploring the area more broadly.

Finally, after these offerings were placed, the Maya covered the context in a large deposit of lithics. I recovered approximately 7,000 pieces of chert, which consisted of unused flakes, many with cortex. I also recovered about 450 pieces of obsidian, including small flakes and intentionally broken spent prismatic blade cores. Chert would have been available locally at La Corona, while obsidian had to be imported. This scarcity of material probably accounts for the difference between the quantity and forms of the chert and obsidian lithics. I estimate that my excavations recovered only about a quarter to a third of the original deposit, and I suspect that the original amount was probably around 20,000 to 30,000 pieces of chert and 1,500 to 2,000 pieces of obsidian.

After the tomb context was buried, the Muk Phase platform of Structure 13R-2 was constructed to approximately 8 meters high, taller than either of its neighbors. Excavations revealed the method of construction, with informal retention walls creating bins of fill. These fills were clearly drawn from different deposits, as they differed in color and their ceramic material also differed slightly in date. Overall, ceramic analysis from the tomb and the fill revealed that the platform was constructed around 600 or possibly slightly later. At the top of the platform a set of red painted stairs was preserved, probably originally leading into the temple's superstructure.

Burials 2 and 6 were similar to each other in terms of construction, ceramic contents, and date. Overall, the Muk Stage of construction probably spanned the last few decades of the sixth century, perhaps ending just after 600. The archaeological record points to these platforms as funerary shrines for high-status members of the La Corona community, probably rulers. This status is indicated by the labor expenditures in carving the tomb chambers and constructing high pyramidal temples; in burying the deceased with high-quality ceramics and aquatic fauna; in covering Burial 6 with a woven mat, indexical of royal authority; and in depositing tens of thousands of lithic flakes over the burial. Such lithic deposits are associated with elite burials at other Classic Maya sites as well (Demarest et al. 2003; Moholy-Nagy 1997). But in spite of the obvious importance of the tomb occupants, it is significant that I did not recover jade in either context and that the quantity of marine shell was also low. Though these materials were important status markers for Maya elites, they were not available locally at La Corona. This indicates that during the period in which Burial 6 was created, La Corona was not highly integrated into regional exchange networks and instead relied on locally available resources such as aquatic fauna from its seasonal lakes. This would seem to suggest that these buried sixth-century rulers were not very politically connected with the greater Maya world.

Looking at the entire construction sequence of the Coronitas temples so far, we can interpret them as a necropolis, slowly built after the death of each subsequent ancestor, beginning with the death of Tahn K'inich and continuing until around 600.

HISTORICAL REFERENCES

There is little historical information about the sixth century in the inscriptions of La Corona. But two later inscriptions did make reference to a ruler from this period. Although his name glyph cannot be read with certainty, it represents a bird with a person in its mouth, possibly a vulture (Martin 2008b). According to Panel 6, Vulture was the first of three La Corona rulers to marry the daughter of a ruler from the Kaan polity in 520 (Martin 2008b). Just over a century later, the Kaan rulers would be based at Calakmul, but during the sixth century they were still located at the previous court, Dzibanche (Martin 2005b; Velásquez García 2004). The woman was named Naah Ek', meaning "House Star," and she was the daughter of Kaan ruler Tuun K'ab Hix. Panel 6 depicted her arrival, standing atop a palanquin platform, which also held the towering effigy of a patron god (Figure 5.10). This scene is similar to those on the lintels of Tikal, described in chapter 4. The god effigy's eye and upturned snout bore a strong resemblance to motifs from the Central Mexican city of Teotihuacan. Lady Naah Ek' herself wore a Teotihuacan-style headdress. Overall, the scene presented her marriage to La Corona's ruler as the beginning of a new era of foreign connections, particularly with the Kaan polity, and by extension with a distant source of authority in Central Mexico.

The other reference to Vulture can be found on Stela 1, carved in 694 (Martin 2008b). The text harkened back to an important calendrical ceremony that Vulture performed in 544 and compared it to contemporary events in the era in which the stela was carved. The text referred to Vulture with the royal title of La Corona, *Sak Wahyis*,[6] with the unusual addition of *k'uhul* "godlike" (Stanley Guenter, personal communication 2008).

Both of these inscriptions, then, considered Vulture a person of great distinction. On Panel 6 his marriage in 520 was described using the verb *huli*, meaning "she arrived here," and was compared to the marriage of two later rulers, both from the Six Nothing lineage. This verb is of particular interest, since it often implied arrivals of great political import (Stuart 2000). At Tikal, for example, this verb was used to refer to the arrival of conquerors from Teotihuacan in the fourth century. At Copan it designated the arrival of the site's first dynastic ruler. Here at La Corona it described the arrival of three different women from the Kaan polity, suggesting a dynastic founding and periodic renewal. The depiction of the towering patron god that accompanied Lady Naah Ek' implies a religious renewal as well. Panel 6 thus demonstrates that the Six Nothing rulers traced their dynastic authority to Vulture and his wife. Stela 1 was also carved by a member of the Six Nothing family, and its account of Vulture's 544 calendar ritual supports the notion that this later ruler saw him as an ancestor.

FIGURE 5.10. *Right side of La Corona Panel 6, showing the arrival of Lady Naah Ek' in 520. She is accompanied by a Teotihuacan-style patron deity effigy.*

In 2017, archaeologists working at La Corona discovered Altar 5, a monument dated to 544 CE and commemorating an important calendar ritual performed by a ruler named Chak Tok Ich'aak (see Stuart et al. 2018 for its archaeological context and epigraphic significance). The same ritual is also recorded on La Corona Stela 1, this time with Vulture as a protagonist, suggesting that these two rulers were either alive at the same time or two names for the same individual. The altar was set into a cut platform floor in front of Str. 13R-2, but it is unclear whether it was placed there originally in 544, or reset there later from a different location. If original to that location, it likely corresponds to the Mam phase and may mark the location to an as-yet undiscovered tomb in the Mam platform. However, it is also possible that this ruler was buried elsewhere at La Corona or possibly El Peru, where he is also named.

Crucially, the altar depicts Chak Tok Ich'aak cradling a ceremonial bar from which emerge the images of two patron deities, each labeled with their name glyphs. On the left is Yaxal Ajaw, depicted as an aspect of the Sun God. I translate Yaxal Ajaw as "Firstborn Lord" after Hull (2005:116). The use of *Ajaw* ("Lord") in his name exemplifies the Classic Maya practice of using rulership tropes to describe and represent patron gods. On the right side is Chak Wayaab Chak ("Red Dreamer Rain God"). Both of these gods were venerated by later rulers of La Corona as well (see below). In the image, Chak Tok Ich'aak is seated upon a large glyph reading Wak Mih Nal Chan Ch'een ("Six Nothing Place City"). This links the ruler to the mythical place of origin that would continue to be of extreme rhetorical importance for later lineage members (see below).

But the textual narrative presented in these inscriptions of a new era of political alliance with the Kaan polity contrasts to the apparent isolation indicated by the remains in Burials 2 and 6. During later periods in which the Six Nothing lineage was firmly established as rulers of La Corona, burials contained lavish exotic material such as carved jades, shells, and pearls (Desailly-Chanson 2011, 2012). As I have already noted, I believe that the Six Nothing lineage, of which Vulture and Chak Tok Ich'aak were a part, was a distinct family from that of Tahn K'inich and his descendants buried in the Muk phase Coronitas tombs. The evidence for this distinction becomes clearer in other inscriptions and in subsequent construction phases. Thus, I reconstruct the sixth century at La Corona as a back-and-forth shift of power. In the early 500s Vulture somehow established himself as ruler of the site rather than the descendants of Tahn K'inich. According to later members of Vulture's lineage, he cemented his authority by forging a marriage alliance with the rulers of the Kaan polity at Dzibanche. But upon upon the death of Chak Tok Ich'aak, authority reverted to the members of Tahn K'inich's lineage, who were buried with locally obtained status symbols and impressive funerary shrines near their ancestor (Baron, Fridberg, and Canuto 2011).

This is the first time in La Corona history when it is possible to see two competing models of hereditary authority: one based on the continued veneration of one's ancestor—a first settler of the community, and the other based on the introduction of foreign symbols of authority—marriage to a foreign princess, the arrival of new patron gods, and the use of imagery from distant Teotihuacan.

THE SEVENTH CENTURY: CIVIL BLOOD

Sak Maas

The historical record of La Corona's rulers is much more detailed during the seventh century, the period in which the Six Nothing lineage dominated the site. Panel 2 records the accession of a La Corona ruler named Sak Maas[7] and links him genealogically to later rulers at the site, including his son and grandson. Sak Maas's own monuments indicated the importance of a renewed alliance with the Kaan polity. In 651 he commissioned a pair of stairway blocks (Elements 35 and 36) that depicted him engaged in a ballgame with Kaan ruler Yuknoom Ch'een (Stuart and Baron 2013:200). This game had taken place in 635, but it was so important politically that it was commemorated not only on the stairway blocks but generations later on a block (Element 33) commissioned by Sak Maas's grandson in 696. The same block recorded the reason this ballgame was probably so politically important: just fifty-four days after it occurred, the Kaan dynasty moved its court to Calakmul from Dzibanche (Stuart 2012b; see also Martin 2005b; Velásquez García 2004). This put it significantly closer to La Corona, just ninety miles to the northeast. The move also had profound repercussions in Maya regional politics—it began a period in which Calakmul accumulated allies and vassals across the southern lowlands, temporarily encircling its rival, Tikal. La Corona was an important part of that network. It formed part of a chain of sites that controlled the Western Peten and stretched all the way to Cancuen, giving Calakmul access to jade, prized quetzal feathers, and obsidian (Canuto and Barrientos 2013). The ballgame in 635 was probably a vital step in a new alliance in which Sak Maas pledged La Corona's support for Calakmul's expanding influence.

By comparing this historical record to that of the Coronitas temples, Sak Maas's accession must have taken place within a few decades, if not

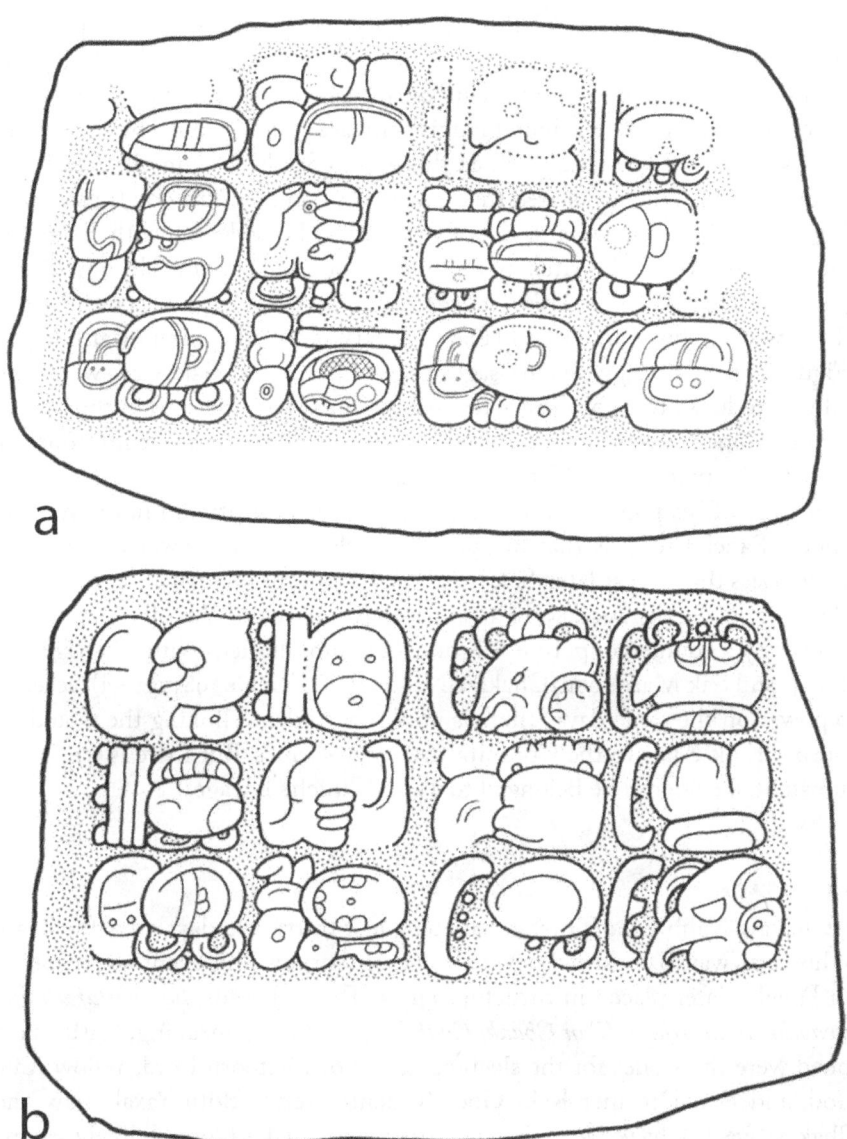

FIGURE 5.11. *Hieroglyphic Stairway blocks mentioning the patron god Ikiiy: a. Sak Maas conjures Ikiiy on Element 11 (after drawing by Nikolai Grube). b. K'inich [?] Yook conjures Ikiiy on Element 44, continuing the work of his grandfather.*

immediately after, the completion of Burial 6. This indicates that he probably came to power at the expense of Tahn K'inich's lineage, and it could explain the appearance of a new patron deity during his rule. The god Ikiiy[8] was mentioned only in the text of a hieroglyphic staircase commissioned by Sak Maas's grandson, but the text clearly linked this god to Sak Maas himself (Stuart and Baron 2013:212). The text stated that Sak Maas "conjured" the god (*tzak*) in 637 (Figure 5.11a), about two and a half years after the ballgame with Yuknoom Ch'een. It compared this ritual to a similar conjuring performed by Sak Maas's grandson but concluded with *utz'akbuil uchabiy umam* "it is the continuation of the work of his grandfather" (David Stuart, personal communication 2012) (Figure 5.11b). These glyphic passages suggest that it was Sak Maas who originally introduced this god. This narrative is similar to those seen in the inscriptions of Copan, where ancestors were specifically credited for the introduction of particular patron gods (Prager 2013:374).

In spite of his political strategies, Sak Maas's authority did not go unchallenged. Panel 2 records that in 655 a new ruler came to power named K'uk' Ajaw.[9] Less than a year later, Sak Maas died "with the edge of a stone" (Grube, Martin, and Zender 2002:85) in an apparent coup d'etat.[10] And it was followed quickly by a countercoup. In 658 K'uk Ajaw himself died "with the edge of a stone," and Sak Maas's son, Chakaw Nahb Chan (Ringle 1985:152–53), acceded to power on the same day.[11] There is no direct evidence linking the would-be usurper K'uk' Ajaw to the Coronitas funerary shrines. But there is strong circumstantial evidence he belonged to Tahn K'inich's lineage.

K'UH STAGE

Chakaw Nahb Chan's first act as ruler, just thirty-five days after the death of his rival, was to construct new patron deity shrines. This event was recorded on Panel 1, later placed in Structure 13R-5. The text reads, *hux patlaj utuunil uwayibil Yaxal Ajaw, K'an Chaak, Chak Wayaab Chaak*, meaning, "thrice fashioned were the stones for the sleeping places of Firstborn Lord, Yellow Rain God, and Red Dreamer Rain God" (Guenter 2005). Both Yaxal Ajaw and Chak Wayaab Chaak were already patron gods of La Corona, likely having been introduced by Chak Tok Ich'aak as depicted on Altar 5. Yet this is the first time in the inscriptions of La Corona that K'an Chaak was mentioned, and the context suggests that Chakaw Nahb Chan, like his father Sak Maas, introduced a new patron god upon his victory over a rival.

When I began excavations in the Coronitas temples, it was with the strong suspicion that the temples for the three gods listed on this monument corresponded to Structures 13R-2, 13R-3, and 13R-4. After all, these temples are immediately adjacent to Structure 13R-5, where Panel 1 was found. Furthermore, they are a set of three temples approximately equal in size, a configuration that is not obvious elsewhere on site. For this reason, I was initially surprised to find tombs under the Muk Stage of these platforms, since burials point to an obvious interpretation as funerary shrines rather than "sleeping places" for patron gods. However, archaeological evidence suggests that, in fact, in the K'uh Stage these structures were repurposed for patron deities. This is indicated by three characteristics of this stage. First, whereas the Muk Stage had consisted of a series of platforms built at separate times, the K'uh Stage was a single continuous architectural program, consistent with three temples dedicated on the same day. Second, this phase showed signs of having been constructed with considerable speed, consistent with a thirty-five-day time frame. Finally, evidence from an accumulated midden indicates that the rituals that took place on these structures after the K'uh Stage differed from those of the earlier Mam Stage.

The K'uh Stage appears as a thin veneer of architecture on the front of Structures 13R-2, 13R-3, and 13R-4. On Structure 13R-2 the top of the platform rose only to a height about 50 centimeters above that of the platform's Muk Phase. Similarly, on Structure 3, a looters' trench cut revealed that the new K'uh Stage floor was less than 50 centimeters higher than that of the previous architecture. In Structure 13R-4 the difference was about 1.5 meters, also observable in a looters' trench. This evened out the differences in height between the structures, so that in the K'uh Stage, Structure 13R-4 was about a meter shorter than 13R-3, which was in turn only about a meter shorter than 13R-2. I identified K'uh Stage staircases on Structures 13R-2 and 13R-3 and a wall feature that may be the north side of the 13R-4 staircase. All of these features were integrated with a single floor that formed a front terrace shared by the three buildings. In addition, the possible north side of the 13R-4 staircase integrated with a frontal terrace of 13R-3, indicating that they were built simultaneously.

The superstructures of the three platforms were almost certainly perishable. I identified low masonry foundation walls on Structures 13R-2 and 13R-3, but no vault stones. I also recovered fragments of daub—used to cover wooden walls—at the summit of Structure 13R-2 and in the collapsed debris behind Structure 13R-4. Even more significant is the fact that I did not identify K'uh Stage architecture on the back terraces of the platforms. Instead, the Muk Stage masonry was left exposed. In fact, many of the Muk Stage facing stones on the back of Structure 13R-4 had been torn out. Although I can't know for certain when these stones were removed, it is possible that they were repurposed on the front of the structure during the hurried construction of the K'uh Stage. Only twelve diagnostic sherds were recovered from the fills of this thin K'uh Stage architecture, but this small sample is consistent with a date in the mid-seventh century.

In a corner formed by the back terraces of Structures 13R-4 and 13R-3, ceramic material had accumulated into a midden. Because the K'uh Stage of construction left the Muk terraces intact in this location, it is difficult to determine stratigraphically when these materials were deposited. However, the soil matrix was a noticeably hard gray material, and at least part of this matrix must have been deposited after the facing stones of the terraces were removed. Of the ceramics themselves, 130 had diagnostic features consistent with a mid-seventh-century date. This evidence indicates that the midden was probably deposited in the years following the K'uh construction of the temple platforms.

The forms of these sherds were particularly significant. While more than half of the Mam Stage midden recovered within Structure 13R-2 had consisted of plates, this K'uh Stage assemblage reflected a greater emphasis on liquids (see Figure 5.5). The identifiable forms included 20 percent vases (a form that was absent from the earlier Mam midden), 49 percent bowls, 17 percent jars, and only 15 percent plates. A Fisher's exact test showed that these two assemblages were significantly different from each other ($p < .001$), reflecting a shift in ritual practices between these two periods.

All of this archaeological evidence demonstrates that Structures 13R-2, 13R-3, and 13R-4 underwent comparatively minor architectural modifications in the mid-seventh century, with an accompanying dramatic change in function. This is consistent with my interpretation of these buildings as repurposed "sleeping places" for patron deities, built by Chakaw Nahb Chan, just thirty-five days after his bloody countercoup and rise to power. The fact that he chose to repurpose these particular buildings is also significant. As funerary shrines of a rival lineage, these temples and the ancestor veneration that took place on them were key aspects of a social model that challenged Chakaw Nahb Chan's new authority. Descendants of Tahn K'inich would have used these veneration rites as indexical signs linking them to the rights and privileges of their ancestors (McAnany 1995). By replacing these funerary temples with *wayibs* of patron gods, Chakaw Nahb Chan challenged this social model and in its place promoted one in which authority was derived from the ruler's close association with community-protecting patron deities. The fact that Chakaw Nahb Chan was in such a hurry to make this change supports the idea that his recently killed rival was also a member of this dangerous rival lineage.

FIGURE 5.12. *Polychrome ceramics with royal titles recovered from the patio of Structure 13R-10 and the lower fill of Structure 13R-9*

UB STAGE

Chakaw Nahb Chan continued the close association with Calakmul that had been initiated by his father, Sak Maas. In 664 his eldest son, K'inich [?] Yook,[12] traveled to Calakmul, staying there until his father's death in 667 (Schele and Grube 1994:128–29). Upon his return, La Corona saw what might have been its first smooth transition of power for quite some time. Many of the known monuments of La Corona date to the reign of K'inich [?] Yook and indicate his continued close relationship to Calakmul. Not only did he return there for a second accession ceremony under the auspices of the Kaan ruler in 675 (Guenter 2005); he became the second La Corona ruler to marry a Kaan princess in 679 (Martin 2008b). The two of them had a son who would later become the La Corona ruler Yajawte' K'inich (Martin 2008b). K'inich [?] Yook's own hieroglyphic staircase emphasized his son's genealogical links to the Calakmul ruler.

K'inich [?] Yook also emphasized devotions to patron deities on his monuments, both those introduced by previous rulers of his lineage as well as a new patron deity, [?] Winik Ub. The *wayib* temple of this god corresponds to the Ub Stage of Structure 13R-5, built over the ancient K'inich Stage funerary shrine. In this case, the platform's change in function is indicated by the accompanying Panel 1,[13] which explicitly stated the temple's new purpose and offers a fascinating look at the ideological discourses that K'inich [?] Yook used to promote his own dynasty at the expense of his rivals.

According to this text, the new *wayib* was dedicated in 677, about ten years after K'inich [?] Yook's original accession (Guenter 2005). Unlike his father's hurried completion of the K'uh Stage, K'inich [?] Yook had the time to see that the Ub Stage was completed with more care. While the previous K'inich Stage of Structure 13R-5 had been a low platform just 30 centimeters high, the new architecture raised the platform an additional 1.5 meters. Its terraces were constructed of carefully cut blocks and extended to both the front and back of the platform. Its superstructure consisted of masonry walls forming a room approximately 7.5 meters wide and 3 meters deep (Canuto 2006). The back wall of this superstructure was nearly 2 meters thick, wide enough to support a vaulted roof, though no vault stones were recovered. This wall was pierced by a window or doorway opening toward the back (east) of the structure. At the base of this opening was a bench into which was set Panel 1. As discussed above, the panel was not placed along the center axis of the new Ub construction but rather above the K'inich Stage tomb below (Canuto 2006).

Other episodes of construction in the Coronitas group also probably correspond to K'inich [?] Yook's reign. Structure 13R-10 saw a major phase of construction around this time, and Structure 13R-9, a pyramidal funerary shrine, was constructed next to it (Ponce Stokvis 2013). Excavations on the patio behind these two structures, as well as in the deeper fill of Structure 13R-9 itself, recovered massive amounts of ceramics and animal bones (Acuña 2006, 2009; Patterson, Garza, and Miguel 2012; Ponce and Cajas 2012). Many of the ceramics were polychromes, and several were recovered with painted texts, including royal titles from La Corona and Calakmul (Figure 5.12). This evidence indicates that the area behind Structures 13R-9 and 13R-10 served as a venue for elite-sponsored feasting activities, in which food and drink were consumed in high-status vessels that were then discarded in a display of conspicuous consumption. This feasting refuse made convenient fill material when the base of Structure 13R-9 was constructed nearby (Cajas 2013:137).

Patron Deities in the Inscriptions of K'inich [?] Yook

K'inich [?] Yook commissioned a lengthy hieroglyphic staircase whose original location is uncertain. Many blocks have been looted, and several were

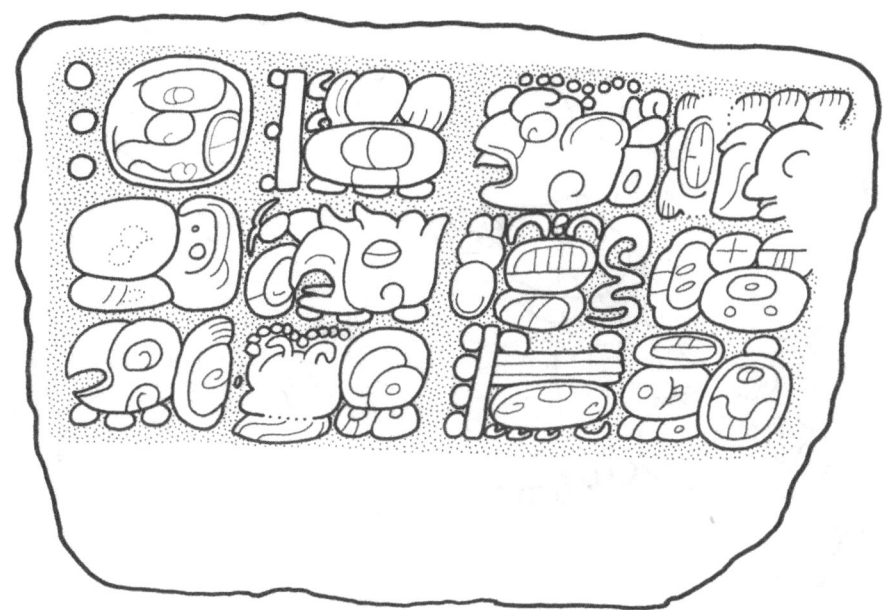

FIGURE 5.13. *Hieroglyphic Stairway block (Element 39) describing a ritual dance by K'inich [?] Yook "in the year of Yaxal Ajaw"*

found on the front of Structure 13R-10, having been mixed with other panels in the mid-eighth century. There is strong possibility that Structure 13R-10 was the original location of the text during K'inich [?] Yook's reign, though the movement of these blocks by looters and the Maya themselves leaves open other possibilities. Enough of the text is preserved to make it clear that the continued veneration of patron gods was an important part of the overall narrative of K'inich [?] Yook's exploits as ruler of La Corona. For example, as mentioned earlier, one block recorded a conjuring ritual (*tzak*) performed by K'inich [?] Yook for the god Ikiiy, first introduced by his grandfather Sak Maas (Stuart and Baron 2013:212) (see Figure 5.11b). Here the god's name was followed by the La Corona place-name, Sak Nikte', perhaps to emphasize the importance of this god to the entire community. The text referred to the god as *ubaah uch'ab yahk'abil K'inich [?] Yook* "K'inich [?] Yook's image, penance, and darkness," a metaphor commonly used to describe the relation between fathers and sons as well as the relationship between ruler and patron god (see chapter 4). But while emphasizing this close relationship between K'inich [?] Yook and the god, the text concluded that this ritual was the "continuation of the work of his grandfather," Sak Maas.

FIGURE 5.14. *Hieroglyphic Stairway block (Element 23) describing K'inich [?] Yook drinking and giving pulque (after photograph by Justin Kerr)*

Another two blocks on the same stairway linked a set of calendar rituals to the patron god Yaxal Ajaw ("Firstborn Lord"), first mentioned on Altar 5 from 544 (Figure 5.13). The text referred to a set of dances occurring one year apart from one another, leading up to an important calendrical juncture in 682 (Stuart and Baron 2013:204). This period of dancing was described as "the year of song of Yaxal Ajaw "(David Stuart, personal communication 2012),[14] suggesting that the god somehow presided over this period in the ritual calendar.

One other block on this stairway may also have referred to patron deity veneration. It recounted an event in 683 in which K'inich [?] Yook drank and gave pulque (Stuart 2008) (Figure 5.14). This passage is highly reminiscent other Classic Maya texts about feeding liquids to patron deities, especially Tortuguero Monument 6, which also makes reference to pulque. And as I will discuss shortly, there is strong archaeological evidence to suggest that liquid offerings were a key aspect of the worship of patron gods at the Coronitas temples as well. These various references to patron deity veneration rituals on

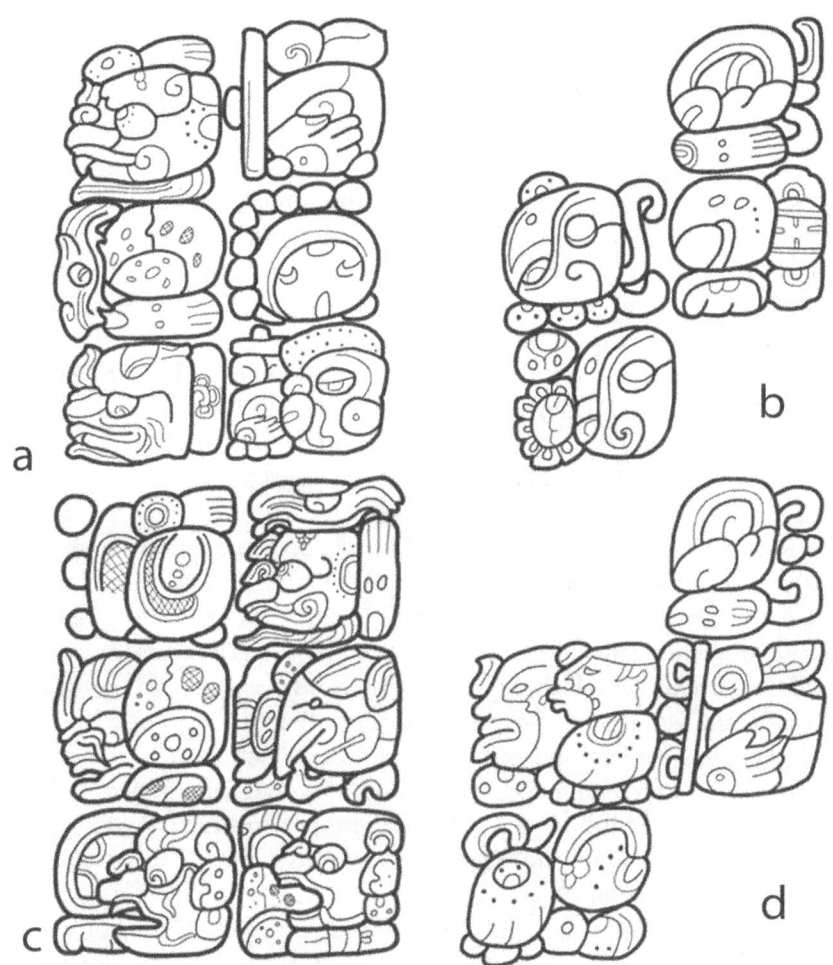

Figure 5.15. *La Corona Panel 1, recovered from the Ub Stage of Structure 13R-5: a. Construction of a wayib temple for the Six Nothing Place god. b. Tahn K'inich comes to La Corona. c. Construction of three wayib temples for three patron gods. d. An ancestor comes to La Corona from the Six Nothing Place in ancient times.*

Structure 13R-10's hieroglyphic staircase, if indeed that is its original location, suggest that the structure functioned not only as an elite residence but also as part of a greater complex for patron deity ritual during the reign of K'inich [?] Yook. The feasting events that took place on the patio behind this structure may also have been related to this ritual purpose.

But of all K'inich [?] Yook's monuments, Panel 1, recovered from the Ub phase of Structure 13R-5, is the most compelling evidence for the importance of patron deity veneration in the ruler's claims to authority. It carried an extensive text, which linked his newly introduced god to the exploits of two ancient historical figures. This text engaged two competing discourses about the history of La Corona, promoting one and minimizing the other.

Of key importance on the panel was the Six Nothing place-name, which I have used already as a label for K'inich [?] Yook's lineage. Aside from Panel 1, this phrase is found on three other La Corona monuments. The earliest is Altar 5, discussed above. Another is Element 19, which depicted Chakaw Nahb Chan and his wife performing a calendar ritual in 662. The text used the typical La Corona royal title, *Sak Wahyis*, but followed it with "Six Nothing Place" as a second title for the ruler. The other inscription, Element 30, is too badly eroded to read or date, but it does contain legible "Six Nothing Place" and *Sak Wahyis* glyphs, in the reverse order from that of Element 19 (Stuart and Baron 2013:192–93).[15] "Six Nothing Place" is not a unique place-name but in fact parallels a whole set of Six [x] Places found in Classic Maya inscriptions (Tokovinine 2008:282–84). For example, the rulers of the site of Naranjo were said to come from the Six Earth Place. These place-names were also painted on polychrome vessels depicting dancing maize gods, each associated with a different Maya polity. Six [x] Places, including Six Nothing Place, can thus be interpreted as ancient mythical places from which the royal lineages of different polities were said to originate. K'inich [?] Yook's use of Six Nothing Place thus presented his lineage as equal in stature to other illustrious dynasties, like those of Calakmul and Naranjo, through its iconic similarity to other mythical places of origin.

Panel 1 recorded six main events (Guenter 2005): (1) the construction of the Ub phase of 13R-5, the *wayib* for the patron god [?] Winik Ub (Figure 5.15a); (2) Tahn K'inich's journey to La Corona in 314, as discussed above (Figure 5.15b); (3) Chakaw Nahb Chan's dedication of three temples for patron gods in 658, also discussed above (Figure 5.15c); (4) a journey by K'inich [?] Yook to Calakmul and various interactions with the Calakmul royal family; (5) K'inich [?] Yook's second accession ceremony under the auspices of the Calakmul ruler; and (6) an ancient journey made by an individual to La Corona from the Six Nothing Place in 3805 BCE (Figure 5.15d). Some of the events at Calakmul were also repeated on K'inich [?] Yook's hieroglyphic staircase, indicating that his relationship with the Kaan polity was important to his status as ruler of La Corona. However, I will focus on the other four events, since they are most revealing about the role of patron deities in his ideological discourse.

The text juxtaposes two historical characters that came to La Corona from other locations. One was Tahn K'inich, whose journey took place in 314. The other's name cannot be read, but he was said to have come in 3805 BCE. Both of these journeys happened on the day 4 K'an in the ritual calendar, which served to iconically link them as parallel events. As I have already noted, Tahn K'inich's journey occurred around the same time that La Corona was first settled, and this historical record, combined with his probable remains in the tomb below, points to him as an early settler or founder of the community. The other character, however, seems like a more mythical figure. Not only does the date of his journey predate any conceivable occupation of La Corona by nearly 4,000 years; he was said to have come from Six Nothing Place, a mythological location associated with K'inich [?] Yook's lineage. While the text thus acknowledges the role of Tahn K'inich in the early history of La Corona, it simultaneously presents the Six Nothing lineage as having been at the site far earlier. By extension, any claims that Tahn K'inich's family may have had by virtue of their veneration of this ancestor would be trumped by the far older claims of the Six Nothing lineage.

It is also significant that the verb used to describe both of these ancient journeys was *tali*, meaning "to come from somewhere." But, as I mentioned previously, arrival events of political import, such as the founding of a new community or dynasty, would typically be recorded using the verb *huli* "to arrive here" (Stuart 2000). In La Corona texts the *huli* verb was used only to describe the arrival of politically important women who married rulers of La Corona. For example, K'inich [?] Yook's hieroglyphic staircase described the arrival of his wife, a Calakmul princess, using the *huli* verb. The choice to use the *tali* verb on Panel 1 was thus more than a semantic distinction. The pragmatic meaning of the text was that neither Tahn K'inich nor the other ancient individual named on the panel established dynastic authority at La Corona. This was achieved only later by the Six Nothing lineage, when its members married Calakmul women and infused their lineage with royal blood from the Kaan polity. The panel thus offers two justifications for the Six Nothing lineage's supremacy over the descendants of Tahn K'inich: not only were they here thousands of years earlier but they descended from high-status rulers of powerful Calakmul.

How did patron gods play a role in this text? The panels commemorated the dedication of the "sleeping place" for a new god, not mentioned in previous La Corona inscriptions. This temple, reflecting the Ub Stage of Structure 13R-5, was described as the "Six Nothing Place" and the god, named [?] Winik Ub,[16] was described as "the Six Nothing Place god." This temple was dedicated on the day 4 K'an, linking him to the two ancient historical characters. The fact that this god was explicitly identified with the Six Nothing Place firmly associates him with the Six Nothing lineage and with the primordial ancestor who came to La Corona long ago. Similarly, his temple recreated the mythical place of origin of the lineage.

Finally, the dedication of his temple was compared to the recent construction of sleeping places for three other patron gods by Chakaw Nahb Chan in 658. The text used the same phrasing to refer to both dedications: *patlaj utuunil uwayibil* . . . "the stone[s] was/were fashioned for the sleeping place[s] of . . ." The archaeological record from Structures 13R-2, 13R-3, and 13R-4 indicates that this 658 dedication repurposed platforms that had previously served as ancestor shrines, probably for members of the rival lineage founded by Tahn K'inich. And the Ub phase of Structure 13R-5, where this panel was found, accomplished the same task, covering over the funerary temple of Tahn K'inich himself. By comparing these two temple dedication events, the text established a recent historical precedent and justified the reuse of Structure 13R-5.

Taken as a whole, the panel emphasized the immense antiquity of the Six Nothing lineage at La Corona as compared with the relatively recent arrival of Tahn K'inich in 314. This claim to primacy at the site justified the repurposing of K'inich's tomb for the benefit of a patron god also from the venerable Six Nothing Place. And this temple replacement was also framed with reference to a recent precedent—the construction of patron deity shrines over other funerary temples by the previous ruler. This text is a clear example of an ideological discourse, which in fact engages three distinct (and often competing) social models. The claims of this specific ruler to authority were linked to his close relationship to protective patron gods and his role in caring for and maintaining their effigies through temple dedications. They were also linked to the competing model of chronological primacy and ancestor veneration— K'inich [?] Yook claimed that his mythical ancestor in fact came to La Corona from the Six Nothing Place long before any other competing lineages. And, finally, his authority to rule was rhetorically associated with his affinal relations with the distant and high-status Kaan dynasty, rulers of Calakmul, an alliance exclusive to the Six Nothing family.

THE EIGHTH AND NINTH CENTURIES: AN ANCIENT GRUDGE

The Historical Record

Upon the death of K'inich [?] Yook, his younger brother, Chak Ak,' became ruler of La Corona for several decades (Schele and Grube 1994:125).[17] He maintained close ties to Calakmul, engaging in several rituals with its ruler

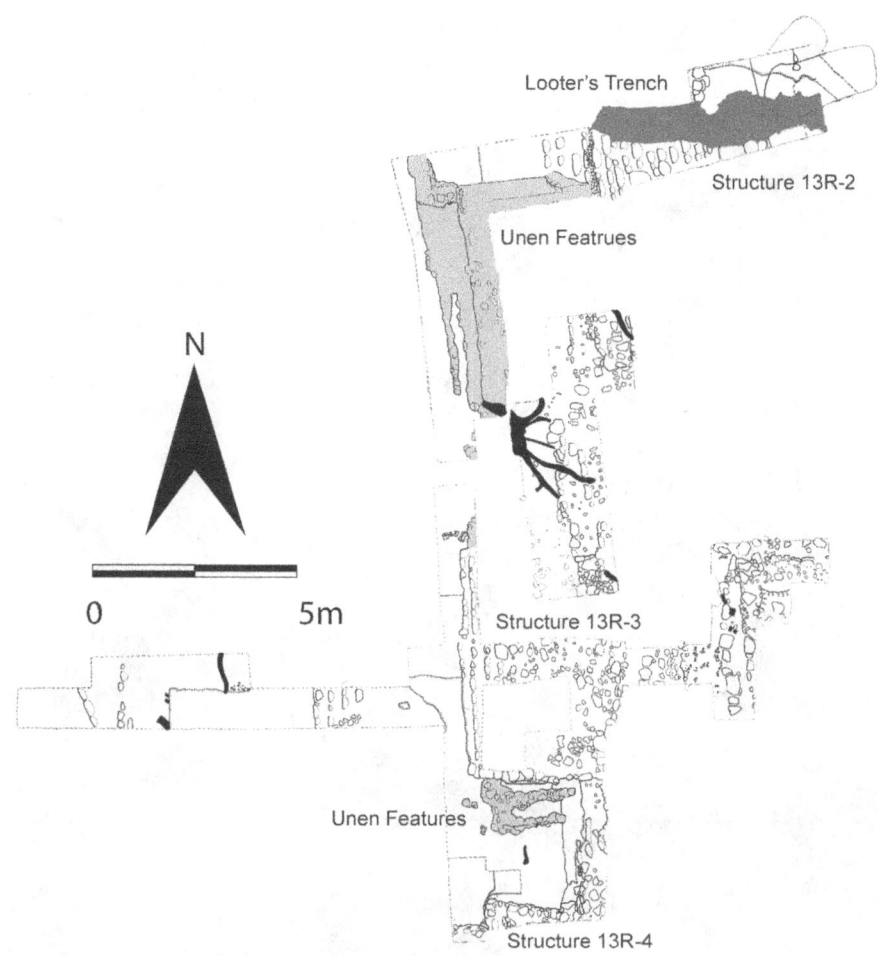

Figure 5.16. *Plan of the front terraces of Structures 13R-2 and 13R-3 showing Unen Stage features*

Yich'aak K'ahk'. A panel from La Corona (Element 56) indicates that he also maintained devotional rites to the patron god Yaxal Ajaw, though the nature of those rites remains unclear (David Stuart, personal communication 2015).

Sometime before 721 K'inich [?] Yook's son, Yajawte'e K'inich, came to power at La Corona. He commissioned Panel 6, a monument I discussed briefly above, which depicted the arrival of Vulture's wife in 520 together with the towering effigy of a Teotihuacan-style patron god. The text of this monument compared her arrival to that of his own mother from Calakmul, followed

FIGURE 5.17. *Unen Stage plaster decoration on the front of Structure 13R-3*

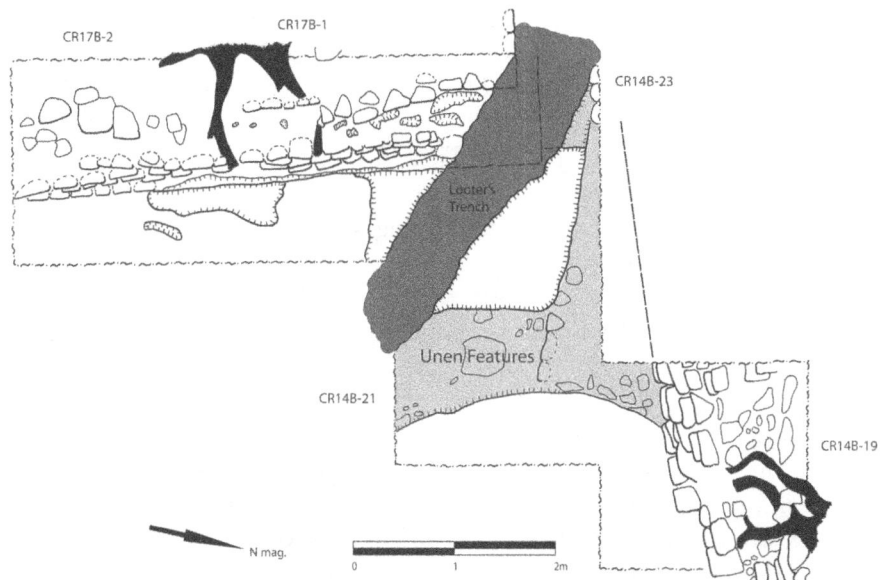

FIGURE 5.18. *Plan of the back terraces of Structures 13R-4 and 13R-5 showing Unen Stage features*

by that of his wife, a third Kaan princess, in 721 (Martin 2008b). This monument also used the *huli* verb to refer to the princess' journeys, indicating that this ruler, like his father, saw Calakmul as the origin of dynastic authority.

Yajawte' K'inich commissioned two other monuments. One is a stairway block (Element 34) that depicted him sitting triumphantly on a throne in front of stacks of tribute payments (Stuart and Baron 2013:198–99). The accompanying text told of a military victory. The other monument is an altar from the La Corona satellite La Cariba, dedicated in 746 (Marken 2010:34–35). The altar depicted both the ruler and his wife in front of a kneeling subject. But Yajawte' K'inich disappeared from the historical record after this time. Not coincidentally, it was in 743 and 744 that Tikal, archrival of Calakmul, attacked and defeated the Calakmul allies El Peru (about a day away from La Corona) and Naranjo (Martin 1996, 2000a) (see chapter 4). It is possible that Yajawte' K'inich also fell victim to the shifting geopolitics of the region.

The historical record resumed in 785 with the dedication of Altar 2. Altar 4 was probably commissioned by the same ruler, whose name cannot be read with certainty. In 791 a woman arrived at La Corona (described with the verb *huli*), but this time she came not from Calakmul, but from its longtime rival Tikal (Barrientos et al. 2011). This indicates an important shift in the politics of La Corona. While rulers from the Six Nothing lineage had rhetorically linked their right to rule to their blood ties to the Kaan dynasty for generations, this ruler was sleeping with their enemy, Tikal. Thus, it seems highly likely that he belonged to a different family, either a resurgent lineage of Tahn K'inich or some other faction. The latter part of the eighth century, therefore, represents yet another power shift in the local politics of La Corona.

The dedication of Altar 4 in 805 is the last known historical date at the site. As at so many other Classic Maya communities, the collapse of royal authority probably came soon after.

Unen Stage

After the completion of the K'uh and Ub Stages of Structures 13R-2, 13R-3, 13R-4, and 13R-5, a series of minor modifications was made on each of these temples. Stratigraphically, these features cannot be connected to one another, nor have sufficient ceramics been recovered to positively date them. I tentatively propose that they were eighth-century modifications, since they do not fit the planned architectural programs of these structures. However, it is possible that they could have been made in the late seventh century as well.

On the south side of the front stairs of 13R-3, I discovered two thin walls, designed to support decorative molded stucco (Figure 5.16). The only piece left intact represented a vegetal motif (Figure 5.17). On the north side of the same staircase a low platform was constructed that connected the stairs to those of Structure 13R-2. I also recovered chunks of molded stucco along the base of this platform near the 13R-3 staircase, but if there was a wider function of this new platform, it cannot be identified. Recent excavations carried out by other archaeologists at La Corona have revealed the presence of an Unen phase staircase on the front of Str. 13R-2 as well as a new building at its base, Str. 13R-45. This new building was constructed over Altar 5, which had previously been open to the sky (Stuart et al. 2018; Marcello Canuto, personal communication 2019).

On the back of Structure 13R-5 I identified another new set of walls (Figure 5.18). One connected the back terraces of 13R-5 to those of 13R-4. In addition, some sort of low foundation wall was constructed that attached to the southeast corner of the 13R-4 platform and continued to the south. This set of features formed an enclosed space immediately behind Structure 13R-5, also of unknown function. Within this area a small midden formed from ceramics discarded off the back of the temple. Ceramics from this midden included Chablekal Fine Grays, usually dated to after 760. Importantly, the assemblage of this midden closely matches that of the K'uh Stage midden discussed earlier. The main difference between them was that the K'uh Stage midden contained vases, a form of drinking vessel associated with elites. In the Unen Stage midden this function was taken by Fine Gray bowls, which made up a similar percentage of the assemblage (see figure 5.5). Assuming a functional equivalence between Fine Grays and cylinder vases, a Fisher's exact test revealed that the K'uh and Unen middens were not significantly different from each other (p = .653), while the Unen midden, like the K'uh midden, was significantly different from the earlier Mam Stage midden (p < .001). This is evidence that, even after the construction of the late Unen Stage walls behind Structure 13R-5, it continued to serve as a patron deity shrine.

Elsewhere in the Coronitas group other architectural modifications were made to Structures 13R-9 and 13R-10. Walls were added to the front façades of both, and the interior rooms of 13R-10 were changed, perhaps to add privacy (Ponce Stokvis 2013). In addition, sometime in the late history of the site, the hieroglyphic stairway of the structure was modified by adding a series of panels originally from other locations around La Corona (Ponce Stokvis 2013). Reassembled on Structure 13R-10, they formed no coherent order, and two were even placed upside down on either side of the new bottom step. To make matters worse, the context was looted in the 1960s, leaving only the bottom step in place. This made it difficult to reconstruct the stratigraphy of the context. During the ninth century a series of additional wall features was added to the basal platform in front of Structure 13R-10. These may represent residential structures built after dynastic authority at the site had collapsed (Ponce Stokvis 2013). Each of these eighth- and ninth-century architectural modifications was accompanied by evidence of significant ritual activities in and around Structure 13R-10. These indicate that even as La Corona saw dramatic political changes, the Coronitas group was still a venue for rituals.

PATRON DEITY VENERATION IN THE ARCHAEOLOGICAL RECORD

As I have alluded to throughout this chapter, there are multiple contexts throughout the entire Coronitas group that have yielded evidence for extensive ritual activities. These include deposits on and around the temples themselves as well as other areas on Structures 13R-7, 13R-9, 13R-10, and surrounding platform.

I identified three middens behind the temples that were formed after the refuse from ritual activities was discarded off the back of the platforms. The earliest of these was associated with the Mam Stage platform in Structure 13R-2 and thus probably accumulated from ancestor veneration activities. Another midden was located in a corner created by the back terraces of Structure 13R-3 and 13R-4 and corresponds to a period in which the temples were used as "sleeping places" for patron gods. The third was located behind Structure 13R-5, which by this time was also used as a patron deity shrine. As I have noted, the two middens associated with patron deity ritual are both significantly different from that associated with ancestor veneration, while they are statistically indistinguishable from one another. The major difference between these K'uh and Unen middens was that in the late eighth century high-status vases were replaced by Fine Gray bowls as an elite vessel for liquid consumption (Figure 5.5).

It is clear from the percentages of vessel forms in these two middens that primarily liquids were consumed on the patron deity temple platforms. Plates made up only a small portion of the assemblage (15 percent and 9 percent, respectively). Bowls were far more abundant (49 percent and 62 percent). These ranged from small, probably individual serving bowls less than 10 centimeters in diameter to larger basins of a maximum 54 centimeters wide. They also included a range of surface treatments, from polychromes and an incised text, probably belonging to elites, to more plain decoration, probably belonging to lower-status individuals. In the Ub Stage midden, Fine Gray bowls averaging 16 centimeters in diameter made up 15 percent of the assemblage and replaced similar-sized polychrome vases, which made up 20 percent of the earlier K'uh midden. These forms are also associated with elite use. Also common were undecorated jars (17 percent and 15 percent, respectively), whose lack of surface treatment may also point to use by lower-status individuals. In sum, these middens were made up primarily of vessels used to transport and serve liquids (85 percent and 91 percent, respectively), though the original owners of those containers varied considerably.

It is also possible to compare these two midden contexts with the remains found on the front of the Coronitas temples. When the site was abandoned, various vessels were left *in situ* sitting on the wide front terrace shared by Structures 13R-2, 13R-3, and 13R-4. These vessels also show an emphasis on liquids, but with a markedly different collection of forms. In all, I recovered 278 sherds, of which 72 percent of the identifiable forms were jars, most of which were undecorated and with an average diameter of 15 centimeters. Another 21 percent were bowls ranging from 10 to 32 centimeters across with both high-status and plain surface treatment. One sherd of a Fine Gray bowl was recovered here (1 percent), along with a small percentage (6 percent) of plate sherds (see figure 5.5).

From these ceramics, I reconstruct a pattern of temple use in which members of the La Corona community carried primarily liquid offerings to patron gods in bowls, vases, and jars (and the occasional plate), which were later discarded off the back of the temple after the ritual was complete. This is consistent with the evidence presented in chapters 3 and 4 that patron gods were sustained with ritual liquids such as chocolate, pulque, stews, and human blood. The varying surface treatment on these discarded vessels points to participation by differing social strata, not just elites. It is not clear whether community members themselves were allowed to approach the god effigies within their sanctuaries, but the midden assemblages do point to individualized offerings from a variety of different devotees. I speculate that the ritual liquid used in these offerings was served from the large jars found on the wide terrace platform in front of the temples. Perhaps this was the only officially sanctioned liquid, or possibly it was simply provided for free to poorer supplicants. The hieroglyphic stairway block that told of K'inich [?] Yook giving pulque may have referred to this practice.

Deposits on other La Corona structures also point to ritual food consumption. Large quantities of ceramics, many of them polychromes, were discarded on the platform behind Structure 13R-9 during the seventh century, and these refuse deposits were also used in the construction of the basal fill layer of Structure 13R-10 (Acuña 2006, 2009; Patterson, Garza, and Miguel 2012; Ponce and Cajas 2012). In the eighth century the inhabitants of Structure 13R-10 also excavated a pit into bedrock behind the structure and buried over 6,000 ceramic sherds, including undecorated storage vessels, polychrome serving vessels, and ceramic drums (Fernández 2011; Fridberg and Cagnato 2012; Caroline Parris, personal communication 2012). Sherds from different depths of this deposit refit with one another, indicating that they were dumped in a single massive episode (Parris 2014). The good preservation and absence of rodent gnaw marks on the animal bones also supported this conclusion (Fridberg and Cagnato 2012). Also recovered were over 1,100 animal bones, including those of deer, turtle, bird, domestic dog, opossum, large rodent, fish, and mollusks. Botanical remains included maize, possibly chile seeds, amaranth seeds, leafy greens, and legumes (Fridberg and Cagnato 2012). A similar deposit was also identified beside Structure 13R-7, probably another elite residence (Perla Barrera 2013). Both middens contained Chablekal Fine Gray sherds, indicating a date after 760 and roughly contemporaneous with the Unen Stage midden behind Structure 13R-5.

An even later deposit was also identified behind Structure 13R-10 (Fernández 2011), which included over 400 sherds, many of them large water jars and basins.

Over 700 animal bones were recovered, identified as deer, peccary, opossum, birds, turtles, and mollusks (Fridberg and Cagnato 2012). Fine Orange sherds date this deposit to sometime after 830, probably after royal authority at La Corona had collapsed. Excavations within Structure 13R-10 recovered numerous artifacts, among them four manos and five metates, stone mortars used for food preparation (Ponce Stokvis and Nájera 2012). Analysis on one of the metates revealed starch from maize as well as the family *Euforbiacea*, to which manioc belongs (Fridberg and Cagnato 2012).

Archaeological evidence thus points to food preparation and consumption on a grand scale around the other buildings of the Coronitas group. While the ceramics on the temples themselves are consistent with an emphasis on liquids, these other contexts indicate that La Corona's populace consumed all different kinds of foods, including meats and vegetables, in the other areas. This is consistent with historical and ethnographic references to food consumption by human beings during patron deity festivals. "You must carry them, feed them, and eat with them," urges the Annals of the Kaqchikels in reference to commensal meals with patron gods (Otzoy 1999:156). Some of these events may have been exclusive to the elites, as indicated by the high quantity of polychrome vessels, including some with royal titles. But other events may have also included the whole community, as evidenced by the massive amounts of food remains.

SUMMARY

The archaeological and epigraphic record at La Corona offers a unique view of the relationship between patron deity veneration and the institution of rulership among the Classic Maya. The history of the site was characterized by the struggle of at least two elite lineages to claim royal authority using different semiotic strategies. The descendants of Tahn K'inich, an early settler of La Corona, used ancestor veneration to indexically signify their entitlement to the privileges of the first founder. These privileges apparently included access to locally acquired wealth, social status, and political authority over other lineages. As each generation of this family died, subsequent members built more and more elaborate funerary shrines in order to maintain these hereditary claims.

The veneration and glorification of ancestors was an important element of the ideological discourses recorded in the monuments of the Six Nothing lineage as well. For example, Panel 1 pushed this family's mythical ancestor back thousands of years into the past to establish primacy over Tahn K'inich. And Stela 1 referred to the sixth century Vulture as a "godlike" ruler of La

Corona, comparing him to his descendant over a century later. But these rulers also used patron deity veneration as a strategy to supersede the claims of their rivals. Each time the Six Nothing lineage seized power, it introduced a new patron god: first in 520, when Vulture married a woman from the Kaan dynasty and introduced a Teotihuacan-style god; next, in the early seventh century, when Sak Maas introduced Ikiiy after taking over from the descendants of Tahn K'inich, who were buried in the Coronitas temples; and again in 658, after K'uk' Ajaw's short-lived coup d'etat, when Chakaw Nahb Chan introduced a new god just thirty-five days after his bloody rise to power. This time, the patron deity cults were initiated at the direct expense of his rival lineage—Chakaw Nahb Chan rapidly constructed new *wayib* temples on top of these competing funerary shrines. This act severed the indexical ties between entombed ancestors and their descendants while simultaneously promoting Chakaw Nahb Chan's exclusive relationship with protective patrons. His son, K'inich [?] Yook, introduced yet another new god in 677, though this time after a decade of rule.

The strategy of introducing new gods relied on the belief in their efficacy among the general population. As I argued in chapter 4, these deities were believed to confer protective powers on their home communities, such as success in war and safety from misfortune or death. As unique intermediaries with these gods, rulers claimed rights to tribute and authority that superseded the claims of all other elites. Once a ruler successfully promoted a new god, that deity entered the local pantheon, and its proper veneration was essential for the community's well-being, even after the death of the ruler who introduced it. This process led to the gradual accumulation of gods observed in the inscriptions of many Maya sites, including La Corona. Even as rulers like K'inich [?] Yook promoted new patron gods, they continued to venerate others introduced by previous rulers.

The archaeological evidence in the Coronitas group demonstrates that the inhabitants of La Corona readily supported the veneration of patron gods, providing ritual liquid offerings and attending feasts from the mid-seventh century all the way until the site was abandoned. In fact, they continued to show devotion to the gods introduced by the Six Nothing lineage even after this family was probably deposed in the mid-eighth century. This indicates that their offerings to gods were not made simply to appease the Six Nothing lineage, but because these gods had been truly "domesticated." For the supernatural protection of La Corona, it was not especially important *who* was ruler of the site so long as he continued to maintain the deities and sponsor their veneration.

The institution of rulership itself underwent dramatic changes at the beginning of the ninth century, as the Maya world entered the Terminal Classic period and many sites in the southern lowlands declined and were abandoned. Hereditary rule continued in the northern lowlands and in the highlands to the south, though often with distinct organizational structures and differing ideological discourses. However, as I demonstrated in chapter 4, patron deity veneration continued to play a major role in the constitution of political institutions among the Postclassic Maya and other Mesoamerican peoples. At La Corona the transition to the Terminal Classic is marked by the cessation of carved monuments after 805, though the site continued to be occupied until at least 830, if not later. Feasting activity continued in the Coronitas group during that time, very likely as part of continued efforts to properly venerate the community's gods. Did the sponsorship of these rituals become a democratic process taken on by all community members? Did leaders emerge to fill this role even when the external trappings of rulership were inaccessible? When the last of the site's inhabitants left, they either destroyed their gods or carried them to their next destination.

I believe that La Corona is illustrative of Classic Maya communities and their relationships with patron gods. While each site has its own unique pantheon, dynastic history, and historical narratives, the institution of rulership was maintained and transformed through practices and discourses related to patron deity veneration. Therefore, the political organization of the Classic Maya cannot be understood apart from semiotic acts such as building temples, offering bowls of pulque, or publicly declaring one's devotion to a town's supernatural protector. In this way, both rulers and subjects defined their social world and their places within it.

NOTES

1. An interesting problem in La Corona epigraphy is that several inscriptions contain mathematical errors in the calculations of their dates. In some cases this makes it difficult to reconstruct when exactly events occurred. However, most of the events discussed in this chapter are associated with unproblematic calendrical information.

2. Stephen Houston (personal communication 2008) favors the former reading, proposing that Lajua' refers in fact to "Ten Lakes," possibly the individual's place of origin. Zender (2011) prefers the latter interpretation, reading the first glyph in the sequence as *ahneel*, perhaps indicating that the individual "came running" to La Corona.

3. All the ceramics from the Coronitas temples were analyzed by Caroline Parris in 2012.

4. In addition to recent looting, the interpretation of La Corona monuments is also challenging because the Maya themselves moved portable panels around the site, probably in the eighth century (Marcello Canuto, personal communication 2015). The monuments that were moved were often reset in seemingly haphazard order and often divorced from their original architectural context. This contrasts with Panel 1, which forms a complete set of two panel halves, apparently intentionally set above a fourth-century tomb. Thus, while current evidence suggests that Panel 1 was indeed recovered in its original 677 location, the possibility remains that it was moved as well.

5. Unfortunately, too few diagnostic sherds were recovered from this context for an accurate analysis of the assemblage's vessel forms.

6. Roughly "white spirit companion." *Wahy* creatures have been recognized as the Maya equivalent of the Aztec Nahual, a kind of supernatural alter-ego that belonged to a person and whose fate was bound to his (Houston and Stuart 1989).

7. "White Worm" or "White Cricket" (David Stuart, personal communication 2012).

8. The name of this god cannot be positively translated.

9. "Quetzal Lord."

10. The panel actually records Sak Maas's death first before continuing to tell of K'uk' Ajaw's accession. The accompanying dates, however, reverse the order of the events. This may be one of various calendrical errors found in some La Corona monuments, or the order of the account may have been intentionally reversed for rhetorical effect.

11. Chakaw Nahb Chan means "Red Pool Snake."

12. "Radiant [?] Dog."

13. It is also indicated by the contents of the later Ub Stage midden (see below).

14. David Stuart also pointed out to me (personal communication 2012) that the same phrase appears on Comalcalco Pendant 15B, where it also refers to a god and 365-day cycles.

15. A newly recovered panel from La Corona (Element 56) also contains a reference to "Nothing" in relation to the ruler Chak Ak', although the precise function is still unclear (David Stuart, personal communication 2015).

16. A translation of this god's name is difficult. The unknown first glyph is read by Guenter as *K'uhul* "godlike," but this would be an unusual element for a god's proper name, and the glyph in fact differs from the characteristic *k'uh* glyph I discussed in Chapter 3. I prefer to leave it untranslated. *Winik* has the alternative meanings of "person" or "twenty," while *Ub*, spelled out phonetically, is a complete mystery.

17. Chak Ak' means "Great Turkey." This ruler's full name is now read Chak Ak' Paat Yuk (Stuart 2015).

6

The Classic Maya Polity

At the beginning of this book I sought to investigate the nature of Classic Maya polities. I proposed that a semiotic analysis of specific social phenomena—in this case patron deity veneration—offers archaeologists a way of examining the creation and dissemination of social norms, status, and entitlements in ancient societies. These features are at the core of political institutions—the way social collectivities frame long-term regularities of hierarchies and claims to resources. I have shown that the Classic Maya manipulated objects, rituals, and discourses related to patron deity veneration as signs in their wider negotiation of social differences. Studies of Classic Maya politics have focused on two different levels of social hierarchies. One level consists of relationships within particular kingdoms—social units ruled by an *ajaw* (lord). The other "superstate" level refers to relationships among these different kingdoms. As I have shown, patron deities operated as signs at both of these levels.

KINGDOMS AND THEIR GODS

Historical records from the Classic period as well as ethnohistoric information from later periods of Maya history are replete with metapragmatic discourses, promoted by elites, that framed the upkeep of physical deity effigies as indexical of positive outcomes of stochastic events. In other words, outcomes such as good luck, agricultural success, the safe passage of time, and

DOI: 10.5876/9781607325185.c006

success in battle were signs that the gods were well maintained, and rituals of deity maintenance were signs of future success that could be acted upon accordingly. This indexical relationship between effigy and fortune was established through just the kinds of metapragmatic language fragments that have survived to us in written form. They doubtless circulated as speech acts as well. Under these circumstances, the absence or poor execution of deity maintenance rituals could thus be indexical of future misfortune, and vice versa. As long as these discourses circulated widely and consistently within Maya communities, the social consequences (interpretants) for failing to adequately care for gods by feeding, bathing, clothing, and housing them would have been dire. At La Corona archaeological evidence suggests that these were indeed widely circulating discourses. Community members from all social classes participated in deity feeding rituals, bringing liquid offerings to their temples and engaging in commensal feasts with them over several generations.

Rulers promoted these metapragmatic discourses because of their own place within these indexical relations. Rulers claimed credit for acts of deity veneration such as dressing, bathing, and temple building. They also framed their relationship to gods as similar to that between loving parents and children and described the gods' happy emotional states—"satisfied hearts." Artistic representations depicted rulers handling deity effigies. All these discursive and representational strategies also served to create strong indexical linkages between rulers and deity effigies, suggesting that without the intervention of elites, the gods would go unsatisfied and misfortune would follow.

Just as events related to good fortune and agricultural success were framed as indexical of satisfied patron gods, so rulers claimed that political events such as accessions and heir designation ceremonies were also approved by deities, who "oversaw" them or "made them happen." This iconic similarity between events of obvious community-wide benefit and events normalizing status differentials is an example of an ideological discourse, in which access to particular entitlements were framed as divine will.

The role of patron gods in the formulation of social relationships at the polity level was of course an ongoing process, in which rituals and speech acts were linked to one another over the long term. This discursive mediation could occur in large public events like patron deity feasts in which many participants could rapidly contribute to the semiotic chaining of signs and interpretants. But patron deity veneration played a role in political relationships not only in public theatrical settings. Even intimate interactions—such as exclusive ceremonies or private conversations—could initiate or perpetuate new semiotic chains as well. Each individual semiotic event contributed to or challenged the regularities of political life. The institution of the *ajaw*, like all political institutions, was thus not a monolithic or stable set of laws but a dynamic set of social norms that were simply *promoted* as timeless by Classic Maya rulers.

These social norms were challenged by at least one competing model of social entitlement—that of ancestor veneration (McAnany 1995). According to this discourse, differential access to wealth or social status was a product of indexical links to ancestors, not patron deities. Though rulers themselves emphasized relationships with their own ancestors, the ancestor veneration model ultimately challenged the *ajaw*'s claims to social entitlement by suggesting that he had claim only to his own ancestor's privileges rather than those of the whole kingdom. As this conflict played out at La Corona, the Six Nothing lineage had to take steps to neutralize the competing claims of a rival family. Chakaw Nahb Chan accomplished this by severing the rival family's indexical links to deceased ancestors—replacing old funerary shrines with those of new patron deities that he himself introduced.

At La Corona the introduction of new gods throughout the kingdom's history led to the gradual accumulation of deities over time. The Six Nothing *ajaw*s intended to establish strong indexical links between themselves and deity effigies whose care and maintenance was a sign of overall community well-being. Each time civil strife weakened the Six Nothing lineage's claims on social entitlements, they were forced to adopt new patron gods to promote themselves again. Furthermore, as indicated by Panel 1, Chakaw Nahb Chan's son, K'inich [?] Yook, also adopted discourses related to ancestor veneration. He claimed exceptional antiquity for the founding ancestor of the Six Nothing lineage, who was framed as iconically similar to La Corona's actual founder through parallel verb choice and calendar manipulation. K'inich [?] Yook's devotion to the Six Nothing Place god through the construction of a new temple (conveniently severing his rivals' indexical links to their buried ancestor below) was thus metapragmatically framed as a justification for his social privileges.

La Corona was not unique in seeing the gradual accumulation of new patron deities. And although the appearance of these new gods is observable in the historical record, the variety of responses by different Classic Maya communities in different historical circumstances to the introduction of different patron gods is not yet analyzable. At La Corona the veneration of new gods was apparently supported by the community, but it can only be assumed that this reaction varied widely across different social contexts. Perhaps only the deities that were successfully promoted ever made it into the records of carved stone monuments.

What can I conclude about the nature of Classic Maya politics on the level of particular kingdoms, especially in relation to patron deities? The kingdom was the social group that oriented itself toward the care and maintenance of the same patron gods. These political communities had a geographic component, in that patron gods were associated with particular places on the landscape and the people who lived there. But, at the same time, lists of patron gods were constantly changing. Thus the kingdom itself—as a semiotic artifact—was in a constant state of flux and was constantly renegotiated through discourses and ritual acts.

Supracommunity Networks

I have given several examples in this book of rulers who used patron deities as indices of social relationships between different communities and kingdoms. Frequently, such discourses appeared in the context of wars between kingdoms in which patron gods were destroyed or captured, indexing the subordination of one kingdom under another. But rulers also used patron gods in friendly interactions of suprapolity network maintenance such as accessions and gatherings. The rulers of the Kaan polity, based at Dzibanche in the Early Classic and at Calakmul in the Late Classic, were especially keen on this semiotic strategy.

The Kaan lords gathered the most extensive network of client kingdoms of any Classic Maya polity. La Corona was just one of its many subordinates. Panel 6 shows the arrival of a Kaan princess at La Corona in 520, accompanied by the towering effigy of a deity. This suggests that the forging of this alliance between the two kingdoms was accompanied by the introduction of a new god of foreign origin. This narrative echoes that of Tikal's god, Waxaklajun Ubaah Kaan, the war deity from Teotihuacan that was introduced in the fourth century. Both examples substitute a deity from a far-off geographical locale for the more typical god of the local landscape.

A different narrative appears in texts from Caracol, which discuss a new effigy for an old Caracol patron god. This new effigy was given as a gift by the Kaan *ajaw* to the lord of Caracol. This narrative is also atypical of Classic Maya discourses related to patron deity veneration. Ordinarily, rulers claimed their indexical linkages to patron gods by taking responsibility for their care and maintenance themselves. In this case, a foreign overlord has inserted his own indexical claim to this local god cult, suggesting a similarity or equivalence between the role of the Caracol ruler and that of his political patron.

On Cancuen Panel 1, a different discourse was promoted, again by the local ruler of Cancuen. In this case, the text recounts how the lord of Cancuen acceded to rulership under the auspices of Calakmul's patron gods, rather than his own. So here an equivalence is suggested between the local patron gods and those of far-off Calakmul, perhaps even implying that these foreign gods were somehow responsible for the well-being of Cancuen's populace. Finally, a fragment of a text from a carved block at Calakmul mentions the "gathering together" of the patron gods of Calakmul and El Peru, another client kingdom. The text does not indicate where this gathering took place, but this may be an attempt to discursively fuse the two political communities, with the relationship between the two gods suggesting an iconic equivalence to the relationship between the two kingdoms.

Textual narratives at Tikal and Chichen Itza also describe the capture of foreign gods and their "domestication" through rituals usually performed for a kingdom's own patrons. Here there may be an attempt to discursively widen the landscape for which the Tikal and Chichen Itza lords were responsible—the area within which particular hierarchical relationships could be mediated through patron deity veneration. The Calakmul lords, whose god was captured by the Tikal ruler, contested this narrative and constructed a new effigy at home to replace the one that had been captured.

These examples can be compared as well with the K'iche' Popol Vuh, in which the lords fasted and prayed fervently on behalf of all their vassals and servants—their own people and all the other peoples that they had conquered. In exchange for this supplication of their own deity, Tohil, on behalf of the conquered nations, they received riches such as feathers and precious stones. These other nations already had their own patron gods, but the K'iche' lords framed their hierarchical relationship to these conquered peoples in the same terms as hierarchical relationships within the K'iche' polity.

So what did Maya politics entail at the supracommunity level, especially in relation to patron deities? In my view, it represents an attempt by certain rulers to discursively extend the norms and hierarchies in circulation within the local kingdom to a broader political community. This meant somehow creating indexical links between the dominant patron lord and local patron gods—either by taking over the role of local ruler in maintaining effigies (in the case of Caracol's new effigy or the Tikal lord's devotions to foreign gods) or by inserting the gods of the overlord into the role of the local deity effigies (in the case of the Cancuen lord's accession or La Corona's new patron deity). But these attempts at the creation of stable political relationships beyond the kingdom itself were ultimately abortive. Calakmul's extensive network was in a constant state of flux and ultimately collapsed after just a few generations.

CONTRADICTIONS OF RECIPROCITY

So what was the Classic Maya polity? The short answer is that there was no Classic Maya polity. Named institutions like these, although they appear monolithic and stable, are in fact patterned precipitates of semiotic activities, constructed and dismantled one semiotic event at a time. But to the extent that these patterns existed—that there were observable regularities in political action and discourse—it is possible to propose causes and consequences of those regularities (Pauketat 2007:40). In this sense the Classic Maya polity of the southern lowlands was made up of norms of reciprocity. At the local level this meant that people living within a particular geographic locale owed offerings and physical care to patron gods, who in return protected them from harm. *Ajaws* mediated these relationships, taking responsibility for godly maintenance and claiming material rewards in return. In Postclassic narratives this triangle of reciprocity between people, ruler, and god was explicitly stated, as in "[the lords] fasted for long periods of time, and sacrificed before the faces of their gods . . . pleading for the light and the lives of their vassals and servants. . . . Great was the price that the nations gave in return" (Christenson 2003:288–91). Statements like these constitute arguments (in the Peircian sense). In other words, they explicitly formulate norms. Such arguments and all the individual instances in which their formulated norms are upheld instantiate and perpetuate the discursive patterns we call "institutions," or, in this case, the Maya polity.

Over the course of the Late Classic period, more influential *ajaws* attempted to extend this discourse of reciprocity beyond the local kingdom. Referring to themselves as *k'uhul* "godlike" while leaving their enemies and subordinates without such adjectives, these rulers claimed an iconic resemblance between themselves and their powerful supernatural patrons. They simultaneously compared gods in text and image to *ajaws*. This comparison is echoed in the Postclassic Aztec empire: "You [emperor Ahuitzotl] will carry the same burden as does the god Huitzilopochtli, which is to provide and maintain this world order, that is, to provide the sustenance, the food and drink for your people" (Duran 1994:313). Through differential claims to *k'uhul* status, influential Classic Maya lords attempted to widen the extent of reciprocal relationships. But this discourse was inherently contradictory.

The whole basis of using patron deity veneration as a political strategy relied on the widespread circulation of discourses relating patron gods to the well-being of particular communities in particular geographical locations. Community success was interpreted as indexical of godly satisfaction, and rituals to please local gods were interpreted as indexical of future success. The *ajaw*'s responsibility, which he so loudly promoted, was to administer rituals to assure supernatural appeasement. How could one lord care for his kingdom's own numerous gods—which he described as similar to a mother's care for her children—while simultaneously caring for those of all his client kingdoms? How could a local community trust that a far-off god, whom they had never seen, never fed, and who had no ties to the local landscape, would actually protect them? And how, if that deity failed to do so, could they possibly make their grievances known to a distant overlord? The central place of patron deity veneration in the discursive formulation of local hierarchical relationships ultimately made the extension of those relationships a difficult task. As a consequence, the semiotic acts and narratives that patterned hierarchical relationships within the community were ultimately distinct from those that mediated patron-client relationships between *ajaw*s. The result was a dynamic, and ultimately fragile, political system.

I have examined only semiotic activities related to patron deities in this book. As I noted in chapter 1, the universe of Classic Maya political strategies was vast, and there are doubtless many other factors that contributed to patterns of political discourse observable in this particular time and place. I have not even touched upon subsistence or political economies or even on the many other facets of complex Maya religion. But the same approach that I have used here can be applied to these other features of Maya culture or indeed any ancient society. In order to comprehend ancient political life, it is necessary to focus on the particular semiotic acts—whether economic or transcendental—that shaped long-term regularities of status differentials and entitlements.

If there is no such thing as "the Classic Maya polity" in the sense of a monolithic and stable institution, much less are there cross-cultural political typologies into which ancient peoples can be squeezed. A semiotic approach to politics is necessarily an interpretive approach to specific cultural and historical moments. It is these specifics that reveal the reasons that people in the past made the choices that they did. Does this diminish the comparative project that has traditionally been the task of anthropology? Not if one recognizes that there is a vast difference between cross-cultural comparison on the one hand and the search for human universals on the other (Agha 2007:340–41). Comparison itself remains at the core of the anthropological (and archaeological) project. Without an awareness of the vast range of human difference across time and space, one assumes that other people—deep down—have similar goals and values. Archaeologists have grappled with this interpretive bias for generations, either trying to banish it or to come to terms with it. Cross-cultural comparison without an assumption of universal or predictive similarity prepares the archaeologist to encounter different realms of human experience (Orme 1981). This is what anthropology and archaeology contribute as academic disciplines—the recognition of human difference.

Appendix

*Patron Deities of
Classic Maya Sites*

Site Name	God Name	Inscriptions	Dates (CE)	Further Reading
Balakbal	"Jaguar Paddler"	Stela 5	406	
	"Stingray Paddler"	Stela 5	406	
Calakmul	Yajaw Maan	Cancuen Panel, Tikal Temple I Lintel 3, Stela 54, Stela 89?, Stela 58, carved block	656–771	(Guenter 2002; Martin 2000a; 2000b; 2008a; Schele and Grube 1994)
	Yax Ha'al Chaak	Cancuen Panel, Stelae 54, 58	656–771	(Guenter 2002)
	Ho Kohkan K'uh	Cancuen Panel	656	(Guenter 2002)
	Bolon [?] Tuun(?)-wa	Stelae 54, 58	741–771	(Martin 2009)
	Bolon Yookte'	Stela 54	741	(Martin 2009)
	Yax Chit Hu'n Witz' Naah Kaan ("Water Lily Serpent")	Stela 54, carved block?	741	(Martin 2009)
Caracol	[?]-Hix	Stelae 13, 16, 14	514–554	
	Hux "vulture-eating-man"	Stelae 16, 14, 3, 22? Naranjo Hieroglyphic Stairway, Stelae 19, 17	534–820	(Grube 1994; Martin 2009)

continued on next page

APPENDIX—*continued*

Site Name	God Name	Inscriptions	Dates (CE)	Further Reading
Caracol (*contd.*)	"Sun Eagle Lord"	Stelae 16, 14	534–554	
	"Jaguar God of the Underworld"	Stelae 16, 14	534–554	
	"Akbal Skull"	Stela 14	554	
	"Jaguar Paddler"	Stela 3, Naranjo Hieroglyphic Stairway, Stela 19	618–820	
	"Stingray Paddler"	Stela 3, Naranjo Hieroglyphic Stairway, Stela 19	618–820	
Chichen Itza	"Hieroglyphic Jamb god"	Hieroglyphic Jamb	832	(Boot 2005; Grube, Lacadena, and Martin 2003)
	Te' Uchok	Casa Colorada	869	(Boot 2005; Grube, Lacadena, and Martin 2003)
	Yax Uk'uk'um K'awiil	Casa Colorada, Halakal Lintel, Initial Series Lintel, Las Monjas Lintel 6, Stela 2	869–889	(Boot 2005; Grube, Lacadena, and Martin 2003)
	"Halakal Lintel god"	Halakal Lintel	870	(Boot 2005; Grube, Lacadena, and Martin 2003)
	Yax Ha'al Chak	Yula Lintel 1	874	(Boot 2005; Grube, Lacadena, and Martin 2003)
	Pomun Chak	Yula Lintel 1	874	(Boot 2005; Grube, Lacadena, and Martin 2003)

continued on next page

APPENDIX—*continued*

Site Name	God Name	Inscriptions	Dates (CE)	Further Reading
Chichen Itza (*contd.*)	K'uh [?]-il 9-ti-[?]	Initial Series Lintel	878	(Boot 2005; Grube, Lacadena, and Martin 2003)
	Yax Chich Kan ("Water Lily Serpent?")	Initial Series Lintel, Las Monjas Lintel 2, Temple of the 4 Lintels 1, 4, Caracol Stela, Caracol Frieze	878–889	(Boot 2005; Grube, Lacadena, and Martin 2003)
	Bah Sabak Ahaw	Las Monjas Lintel 2	880	(Boot 2005; Grube, Lacadena, and Martin 2003)
	Uchoch Yokpuy	Temple of the 4 Lintels 3	881	(Boot 2005; Grube, Lacadena, and Martin 2003)
Chinikiha	Ix Tzak Ko-?-w	Dumbarton Oaks panel	800	(Stuart, Houston, and Robertson 1999)
	Ix Bolon Ilaj	Dumbarton Oaks panel	800	(Stuart, Houston, and Robertson 1999)
Comalcalco	Chan Hut Jol	Pendants 1A, 1B	765	(Zender 2004)
	Yax Bul Chan	Pendants 3A–3B	767	(Zender 2004)
	Ahkal Kab [?] Chaak	Pendants 4A–4B	768	(Zender 2004)
	Hix [?]	Pendants 6A–6B	770	(Zender 2004)
	[?] Chaak	Spine 2, Pendants 7A–7B	771	(Zender 2004)
	Unen K'awiil	Spine 2, Pendants 8A–8B	771	(Zender 2004)
	Ix Pakal Tuun	Pendants 8A–8B	771	(Zender 2004)
	Nat Hut Jol	Pendants 9A–9B	771	(Zender 2004)

continued on next page

Appendix—*continued*

Site Name	God Name	Inscriptions	Dates (CE)	Further Reading
Comalcalco (*contd.*)	Jolow Chan [?]	Pendants 10A–10B	772	(Zender 2004)
	K'anal Chaak	Pendants 11A–11B	773	(Zender 2004)
	Yaxkul Chan	Pendants 13A–13B	774	(Zender 2004)
	Chak Xib Chaak	Pendants 15A–15B, Spine 15	776	(Zender 2004)
Copan	9 ?-s	xukpi stone	437	
	Huk Ajaw Huun?	xukpi stone	437	
	Wak Bikaah Nal	xukpi stone	437	
	unnamed god	Papagayo Step	ca. 500	
	Chante' Ch'oktaak	Ante Step, Stelae 7, I, 6, Altar U	542–793	
	Bolon K'awiil	Ante Step, Stela 7, Altar X, Stelae P, 12, 2, 13, I, J, Temple 22 façade, Temple 11 step, Altar R, Temple 21a bench, El Palmar stairway	542–763–?	(Tsukamoto 2014)
	Chante' Ajaw	Stela 7, Altar X, Stelae P, 12, 2, 13, 6, J, Temple 22 façade, Quirigua Stela I, Temple 11 step, Altar U, Temple 21a bench, El Palmar stairway	613–793–?	(Houston and Stuart 1996; Looper 1999; Tsukamoto 2014)
	"Wind God"	Stela 7	613	(Schele 1987)
	[?] Kab [?]	Stela 7	613	(Schele 1987)
	"Jaguar Paddler"	Stelae 7, P, 2, 13, 1, I, 6, I'	613–692	(Schele 1987)

continued on next page

APPENDIX—*continued*

Site Name	God Name	Inscriptions	Dates (CE)	Further Reading
Copan (*contd.*)	"Stingray Paddler"	Stelae 7, P, 2, 13, 1, I, 6, I'	613–692	(Schele 1987)
	"Maize God"	Stela P	623	
	"Star Born Water Lily Serpent"	Stelae P, J	623–702	
	Chanal K'uh ("sky gods")	Stelae 7[?], 10, B	613–731	(Houston, Stuart, and Taube 2006)
	Kabal k'uh ("earth gods")	Stelae 7, 10, B	613–731	(Houston, Stuart, and Taube 2006)
	Bolonte' Witz	Stela I	676	
	Lajcha' Chuwen	Stela 6	682	
	Waxaklajun Ubaah Kaan	Stelae 6, 11	682–810	
	Winik Ub	Temple 22 façade	715	
	Winik [?] Pohp	Temple 22 façade	715	
	K'uy Saak? Ajaw	Temple 22 façade, Stela 4, Quirigua Stela I, Temple 11 doorjamb, Temple 11 step, Altar R, Temple 21a bench, El Palmar stairway	715–783–?	(Houston and Stuart 1996; Looper 1999; Schele and Grube 1990; Tsukamoto 2014)
	Mo' Witz Ajaw	Temple 22 façade, Stela B, Temple 11 doorjamb, Temple 11 step, Altar R, Temple 21a bench	715–783–?	(Schele and Grube 1990)
	Yax [?]	Stela F	721	
	K'ahk' K'in? [?] Naah Kaan	Stela N	761	
	Tukun Witz Ajaw	Temple 11 step, Altar R, Temple 21a bench	763–?	(Schele and Grube 1990)
	Chan Bate'	Altar U	793	
	Ahkul ya-[?]-mo	Altar R	?	
	[?] Chak Ek'	Altar R	?	

continued on next page

APPENDIX—*continued*

Site Name	God Name	Inscriptions	Dates (CE)	Further Reading
Copan (*contd.*)	ya-ti-ja-lu	Altar R	?	
	Bolon Yookte'*	god house model	?	(Grube and Schele 1990; Stuart, Houston, and Robertson 1999)
	Ixim K'ahk' [?]*	god house model CPN 2845, incensario	?	(Grube and Schele 1990; Stuart, Houston, and Robertson 1999)
	Yax K'amlay [?] Chan*	god house model CPN 21141, god house model CPN 19094, incensario CPN 22350, incensario CPN 22351, incensario CPN 266, Temple 22a stone, Altar U	763–792	(Bardsley 1990; Grube and Schele 1990; Stuart 1986; Stuart, Houston, and Robertson 1999)
	Nun Yajaw Chan Aj Jol*	incensario CPN 22079, incensario CPN 22342, Temple 22a stone, Altar GI, Altar T	763–795	(Bardsley 1990; Grube and Schele 1990; Stuart, Houston, and Robertson 1999)
	Uyaak' Chaak*	Altar F', Altar G', CPN 19649	775–788	(Schele 1993; Stuart, Houston, and Robertson 1999)
	*These characters all appeared within the reign of Copan's last ruler. The inscriptions are unusual, and it is possible that they were nobles rather than gods.			

continued on next page

APPENDIX—*continued*

Site Name	God Name	Inscriptions	Dates (CE)	Further Reading
Dos Pilas	"Jaguar Paddler"	Dos Pilas Stelae 14, 8	698–727	(Schele and Freidel 1990; Stuart 1984a)
	"Stingray Paddler"	Dos Pilas Stelae 14, 8	698–727	(Schele and Freidel 1990; Stuart 1984a)
	"Glyph Y god"	Dos Pilas Stela 8	698–727	(Schele and Freidel 1990)
	K'an Tuun Chaak	Dos Pilas Stela 8	698–727	(Schele and Freidel 1990)
El Peru	Version of Akan	Stela 16, Stela 44, Tikal Temple IV Lintel 3, Calakmul Hieroglyphic Stairway	458–743	(Guenter n.d.; Pérez et al. 2014; David Stuart, personal communication 2013)
	K'inich Ajaw	Stela 16	458	(Guenter n.d.)
	"Wind God"	Stela 16	458	(Guenter n.d.)
El Zapote	[?] Chaak	Stela 1	426	
La Corona	Teotihuacan-style god	Panel 6	520	
	Yaxal Ajaw	Altar 5, Panel 1, Hieroglyphic Stairway A, Element 56	544–681	(Guenter 2005; Stuart et al. 2018)
	Chak Wayaab Chaak	Altar 5, Panel 1	544–658	(Guenter 2005; Stuart et al. 2018)
	Ikiiy	Hieroglyphic Stairway A	637–678	(Stuart and Baron 2013)
	K'an Chaak	Panel 1	658	(Guenter 2005)
	[?] Winik Ub	Panel 1	(662)–677	(Guenter 2005)
La Mar	Ahkal Ichiiy	Stela 1	771	
	A?-[?]-Xukub	Stela 1	771	

continued on next page

APPENDIX—*continued*

Site Name	God Name	Inscriptions	Dates (CE)	Further Reading
La Mar (*contd.*)	Bolon Ookte'	Stela 1	771	
Moral Reforma	Yax Ajaw	Stela 2	729	
	Yax Bahlam	Stelae 2, 1	729–756	
	[?] K'awiil	Stela 2	729	
	"Jawless Jaguar"	Stela 2	729	
	[?] Chaak	Stela 1	756	
	Hu'n Ajaw	Stela 1	756	
Naranjo	Saak? [?] K'in Hix Ik' Huun	polychrome vessel, Tikal Temple IV Lintel 2	6th century–744	(Martin 1996)
	Lem Aat (same god as above?)	Aurora Frieze	early 6th century	(Tokovinine and Fialko 2019)
	"Jaguar God of the Underworld"	Altar 1, Stelae 30, 21, 11, 33, 8, 12, 35	593–800	
	Bolon Ajaw [?] "JGU"	Stelae 30, 6, 19, 12, 32	695–820	(Martin 2005a)
	Kab K'uh	Altar 1	593	
	"Jaguar Paddler"	Stelae 2, 23, 19, 13	692–780	
	"Stingray Paddler"	Stelae 2, 23, 19, 13	692–780	
Palenque	"GI"	House C Stairway, Temple of the Inscriptions, Cross Group Temples, Temple XIV, Palace Tablet, Temples XIX, XXI	514–736	(Berlin 1963; Cuevas García and Bernal Romero 1999; Grube 1996; Houston 1996; Lounsbury 1980; Macri 1988; Stuart 2006a; 2006b; 2007b)

continued on next page

APPENDIX—*continued*

Site Name	God Name	Inscriptions	Dates (CE)	Further Reading
Palenque (*contd.*)	Unen K'awiil ("GII")	House C Stairway, Temple of the Inscriptions, Cross Group Temples, Palace Tablet, Temples XIX, XXI	514–736	(Berlin 1963; Cuevas García and Bernal Romero 1999; Grube 1996; Houston 1996; Lounsbury 1980; Macri 1988; Stuart 2006a; 2006b; 2007b)
	"GIII"	House C Stairway, Temple of the Inscriptions, Cross Group Temples, Palace Tablet, Temples XIX, XXI	514–736	(Berlin 1963; Cuevas García and Bernal Romero 1999; Grube 1996; Houston 1996; Lounsbury 1980; Macri 1988; Stuart 2006a; 2006b; 2007b)
	Ek' Wayaab Chaak	Cross Group Temples, Palace Tablet	651–692	(Stuart 2006b)
	Akan	Cross Group Temples, Death's head, Palace Tablet	651–692	(Stuart 2006b)
	Ix [?] Ajaw	Cross Group Temples, Temple XIV, Palace Tablet	651–709	(Stuart 2006b)
	Ahkal Ichiiy Chaak	unprovenienced panel, Cross Group Temples	?–692	
	3-9 Chaak	Cross Group Temples, Dumbarton Oaks Panel	657–692	(Stuart 2006b)
	Unen "Jaguar God of the Underworld"	Cross Group Temples	692	(Stuart 2006b)

continued on next page

APPENDIX—continued

Site Name	God Name	Inscriptions	Dates (CE)	Further Reading
Palenque (*contd.*)	Chanal K'uh	Temple of the Inscriptions	684	
	Kabal K'uh	Temple of the Inscriptions	684	
	"JGU"	Temple XIV	709	
	"Mother of Fire"	Temple XIV	709	
	Sak [?] Naah	Temple XIV	709	
Piedras Negras	K'inich Ajaw	Panel 12	518	(Martin and Grube 2000)
	6-[?]	Panel 12	518	(Martin and Grube 2000)
	Waxak Ha' Naak	Panels 12, 2	518–658	(Martin and Grube 2000; Stuart, Houston, and Robertson 1999)
	Hu'n Ha' Naak	Panel 2	658	(Stuart, Houston, and Robertson 1999)
	Yax Ha'al Chaak	Panel 2	658	(Stuart, Houston, and Robertson 1999)
	"Jaguar God of the Underworld"	Panel 2	658	(Stuart, Houston, and Robertson 1999)
	"Jaguar Paddler"	Stela 3, Altar 1, Stelae 20, 15	711–785	
	"Stingray Paddler"	Stela 3, Altar 1, Stelae 20, 15	711–785	
	"Maize God"?	Stela 3	711	
Sacul/Ixkun	"Jaguar Paddler"	Sacul Stela 1, Ixkun Stelae 2, 1, 5	761–800	(Laporte et al. 2006)
	"Stingray Paddler"	Sacul Stela 1, Ixkun Stelae 2, 1, 5	761–800	(Laporte et al. 2006)

continued on next page

APPENDIX—*continued*

Site Name	God Name	Inscriptions	Dates (CE)	Further Reading
Sak Tz'i'	Ahkal Ich	Caracas Panel	564–706	(Biro 2005; Stuart, Houston, and Robertson 1999)
	A-[?]-Xukub	Caracas Panel	564	(Biro 2005; Stuart, Houston, and Robertson 1999)
	Bolon Ookte'	Caracas Panel	565	(Biro 2005; Stuart, Houston, and Robertson 1999)
Seibal/ Petexbatun	"GI"-K'awiil (various sites)	Dos Pilas Stela 15, Dos Pilas Panel 19, Dos Pilas Hieroglyphic Bench, Aguateca Stela 1, Seibal Hieroglyphic Stairway, Tamarandito Hieroglyphic Stairway 2, Seibal Stela 6, Aguateca Stela 7, La Amelia Hieroglyphic Stairway, Seibal Stela 10, Seibal Stela 3, Seibal Stela 14	721–874	(Houston 1993; Houston and Stuart 1996; LeFort 1998; Schele and Mathews 1998)
	"Painted K'awiil" (Seibal)	Dos Pilas Stela 2, Aguateca Stela 2	735	

continued on next page

APPENDIX—*continued*

Site Name	God Name	Inscriptions	Dates (CE)	Further Reading
Tikal	Sak Hix Muut	Stela 29, El Encanto Stela 1?, Stela 26, Hombre de Tikal, Stela 31, Temple VI façade, Stela 21, Ixlu Altar 1?, Tetitla fragment V70	292–766–879?	(Helmke and Nielsen 2013; Martin 2014; Martin 2015; Martin and Grube 2000; Stuart 2007a)
	"Jaguar God of the Underworld"	El Encanto Stela 1	305	(Martin 2000c)
	K'inich Ajaw	El Encanto Stela 1	305	(Martin 2000c)
	Waxaklajun Ubaah Kaan	Marcador, Temple I Lintel 2	378–695	(Stuart 2000)
	Pik Chanal K'uh (8,000 Sky gods)	Stela 31	406	(Houston, Stuart, and Taube 2006)
	Pik Kabal K'uh (8,000 Earth gods)	Stela 31	406	(Houston, Stuart, and Taube 2006)
	"Jaguar Paddler"	Stelae 31, 40, 24, Ixlu Stelae 1, 2, Ixlu Altar 1, Jimbal Stelae 1, 2	445–889	(Schele 1987; Schele and Freidel 1990; Stuart, Houston, and Robertson 1999)
	"Stingray Paddler"	Stelae 31, 40, 24, Ixlu Stelae 1, 2, Ixlu Altar 1, Jimbal Stelae 1, 2	445–889	(Schele 1987; Schele and Freidel 1990; Stuart, Houston, and Robertson 1999)
	"Wind God"	Stelae 31, 40	445–468	
	"Principal Bird Deity"	Stelae 31, 26?	445	
	"Star Born Water Lily Serpent"	Stelae 31, 40?, 3	445–488	
	Bolon Tz'akbu	Stelae 31, 3	445–488	
	"jaguar head"	Stela 40	468	
	Yajaw Maan (from Calakmul)	Temple I Lintel 3	695	(Martin 2000a)

continued on next page

APPENDIX—*continued*

Site Name	God Name	Inscriptions	Dates (CE)	Further Reading
Tikal (*contd.*)	Akan (from El Peru)	Temple IV Lintel 3	743	(Martin 2000a)
	Saak? [?] K'in Hix Ik' Huun (from Naranjo)	Temple IV Lintel 2	744	(Martin 1996)
	god with torch forehead	Ixlu Stelae 1, 2	849–879	
	god with jaguar mask	Ixlu Stelae 1, 2	849–879	
	"Glyph Y god"	Ixlu Altar 1	(698?)–879	(Schele and Freidel 1990)
	K'an Tuun Chaak	Ixlu Altar 1	(698?)–879	(Schele and Freidel 1990)
Tila	"Jaguar Paddler"	Stela A	830	
	"Stingray Paddler"	Stela A	830	
Tonina	"Jaguar Paddler"	Monuments 56, 8, 134, 139, 63, 136, 165, 110, 138, 43?, 42, 166	628–721 (805)	(Stuart, Houston, and Robertson 1999)
	"Stingray Paddler"	Monuments 56, 8, 134, 139, 63, 136, 165, 110, 138, 43?, 42, 166	628–721 (805)	(Stuart, Houston, and Robertson 1999)
	Ixim Ajaw	Stone Box	ca. 760	(Martin and Miller 2004)
Tortuguero	Ek' Hix	Monument 6	510?–669	(Gronemeyer 2006; Gronemeyer and MacCleod 2010)
	Yax Suutz'	Monument 6	510?–669	(Gronemeyer 2006; Gronemeyer and MacCleod 2010)
	[?]-ji	Monument 8	651	(Gronemeyer 2006)

continued on next page

APPENDIX—continued

Site Name	God Name	Inscriptions	Dates (CE)	Further Reading
Tortuguero (*contd.*)	Chanal Ho Kohkan K'uh	Monument 8	651	(Gronemeyer 2006)
	K'awiil	Monument 8	651	(Gronemeyer 2006)
Ucanal	Ek' [?]	Stela 4	849	
	Ich'aak [?] Jol	Stela 4	849	
	"spear-carrying god"	Stela 4	849	
Xultun	"Singing Jaguar"	Stelae 5, 14, 24, 3, 10, 1, 9, 16, 19, 23, 25, 18	672–863	
	K'awiil	Stelae 5, 3, 10	672–863	
Yaxchilan	Aj K'ahk' O' Chaak	Lintels 35, 25, Dos Caobas Stela 1, Hieroglyphic Stairway 3, Lintel 42, bone from Lady K'abal Xook's tomb, Lintel 10, La Pasadita Lintel 2	537–808	(Houston, Stuart, and Taube 2006; Martin and Grube 2000; Schele 1991; Stuart 2013)
	K'an Wi' JGU	Lintels 35, 10	537–808	(Houston, Stuart, and Taube 2006; Martin and Grube 2000)
	Pa' Chan Bahlam	Lintel 10	808	(Martin and Grube 2000)
	Sak Baak Na [?]	Lintel 10	808	(Martin and Grube 2000)
	Tajal Wahy?	Lintel 10	808	(Martin and Grube 2000)
	Wak Kaban	Lintel 10	808	(Martin and Grube 2000)
	Yax Ajaw	Lintel 10	808	(Martin and Grube 2000)

continued on next page

APPENDIX—*continued*

Site Name	God Name	Inscriptions	Dates (CE)	Further Reading
Yaxchilan (*contd.*)	Yajawte' Took' Ajaw	Lintel 10	808	(Martin and Grube 2000)
Yaxha	Unen "Jaguar God of the Underworld"	Stela 31, Naranjo Stela 35	796–799	(Martin and Grube 2000)
	"Jaguar Paddler"	Stela 3	793	
	"Stingray Paddler"	Stela 3	793	

References Cited

Acuña, Mary Jane. 2006. "CR-ES: Excavaciones de Sondeo en Los Grupos A, B, y C de La Corona." In *Proyecto Arqueológico El Perú-Waka': Sub-Proyecto La Corona, Informe No. 2, Temporada 2006*, edited by Marcello A. Canuto, Mary Jane Acuña, Ellen E. Bell, Stanley H. Guenter, and Damien B. Marken, 34–55. Guatemala City: Report submitted to the Instituto de Antropología e Historia, Guatemala.

Acuña, Mary Jane. 2009. "Operación CR 11A: Limpieza de Trinchera de Saqueo en La Estructura 13R-9." In *Proyecto Regional Arqueológico La Corona: Informe Final Temporada 2008*, edited by Marcello A. Canuto and Tomás Barrientos Q., 109–28. Guatemala City: Report submitted to the Instituto de Antropología e Historia, Guatemala.

Adams, Richard E. W. 1980. "Swamps, Canals, and the Locations of Ancient Maya Cities." *Antiquity* 54 (212): 206–14. http://dx.doi.org/10.1017/S0003598X00043386.

Adams, Richard E. W., and Richard C. Jones. 1981. "Spatial Patterns and Regional Growth among Classic Maya Cities." *American Antiquity* 46 (2): 301–22. http://dx.doi.org/10.2307/280210.

Agha, Asif. 2007. *Language and Social Relations*. Studies in the Social and Cultural Foundations of Language, no. 24. Cambridge: Cambridge University Press.

Anderson, Patricia. 1998. "Yula, Yucatan, Mexico: Terminal Classic Maya Settlement and Political Organization in the Chichen Itza Polity." PhD diss., University of Chicago. http://dx.doi.org/10.1017/S0956536100001917.

DOI: 10.5876/9781607325185.c008

Andrews, V.E. Wyllys. 1990. "Early Ceramic History of the Lowand Maya." In *Vision and Revision in Maya Studies*, edited by Flora S. Clancy and Peter D. Harrison, 1–20. Albuquerque: University of New Mexico Press.

Asher, Robert. 1961. "Analogy in Archaeological Interpretations." *Southwestern Journal of Anthropology* 17 (4): 317–25. http://dx.doi.org/10.1086/soutjanth.17.4.3628943.

Aulie, H. Wilbur, and Evelyn W. Aulie. 1978. *Diccionario Ch'ol-Español, Español-Ch'ol*. Serie de Vocabularios y Diccionarios Indígenas, no. 21. Mexico City: Instituto Lingüístico de Verano, Secretaria de Educación Publica, and Dirección General de Servicios Educativos en el Medio Indígena.

Ball, Joseph W., and Jennifer T. Taschek. 1991. "Late Classic Lowland Maya Political Organization and Central Place Analysis." *Latin American Antiquity* 2 (2): 149–65.

Bardsley, Nikolai. 1990. "Brothers and Others: New Insights from 'New' Incensarios." Copan Note 77.

Barnhart, Edwin Lawrence. 2001. "The Palenque Mapping Project: Settlement and Urbanism at an Ancient Maya City." PhD diss., University of Texas at Austin.

Baron, Joanne. 2013. "Patrons of La Corona: Deities and Power in a Classic Maya Community." PhD diss., University of Pennsylvania, Philadelphia.

Baron, Joanne. 2014. "Metapragmatics in Archaeological Analysis: Interpreting Classic Maya Patron Deity Veneration." *Signs and Society* (Chicago) 2 (2): 249–83. http://dx.doi.org/10.1086/677879.

Baron, Joanne, Diana Fridberg, and Marcello Canuto. 2011. "'Entró El Agua': Utilización de Especies Acuáticas En Contextos Mortuorios de La Corona, Guatemala." Paper presented at the XXI Encuentro Internacional de Investigadores de Cultura Maya, Campeche, Mexico, November 15.

Baron, Joanne, and Caroline Parris. 2013. "'You Must Carry Them, Feed Them, and Eat with Them': Pre-Columbian Patron Deity Veneration and Its Modern Parallels." Paper presented at the Society for American Archaeology Annual Meeting, Honolulu, Hawai'i.

Barrera Vásquez, Alfredo, Juan Ramón Bastarrachea Manzano, and William Brito Sensores. 1980. *Diccionario Maya Cordemex: Maya-Español, Español-Maya*. Mérida, Yucatán, Mexico: Ediciones Cordemex.

Barrientos, Tomás, and Marcello Canuto. 2009. "Proyecto Regional Arqueológico La Corona: Objetivos, Métodos y Antecedentes de La Temporada de Campo 2008." In *Proyecto Regional Arqueológico La Corona: Informe Final Temporada 2008*, edited by Marcello A. Canuto and Tomas Barrientos Q., 1–20. Guatemala City: Report submitted to the Instituto de Antropología e Historia, Guatemala.

Barrientos, Tomás, Marcello Canuto, Joanne Baron, Yann Desailly-Chanson, and Bruce Love. 2011. "El Reino de Sak Nikte': Nuevos Datos Sobre la Historia, Cronologia, Asentamiento y Medio Ambiente en La Corona." In *XXIV Simposio* de Investigaciones Arqueológicas en Guatemala, edited by Barbara Arroyo, Lorena Paiz Aragon, Adriana Linares Palma, and Ana Lucia Arroyave, 153–65. Guatemala City: Ministerio de Cultura y Deportes, Instituto de Antropología e Historia, Asociación Tikal.

Barthel, Thomas. 1968. "El Complejo Emblema." *Estudios de Cultura Maya* 7:159–93.

Baudez, Claude-François. 2002. *Une Histoire de La Religion des Mayas: du Panthéisme au Panthéon*. Paris: Éditions Albin Michel.

Bauer, Alexander A. 2013. "Objects and Their Glassy Essence: Semiotics of Self in the Early Bronze Age Black Sea." *Signs and Society* (Chicago) 1 (1): 1–31. http://dx.doi.org/10.1086/670166.

Becker, Marshall. 1976. "Priests, Peasants, and Ceremonial Centers: The Intellectual History of a Model." In *Maya Archaeology and Ethnohistory*, edited by Norman Hammond and Gordon R. Willey, 3–20. Austin: University of Texas Press.

Beekman, Christopher S. 2016. "Conflicting Political Strategies in Late Formative to Early Classic Central Jalisco." In *Political Strategies in Pre-Columbian Mesoamerica*, edited by Sarah Kurnick and Joanne P. Baron, 97–120. Boulder: University Press of Colorado.

Bell, Catherine. 1992. *Ritual Theory, Ritual Practice*. Oxford: Oxford University Press.

Bell, Ellen E., Robert J. Sharer, Loa P. Traxler, David W. Sedat, Christine W. Carrelli, and Lynn A. Grant. 2004. "Tombs and Burials in the Early Classic Acropolis at Copan." In *Understanding Early Classic Copan*, edited by Ellen E. Bell, Marcello A. Canuto, and Robert J. Sharer, 131–57. Philadelphia: University of Pennsylvania Museum of Archaeology and Anthropology.

Bell, Ellen E., Loa P. Traxler, David W. Sedat, and Robert J. Sharer. 1999. "Uncovering Copan's Earliest Royal Tombs." *Expedition* 41 (2): 29–35.

Berlin, Heinrich. 1951. "El Templo de Las Inscripciones—VI—de Tikal." *Antropología e Historia de Guatemala* 3 (1): 33–54.

Berlin, Heinrich. 1958. "El Glifo 'Emblema' en las Inscripciones Mayas." *Journal de la Société des Américanistes* 47 (1): 111–19. http://dx.doi.org/10.3406/jsa.1958.1153.

Berlin, Heinrich. 1963. "The Palenque Triad." *Journal de la Société des Américanistes* 52 (1): 91–99. http://dx.doi.org/10.3406/jsa.1963.1994.

Binford, L. R. 1967. "Smudge Pits and Hide Smoking: The Use of Analogy in Archaeological Reasoning." *American Antiquity* 32 (1): 1–12. http://dx.doi.org/10.2307/278774.

Biro, Peter. 2005. "Sak Tz'i'" in the Classic Period Hieroglyphic Inscriptions." Mesoweb. http://www.mesoweb.com/articles/biro/SakTzi.pdf.

Blanton, Richard E., Gary M. Feinman, Stephen A. Kowalewski, and Peter N. Peregrine. 1996. "A Dual-Processual Theory for the Evolution of Mesoamerican Civilization." *Current Anthropology* 37 (1): 1–14. http://dx.doi.org/10.1086/204471.

Bolles, John S. 1977. *Las Monjas: A Major Pre-Mexican Architectural Complex at Chichen Itza*. Norman: University of Oklahoma Press.

Boot, Erik. 2005. *Continuity and Change in Text and Image at Chichen Itza, Yucatan, Mexico: A Study of the Inscriptions, Iconography, and Architecture at a Late Classic to Early Postclassic Maya Site*. Leiden, Netherlands: CNWS Publications.

Bourdieu, Pierre. 1972. *Outline of a Theory of Practice*. Translated by Richard Nice. Cambridge: Cambridge University Press.

Bourdieu, Pierre, and Thompson, John B. 1991. *Language and Symbolic Power*. Edited and translated by Gino Raymond and Matthew Adamson. Cambridge, MA: Harvard University Press.

Brintnall, Douglas. 1979. *Revolt against the Dead: The Modernization of a Mayan Community in the Highlands of Guatemala*. New York: Gordon and Breach.

Buikstra, Jane E., T. Douglas Price, Lori E. Wright, and James H. Burton. 2004. "Tombs from the Copan Acropolis: A Life History Approach." In *Understanding Early Classic Copan*, edited by Ellen E. Bell, Marcello A. Canuto, and Robert J. Sharer, 191–214. Philadelphia: University of Pennsylvania Museum of Archaeology and Anthropology.

Bullard, William R. 1960. "Maya Settlement Patterns in Northeastern Peten, Guatemala." *American Antiquity* 25 (3): 355–72. http://dx.doi.org/10.2307/277519.

Bunzel, Ruth. 1959. *Chichicastenango: A Guatemalan Village*. Seattle: University of Washington Press.

Burkhart, Louise M. 1993. "The Cult of the Virgin of Guadalupe in Mexico." In *South and Meso-American Native Spirituality: From the Cult of the Feathered Serpent to the Theology of Liberation*, 198–227. New York: Crossroad.

Cajas, María Antonieta. 2013. "Operaciones CR11D y CR11C: Excavaciones en la Estructura 13R-9, Temporada 2012." In *Proyecto Regional Arqueológico La Corona: Informe Final Temporada 2012*, edited by Tomás Barrientos Q., Marcello A. Canuto, and Jocelyne Ponce, 125–40. Guatemala City: Report submitted to the Instituto de Antropología e Historia, Guatemala.

Callon, Michel. 1986. "The Sociology of an Actor-Network: The Case of the Electric Vehicle." In *Mapping the Dynamics of Science and Technology: Sociology of Science in the Real World*, edited by Michel Callon, John Law, and Arie Rip, 19–34. London: Macmillan. http://dx.doi.org/10.1007/978-1-349-07408-2_2.

Callon, Michel, and Bruno Latour. 1981. "Unscrewing the Big Leviathan: How Actors Macrostructure Reality and How Sociologists Help Them to Do So." In *Advances in Social Theory and Methodology: Toward an Integration of Micro- and Macro-Sociologies*, edited by Karin Knorr-Cetina and Aaron V. Cicourel, 277–303. Boston: Routledge.

Cancian, Frank. 1965. *Economics and Prestige in a Maya Community: The Religious Cargo System in Zinacantan*. Stanford: Stanford University Press.

Canuto, Marcello A. 2006. "CR-Operación 01: Excavaciones de Grupo C, Estra. 05 (Estra. C-5)." In *Proyecto Arqueológico El Perú-Waka': Sub-Proyecto La Corona, Informe No. 2, Temporada 2006*, edited by Marcello A. Canuto, Mary Jane Acuña, Ellen E. Bell, Stanley H. Guenter, and Damien B. Marken, 56–80. Guatemala City: Report submitted to the Instituto de Antropología e Historia, Guatemala.

Canuto, Marcello A., and Tomás Barrientos. 2011. "La Corona: un Acercamiento a las Políticas del Reino Kaan desde un Centro Secundario del Noroeste del Petén." *Estudios de Cultura Maya* 37:11–43. http://dx.doi.org/10.19130/iifl.ecm.2011.37.12.

Canuto, Marcello A., and Tomás Barrientos. 2013. "The Importance of La Corona." *La Corona Notes* 1 (1): 1–5.

Canuto, Marcello A., Stanley Guenter, Evangelia Tsesmeli, and Damien Marken. 2006. "El Reconocimiento de La Corona, 2005." In *Proyecto Arqueológico El Perú-Waka': Informe No. 3, Temporada 2005*, edited by Héctor Escobedo and David A. Freidel, 455–68. Guatemala City: Report submitted to the Instituto de Antropología e Historia, Guatemala.

Carmack, Robert M., and James L. Mondloch. 1983. *El Título de Totonicapán: Texto, Traducción y Comentario*. Mexico City: Universidad Nacional Autónoma de México.

Carrasco, Pedro. 1961. "The Civil-Religious Hieararchy in Mesoamerican Communities: Pre-Spanish Background and Colonial Development." *American Anthropologist* 63 (3): 483–97. http://dx.doi.org/10.1525/aa.1961.63.3.02a00020.

Carrasco, Ramon, and Rogelio Valencia. 2013. "Yukno'm Ihch'aak K'ahk': A Very Contradictory Figure in the History of the Maya Peten." Paper presented at the 10th Annual Tulane Maya Symposium, New Orleans.

Chance, John K., and William B. Taylor. 1985. "Cofradías and Cargos: An Historical Perspective on the Mesoamerican Civil-Religious Hierarchy." *American Ethnologist* 12 (1): 1–26. http://dx.doi.org/10.1525/ae.1985.12.1.02a00010.

Chase, Arlen F., and Diane Z. Chase. 1998. "Late Classic Maya Political Structure, Polity Size, and Warfare Arenas." In *Anatomía de una Civilización: Aproximaciones Interdisciplinarias a la Cultura Maya*, edited by Andrés Ciudad Ruiz, 11–29. Madrid: Sociedad Española de Estudios Mayas, Madrid.

Chase, Arlen F., Diane Z. Chase, and Rafael Cobos. 2008. "Jeroglíficos y Arqueología Maya: ¿Colusión o Colisión?" *Mayab* 20:5–21.

Chase, Arlen F., Diane Z. Chase, and William A. Haviland. 1990. "The Classic Maya City: Reconsidering 'The Mesoamerican Urban Tradition.'." *American Anthropologist* 92 (2): 499–506. http://dx.doi.org/10.1525/aa.1990.92.2.02a00210.

Chimalpahin, Domingo Francisco de San Antón Muñón. 1997. *Codex Chimalpahin: Society and Politics in Mexico and Tenochtitlan, Tlatelolco, Texchoco, Culhuacan, and Other Nahua Altepetl in Central Mexico*, vol.1. Edited by Arthur J. O. Anderson and Schroeder. Norman: University of Oklahoma Press.

Christenson, Allen. 1993. "K'iche'-English Dictionary." http://www.famsi.org/maya writing/dictionary/christenson/.

Christenson, Allen. 2001. *Art and Society in a Highland Maya Community: The Altarpiece of Santiago Atitlán.* Austin: University of Texas Press.

Christenson, Allen. 2003. *Popol Vuh: The Sacred Book of the Maya.* New York: O Books.

Christenson, Allen. 2009. "'There Was Only Joy in Their Hearts'—Ritual Feasting as a Political Strategy in the Maya Highlands." Paper presented at the 14th European Maya Conference, Krakow, Poland.

Christian, William A. 1981. *Local Religion in Sixteenth-Century Spain.* Princeton: Princeton University Press.

Clark, J. Grahame D. 1951. "Folk-Culture and the Study of European Prehistory." In *Aspects of Archaeology in Britain and Beyond*, edited by William F. Grimes, 49–65. London: Edwards.

Clark, J. Grahame D. 1953. "Archaeological Theories and Interpretation: Old World." In *Anthropology Today*, edited by Alfred L. Kroeber, 241–43. Chicago: University of Chicago Press.

Coben, Lawrence S. 2006. "Other Cuzcos: Replicated Theaters of Inka Power." In *Archaeology of Performance: Theaters of Power, Community, and Politics*, edited by Takeshi Inomata and Lawrence S. Coben, 223–59. Lanham, MD: AltaMira Press.

Coe, Michael D. 1965. "A Model of Ancient Community Structure in the Maya Lowlands." *Southwestern Journal of Anthropology* 21 (2): 97–114. http://dx.doi.org/10.1086/soutjanth.21.2.3629386.

Coe, Michael D. 1972. "Olmec Jaguars and Olmec Kings." In *The Cult of the Feline: A Conference in Pre-Columbian Iconography*, edited by Elizabeth P. Benson, 1–12. Washington, DC: Dumbarton Oaks Research Library and Collection.

Coe, Michael D. 1999. *Breaking the Maya Code.* New York: Thames and Hudson.

Craine, Eugene R., and Reginald C. Reindorp. 1970. *Chronicles of Michoacán.* Norman: University of Oklahoma Press.

Crossland, Zoë. 2014. *Ancestral Encounters in Highland Madagascar: Material Signs and Traces of the Dead.* Cambridge: Cambridge University Press.

Cuevas García, Martha. 2000. "Los Incensarios del Grupo de Las Cruces, Palenque." *Arqueología Mexicana* 8 (45): 54–61.

Cuevas García, Martha, and Guillermo Bernal Romero. 1999. "P'uluut K'uh, 'Dioses Incensario': Aspectos Arqueológicos y Epigráficos de los Incensarios Palencanos." In *La Organización Social entre Los Mayas Prehispánicos, Coloniales y Modernos: Memoria de la Tercera Mesa Redonda de Palenque*, edited by Vera Tiesler Blos, Rafael Cobos, and Merle Green Robertson, 376–400. Mexico City: Instituto Nacional de Antropología e Historia, Universidad Autónoma de Yucatán.

Culbert, Patrick T. 1988. "Political History and the Decipherment of Maya Glyphs." *Antiquity* 62 (234): 135–52. http://dx.doi.org/10.1017/S0003598X00073622.

Culbert, Patrick T. 1991. "Maya Political History and Elite Interaction: A Summary View." In *Classic Maya Political History: Hieroglyphic and Archaeological Evidence*, edited by Patrick T. Culbert, 311–46. Cambridge: Cambridge University Press.

Davis, Virginia D. 1978. "Ritual of the Northern Lacandon May." PhD diss., Tulane University, New Orleans.

De Ara, Fr. Domingo. 1986. *Vocabulario de Lengua Tzeldal Según el Orden de Copanabastla*. Edited by Mario Humberto Ruz. Fuentes Para El Estudio de La Cultura Maya, 4. Mexico City: Universidad Nacional Autónoma de México.

Deetz, James. 1967. *Invitation to Archaeology*. Garden City, NJ: Natural History Press.

Demarest, Arthur. 1992. "Ideology in Ancient Maya Cultural Evolution: The Dynamics of Galactic Polities." In *Ideology and Pre-Columbian Civilization*, edited by Arthur A. Demarest and Geoffrey Conrad, 135–57. Santa Fe: School of American Research Press.

Demarest, Arthur, Kim Morgan, Claudia Wolley, and Héctor Escobedo. 2003. "The Political Acquisition of Sacred Geography: The Mucielagos Complex at Dos Pilas." In *Maya Palaces and Elite Residences: An Interdisciplinary Approach*, edited by Jessica J. Christie. 120–53. Austin: University of Texas Press.

Desailly-Chanson, Yann. 2011. "Operaciones CR33 y CR35: Excavaciones en las Estructuras 13Q-3 y 13Q-5." In *Proyecto Regional Arqueológico La Corona: Informe Final Temporada 2010*, edited by Tomás Barrientos, Marcello A. Canuto, and Mary Jane Acuña, 211–48. Guatemala City: Report submitted to the Instituto de Antropología e Historia, Guatemala.

Desailly-Chanson, Yann. 2012. "Operación CR33: Excavación del Entierro 3, Estructura 13Q-3." In *Proyecto Regional Arqueológico La Corona: Informe Final Temporada 2011*, edited by Tomás Barrientos, Marcello A. Canuto, and Jocelyne Ponce, 201–30. Guatemala City: Report submitted to the Instituto de Antropología e Historia, Guatemala.

Duran, Fray Diego. 1971. *Book of the Gods and Rites and the Ancient Calendar*. Translated by Fernando Horcasitas and Doris Heyden. Norman: University of Oklahoma Press.

Duran, Fray Diego. 1994. *The Histories of the Indies of New Spain*. Translated by Doris Heyden. Norman: University of Oklahoma Press.

Durkheim, Emile. 1933. *The Division of Labor in Society*. Translated by George Simpson. Glencoe, IL: Free Press.

Eco, Umberto. 1979. *A Theory of Semiotics*. Bloomington: Indiana University Press.

Eliade, Mircea. 1964. *Shamanism: Archaic Techniques of Ecstasy*. Translated by Williard R. Trask. New York: Bollingen Foundation and Pantheon.

Farriss, Nancy M. 1984. *Maya Society under Colonial Rule: The Collective Enterprise of Survival*. Princeton: Princeton University Press.

Fash, William L., and Robert J. Sharer. 1991. "Sociopolitical Developments and Methodological Issues at Copan, Honduras: A Conjunctive Perspective." *Latin American Antiquity* 2 (2): 166–87. http://dx.doi.org/10.2307/972276.

Fernández, Carlos Enrique. 2011. "Operación CR16: Excavaciones en la Estructura 13R-10." In *Proyecto Regional Arqueológico La Corona: Informe Final Temporada 2010*, edited by Tomás Barrientos, Marcello A. Canuto, and Mary Jane Acuña. 277–304. Guatemala City: Report submitted to the Instituto de Antropología e Historia, Guatemala.

Fernández, Miguel Ángel. 1985. "Ofrendas del Templo del 'Sol,' de la 'Cruz Enramada': Temporada de Trabajos en La Zona Arqueológica de Palenque, Chiapas, del 25 de Mayo al 10 de Septiembre de 1942." In *Palenque 1926–1945*, edited by Roberto García Moll, 180–226. Mexico City: Instituto Nacional de Antropología e Historia.

Fields, Virginia. 1989. "The Origins of Divine Kingship among the Lowland Classic Maya." PhD diss., University of Texas at Austin.

Fields, Virginia, and Dorie Reents-Budet, eds. 2005. *Lords of Creation: The Origins of Sacred Maya Kingship*. Los Angeles and London: Los Angeles County Museum of Art and Scala Publishers.

Fitzsimmons, James. 1998. "Classic Maya Mortuary Anniversaries at Piedras Negras, Guatemala." *Ancient Mesoamerica* 9 (2): 271–78. http://dx.doi.org/10.1017/S0956536100000198X.

Fitzsimmons, James. 2002. "Death and the Maya: Language and Archaeology in Classic Maya Mortuary Ceremonialism." PhD diss., Harvard University, Cambridge, MA.

Flannery, Kent V., and Joyce Marcus. 1996. "Cognitive Archaeology." In *Contemporary Archaeology in Theory*, edited by Robert W. Preucel and Ian Hodder, 350–63. Malden, MA: Blackwell Publishers.

Fogelin, Lars. 2014. "Material Practice and the Metamorphosis of a Sign: Early Buddhist Stupas and the Origin of Mahayana Buddhism." *Asian Perspective* 51 (2): 278–310. http://dx.doi.org/10.1353/asi.2014.0005.

Foucault, Michel. 1982. "The Subject and Power." *Critical Inquiry* 8 (4): 777–95. http://dx.doi.org/10.1086/448181.

Freidel, David A., and Linda Schele. 1988. "Kingship in the Late Preclassic Maya Lowlands: The Instruments and Places of Ritual Power." *American Anthropologist* 90 (3): 547–67. http://dx.doi.org/10.1525/aa.1988.90.3.02a00020.

Freidel, David A., Linda Schele, and Joy Parker. 1993. *Maya Cosmos: Three Thousand Years on the Shaman's Path*. New York: William Morrow.

Fridberg, Diana, and Clarissa Cagnato. 2012. "Estudios de Plantas e Animales en La Corona." Paper presented at the XXVI Simposio de Investigaciones Arqueológicas en Guatemala, Guatemala City, July 16.

Furst, Peter T. 1976. "Shamanic Survivals in Mesoamerican Religion." In *Actas, XLI Congreso Internacional de Americanistas, México, 2 Al 7 de Septiembre de 1974*, 2:151–57. Mexico City: Comisión de Publicación de las Actas y Memorias.

Gardin, Jean-Claude. 1992. "Semiotic Trends in Archaeology." In *Representations in Archaeology*, edited by Jean-Claude Gardin and Christopher Peebles, 87–104. Bloomington: Indiana University Press.

Geertz, Clifford. 1973a. "Politics Past, Politics Present: Some Notes on the Uses of Anthropology in Understanding the New States." In *The Interpretation of Cultures*, 327–41. New York: Basic Books.

Geertz, Clifford. 1973b. "Thick Description: Toward an Interpretive Theory of Culture." In *The Interpretation of Cultures*, 3–32. New York: Basic Books.

Geertz, Clifford. 1980. *Negara: The Theater State in Nineteenth-Century Bali*. Princeton: Princeton University Press.

Giddens, Anthony. 1979. *Central Problems in Social Theory: Action, Structure, and Contradiction in Social Analysis*. Los Angeles: University of California Press. http://dx.doi.org/10.1007/978-1-349-16161-4.

Giddens, Anthony. 1984. *The Constitution of Society*. Los Angeles: University of California Press.

Gonlin, Nancy. 2007. "Ritual and Ideology among Classic Maya Rural Commoners at Copan, Honduras." In *Commoner Ritual and Ideology in Ancient Mesoamerica*, edited by Nancy Gonlin and Jon C. Lohse, 83–121. Boulder: University Press of Colorado.

Graham, Ian, and Eric Von Euw. 1977. *Corpus of Maya Hieroglyphic Inscriptions*. Vol. 3, pt. 1: *Yaxchilan*. Cambridge, MA: Peabody Museum of Archaeology and Ethnology, Harvard University.

Graham, Ian. 1979. *Corpus of Maya Hieroglyphic Inscriptions*. Vol. 3, pt. 2: *Yaxchilan*. Cambridge, MA: Peabody Museum of Archaeology and Ethnology, Harvard University.

Graham, Ian. 1997. "Mission to La Corona." *Archaeology Magazine* 50 (5): 46.

Grierson, Philip. 1959. "Commerce in the Dark Ages: A Critique of the Evidence." *Transactions of the Royal Historical Society* (fifth series) 9: 123–40.

Gronemeyer, Sven. 2006. *The Maya Site of Tortuguero, Tabasco, Mexico: Its History and Inscriptions*. Acta Mesoamericana 17. Markt Schwaben, Germany: Anton Saurwein.

Gronemeyer, Sven, and Barbara MacCleod. 2010. "What Could Happen in 2012: A Re-Analysis of the 13-Bak'tun Prophecy on Tortuguero Monument 6." *Wayeb Notes* 34:1–68.

Grube, Nikolai. 1994. "Epigraphic Research at Caracol, Belize." In *Studies in the Archaeology of Caracol, Belize*, edited by Diane Z. Chase and Arlen F. Chase, 83–122. Monograph 7. San Francisco: Pre-Columbian Art Research Institute.

Grube, Nikolai. 1996. "Palenque in the Maya World." In *Eighth Palenque Roundtable, 1993*, edited by Martha Macri and Jan McHargue, 1–13. San Francisco: Pre-Columbian Art Research Institute.

Grube, Nikolai. 1997. "The Auguries." In *Notebook for the XXIst Maya Hieroglyphic Forum at Texas*, 79–88. Austin: University of Texas.

Grube, Nikolai, Ekkehardt-Wölke Haase, and Mareike Sattler. 1990. "Vier Neue Archäologische Fundorte Im Nordwestlichen Peten." *Mexicon* 12 (3): 46–49.

Grube, Nikolai, Alfonso Lacadena, and Simon Martin. 2003. *Chichen Itza and Ek' Balam: Terminal Classic Inscriptions from Yucatan*. Proceedings of the Maya Hieroglyphic Workshop. Austin, TX: University of Texas at Austin.

Grube, Nikolai, Simon Martin, and Marc Zender. 2002. *Proceedings of the Maya Hieroglyphic Workshop: Palenque and Its Neighbors*. Edited by Phil Wanyerka. Austin: University of Texas.

Grube, Nikolai, and Linda Schele. 1990. "Royal Gifts to Subordinate Lords." Copan Note 87.

Grube, Nikolai, Linda Schele, and Federico Fahsen. 1991. "Odds and Ends from the Inscriptions of Quirigua." *Mexicon* 13 (6): 106–12.

Guenter, Stanley. 2002. "A Reading of the Cancuén Looted Panel." Mesoweb. http://www.mesoweb.com/features/cancuen/Panel.pdf.

Guenter, Stanley. 2005. "La Corona Find Sheds Light on Site Q Mystery." *PARI Journal* 6 (2): 16–18.

Guenter, Stanley. n.d. "The Epigraphy of El Peru-Waka." Unpublished paper in possession of the author.

Guernsey, Juila. 2006. *Ritual and Power in Stone: The Performance of Rulership in Mesoamerican Izapan Style Art*. Austin: University of Texas Press.

Hammond, Norman. 1974. "The Distribution of Late Classic Maya Major Ceremonial Centers in the Central Area." In *Mesoamerican Archaeology: New Approaches*, edited by Norman Hammond, 313–34. Austin: University of Texas Press.

Hammond, Norman. 1981. "Pom for the Ancestors." *Mexicon* 3 (5): 77–79.

Hammond, Norman. 1991. "Inside the Black Box: Defining Maya Polity." In *Classic Maya Political History: Hieroglyphic and Archaeological Evidence*, edited by Patrick T. Culbert, 253–84. Cambridge: Cambridge University Press.

Hawkes, Christopher. 1954. "Archaeological Theory and Method: Some Suggestions from the Old World." *American Anthropologist* 56:155–68. http://dx.doi.org/10.1525/aa.1954.56.2.02a00020.

Hellmuth, Nicholas. 1987. *Monster und Menschen in der Maya-Kunst: Eine Ikonographie der Alten Religionen Mexikos und Guatemalas*. Graz, Austria: Akademische Druck und Verlagsanstalt.

Helmke, Christophe, Harri Kettunen, and Stanley Guenter. 2006. "Comments on the Hieroglyphic Texts of the B-Group Ballcourt Markers at Caracol, Belize." *Wayeb Notes* 23:1–27.

Helmke, Christophe, and Jesper Nielsen. 2013. "The Writing on the Wall: A Paleographic Analysis of the Maya Texts of Tetitla, Teotihuacan." In *The Maya in a Mesoamerican Context: Comparative Approaches to Maya Studies: Proceedings of the 16th European Maya Conference, Copenhagen, December 5–10, 2011*, edited by Jesper Nielsen and Christophe Helmke, 123–66. Acta Mesoamericana 26. Markt Schwaben, Germany: Anton Saurwein.

Hernandez, Martinez Juan, ed. 1929. *Diccionario de Motul Maya-Español Atribuido a Fray Antonio de Ciudad Real y Arte de Lengua Maya por Fray Juan Coronel*, vol.2. Mérida, Yucatán, Mexico: Talleres de la Compañía Tipográfica Yucateca.

Herzfeld, Michael. 1992. "Metapatterns: Archaeology and the Uses of Evidential Scarcity." In *Representations in Archaeology*, edited by Jean-Claude Gardin and Christopher S. Peebles, 66–86. Bloomington: Indiana University Press.

Hill, Robert M., II. 1986. "Manteniendo el Culto a los Santos: Aspectos Financieros de las Instituciones Religiosas en el Altiplano Colonial Maya." *Mesoamerica* (Antigua, Guatemala) 7 (11): 61–77.

Hodder, Ian. 1982a. *Symbols in Action: Ethnoarchaeological Studies of Material Culture*. Cambridge: Cambridge University Press.

Hodder, Ian. 1982b. "Theoretical Archaeology: A Reactionary View." In *Symbolic and Structural Archaeology*, edited by Ian Hodder, 1–16. Cambridge: Cambridge University Press. http://dx.doi.org/10.1017/CBO9780511558252.002.

Hodder, Ian. 1987. *The Archaeology of Contextual Meanings*. Cambridge: Cambridge University Press.

Hodder, Ian. 1989. "Post-Modernism, Post-Structuralism and Post-Processual Archaeology." In *The Meaning of Things: Material Culture and Symbolic Expression*, edited by Ian Hodder, 64–78. London: Unwin Hyman Ltd.

Hodder, Ian. 1992. *Theory and Practice in Archaeology*. New York: Routledge.

Houston, Stephen D. 1993. *Hieroglyphs and History at Dos Pilas: Dynastic Politics of the Classic Maya*. Austin: University of Texas Press.

Houston, Stephen D. 1996. "Symbolic Sweatbaths of the Maya: Architectural Meaning in the Cross Group at Palenque, Mexico." *Latin American Antiquity* 7 (2): 132–51. http://dx.doi.org/10.2307/971614.

Houston, Stephen D. 2004. "Review: *Une Histoire de La Religion des Mayas: Du Panthéisme au Panthéon* by Claude-Francois Baudez." *Ethnohistory* (Columbus, OH) 51 (2): 445–48. http://dx.doi.org/10.1215/00141801-51-2-445.

Houston, Stephen D. 2006. "Impersonation, Dance, and the Problem of Spectacle among the Classic Maya." In *Archaeology of Performance: Theaters of Power, Community, and Politics*, edited by Takeshi Inomata and Lawrence S. Coben, 135–55. Lanham, MD: AltaMira Press.

Houston, Stephen D., Héctor Escobedo, Mark Child, Charles W. Golden, and Rene Munoz. 2003. "The Moral Community: Maya Settlement Transformation at Piedras Negras, Guatemala." In *The Social Construction of Ancient Cities*, edited by Monica L. Smith, 212–53. Washington, DC: Smithsonian Institution.

Houston, Stephen D., and Takeshi Inomata. 2009. *The Classic Maya*. Cambridge World Archaeology. Cambridge: Cambridge University Press.

Houston, Stephen D., and Peter Mathews. 1985. *The Dynastic Sequence of Dos Pilas*. PARI Monograph, no. 1. San Francisco: Pre-Columbian Art Research Institute.

Houston, Stephen D., John Robertson, and David Stuart. 2000. "The Language of Classic Maya Inscriptions." *Current Anthropology* 41 (3): 321–56. http://dx.doi.org/10.1086/300142.

Houston, Stephen D., John Robertson, and David Stuart. 2001. *Quality and Quantity in Glyphic Nouns and Adjectives*. Research Reports on Ancient Maya Writing 47. Barnardsville, NC: Center for Maya Research.

Houston, Stephen D., and David Stuart. 1989. *The Way Glyph: Evidence for "Co-Essences" among the Classic Maya*. Research Reports on Ancient Maya Writing 30. Washington, DC: Center for Maya Research.

Houston, Stephen D., and David Stuart. 1996. "Of Gods, Glyphs, and Kings: Divinity and Rulership among the Classic Maya." *Antiquity* 70 (268): 289–312. http://dx.doi.org/10.1017/S0003598X00083289.

Houston, Stephen D., David Stuart, and John Robertson. 2004. "Disharmony in Maya Hieroglyphic Writing: Linguistic Change and Continuity in Classic Society." In *The Linguistics of Maya Writing*, edited by Soren Wichmann, 83–99. Salt Lake City: University of Utah Press.

Houston, Stephen D., David Stuart, and Karl Taube. 2006. *The Memory of Bones: Body, Being, and Experience among the Classic Maya*. Austin: University of Texas Press.

Houston, Stephen D., Stacey Symonds, David Stuart, and Arthur Demarest. 1992. "A Civil War of the Late Classic Period: Evidence from Hieroglyphic Stairway 4." Unpublished manuscript.

Hull, Kerry. 2005. "An Abbreviated Dictionary of Ch'orti' Maya." Final Report for the Foundation for the Advancement of Mesoamerican Studies, Inc. http://www.famsi.org/reports/03031/03031.pdf.

Inomata, Takeshi. 2006a. "Plazas, Performers, and Spectators: Political Theaters of the Classic Maya." *Current Anthropology* 47 (5): 805–42. http://dx.doi.org/10.1086/506279.

Inomata, Takeshi. 2006b. "Politics and Theatricality in Mayan Society." In *Archaeology of Performance: Theaters of Power, Community, and Politics*, edited by Takeshi Inomata and Lawrence S. Coben, 187–222. Lanham, MD: AltaMira Press.

Inomata, Takeshi, and Lawrence S. Coben. 2006. "Overture: An Inviation to the Archaeological Theater." In *Archaeology of Performance: Theaters of Power, Community, and Politics*, edited by Takeshi Inomata and Lawrence S. Coben, 11–46. Lanham, MD: AltaMira Press.

Jakobson, Roman. 1990. "Shifters and Verbal Categories." In *On Language*, edited by Linda R. Waugh and Monique Movnille-Burston, 386–92. Cambridge, MA: Harvard University Press.

Johnson, Matthew. 1999. *Archaeological Theory: An Introduction*. Oxford: Blackwell Publishers.

Jones, Christopher. 1977. "Inauguration Dates of Three Classic Rulers of Tikal, Guatemala." *American Antiquity* 42 (1): 28–60. http://dx.doi.org/10.2307/279460.

Jones, Christopher, and Linton Satterthwaite. 1982. *The Monuments and Inscriptions of Tikal: The Carved Monuments*. Tikal Reports, no. 33A. Philadelphia: University of Pennsylvania Museum of Archaeology and Anthropology.

Jones, Grant D. 1998. *The Conquest of the Last Maya Kingdom*. Stanford: Stanford University Press.

Joyce, Arthur A., Sarah B. Barber, Jeffrey Brzezinski, Carlo J. Lucido, and Víctor Salazar Chávez. 2016. "Negotiating Political Authority and Community in Terminal Formative Coastal Oaxaca." In *Political Strategies in Pre-Columbian Mesoamerica*, edited by Sarah Kurnick and Joanne P. Baron, 61–96. Boulder: University Press of Colorado.

Joyce, Arthur A., and Errin T. Weller. 2007. "Commoner Rituals, Resistance, and the Classic-to-Postclassic Transition in Ancient Mesoamerica." In *Commoner Ritual and Ideology in Ancient Mesoamerica*, edited by Nancy Gonlin and Jon C. Lohse, 143–84. Boulder: University Press of Colorado.

Joyce, Arthur A., and Marcus Winter. 1996. "Ideology, Power, and Urban Society in Pre-Hispanic Oaxaca." *Current Anthropology* 37 (1): 33–47. http://dx.doi.org/10.1086/204473.

Joyce, Rosemary A. 2007. "Figurines, Meaning and Meaning-Making in Early Mesoamerica." In *Image and Imagination: A Global Prehistory of Figurative Representation*, edited by Colin Renfrew and Iain Morley, 107–16. Cambridge: Mcdonald Institute for Archaeological Research.

Joyce, Rosemary A. 2008. "Practice in and as Deposition." In *Memory Work: Archaeologies of Material Practices*, 25–39. Santa Fe: School for Advanced Research.

Joyce, Rosemary A. 2012. "A Life with Things: Archaeology and Materiality." In *Archaeology and Anthropology: Past, Present and Future*, edited by David Shankland, 119–32. London: Berg.

Kaufman, Terrance. 1976. "Archaeological and Linguistic Correlations in Mayaland and Associated Areas of Meso-America." *World Archaeology* 8 (1): 101–18. http://dx.doi.org/10.1080/00438243.1976.9979655.

Kaufman, Terrance, and John Justeson. 2003. "A Preliminary Mayan Etymological Dictionary." Manuscript.

Kaufman, Terrance, and William Norman. 1984. "An Outline of Proto-Cholan Phonology, Morphology and Vocabulary." In *Phoneticism in Maya Hieroglyphic Writing*, edited by John Justeson and Lyle Campbell, 77–166. Publication 9. Albany: State University of New York.

Keller, Kathryn C., and Placido Luciano. 1997. *Diccionario Chontal de Tabasco (Mayense)*. Serie de Vocabularios y Diccionarios Indígenas, no. 36. Tucson, AZ: Instituto Linguistico de Verano.

Kertzer, David I. 1988. *Ritual, Politics, and Power*. New Haven: Yale University Press.

Kirchoff, Paul. 1943. "Mesoamérica: sus Limites Geográficos, Composición Étnica y Caracteres Culturales." *Acta Americana* 1:92–107.

Klein, Cecilia F., Eulogio Guzmán, Elisa C. Mandell, and Maya Stanfield-Mazzi. 2002. "The Role of Shamanisim in Mesoamerican Art: A Reassessment." *Current Anthropology* 43 (3): 383–419. http://dx.doi.org/10.1086/339529.

Knappett, Carl. 2005. *Thinking Through Material Culture: An Interdisciplinary Perspective*. Philadelphia: University of Pennsylvania Press.

Kurnick, Sarah. 2016. "Paradoxical Politics: Negotiating the Contradictions of Political Authority." In *Political Strategies in Pre-Columbian Mesoamerica*, edited by Sarah Kurnick and Joanne P. Baron, 3–36. Boulder: University Press of Colorado.

La Farge, Oliver. 1994. *La Costumbre en Santa Eulalia, Huehuetenango en 1932*. Guatemala City: Yax Te' Press.

Lacadena, Alfonso, and Soren Wichmann. 2004. "On the Representation of the Glottal Stop in Maya Writing." In *The Linguistics of Maya Writing*, edited by Soren Wichmann, 100–164. Salt Lake City: University of Utah Press.

Laporte, Juan Pedro, Hector Mejia, Héctor Escobedo, and Phil Wanyerka. 2006. "Los Monumentos Esculpidos de Sacul y algunos Aspectos Historicos del Sitio." In *Sacul, Peten, Guatemala: Exploraciones en una Entidad Politica de las Montanas Mayas, 1985–2006*, edited by Juan Pedro Laporte and Hector Mejia, 220–75. Guatemala City: Direccion General del Patrimonio Cultural y Natural, Ministerio de Cultura y Deportes.

Latour, Bruno. 2005. *Reassembling the Social: An Introduction to Actor-Network-Theory*. Oxford: Oxford University Press.
Laughlin, Robert M. 1975. *The Great Tzotzil Dictionary of San Lorenzo Zinacantán*. Smithsonian Contributions to Anthropology series, #19. Washington, DC: Smithsonian Institution Press; US Government Printing Office.
Law, John. 1986. "On the Methods of Long-Distance Control: Vessels, Navigation and the Portuguese Route to India." In *Power, Action and Belief: A New Sociology of Knowledge?*, edited by John Law, 234–63. Sociological Review Monograph 32. London: Routledge.
LeFort, Genevieve. 1998. "Gods at War: Of War Protectors, Effigy Idols and Battle Banners among the Classic Maya." *Mayab* 11:12–22.
Lele, Veerendra P. 2006. "Material Habits, Identity, Semeiotic." *Journal of Social Archaeology* 6 (1): 48–70. http://dx.doi.org/10.1177/1469605306060561.
Leone, Massimo, and Richard Parmentier. 2014. "Representing Transcendence: The Semiosis of Real Presence." *Signs and Society* (Chicago) 2 (S1): 1–22. http://dx.doi.org/10.1086/674529.
Levi-Strauss, Claude. 1963. *Structural Anthropology*. Translated by Claire Jacobson and Brooke Grundfest Schoepf. New York: Basic Books.
Lind, Michael. 2015. *Ancient Zapotec Religion: An Ethnohistorical and Archaeological Perspective*. Boulder: University Press of Colorado.
Lockhart, James. 1992. *The Nahuas after the Conquest: A Social and Cultural History of the Indians of Central Mexico, Sixteenth through Eighteenth Centuries*. Stanford: Stanford University Press.
Looper, Matthew. 1999. "New Perspectives on the Late Classic Political History of Quirigua, Guatemala." *Ancient Mesoamerica* 10 (02): 263–80. http://dx.doi.org/10.1017/S0956536199101135.
Lopez Lujan, Leonardo, and Xavier Noguez. 2011. "The Codex Teotenantzin and the Pre-Hispanic Images of the Sierra de Guadalupe, Mexico." *Res: Anthropology and Aesthetics* 59/60:93–108.
Lounsbury, Floyd G. 1973. "On the Derivation and Reading of the 'Ben-Ich' Prefix." In *Mesoamerican Writing Systems*, edited by Elizabeth P. Benson, 99–143. Washington, DC: Dumbarton Oaks Research Library and Collection.
Lounsbury, Floyd G. 1976. "A Rationale for the Initial Date of the Temple of the Cross at Palenque." In *The Art, Iconography, and Dynastic History of Palenque. Part III: Proceedings of the Segunda Mesa Redonda de Palenque*, edited by Merle Green Robertson, 211–22. Pebble Beach, CA: Robert Louis Stevenson School.
Lounsbury, Floyd G. 1980. "Some Problems in the Interpretation of the Mythological Portion of the Hieroglyphic Text of the Temple of the Cross at Palenque." In

Third Palenque Round Table, 1978, edited by Merle Green Robertson, 99–115. Austin: University of Texas Press.

Lounsbury, Floyd G. 1985. "The Identities of the Mythological Figures in the Cross Group Inscriptions of Palenque." In *Fourth Palenque Round Table*, edited by Elizabeth P. Benson, 45–58. San Francisco: Pre-Columbian Art Research Institute.

Love, Bruce. 1987. "Glyph T93 and Maya 'Hand-Scattering' Events." *Research Reports on Ancient Maya Writing* 5:7–16.

Lucero, Lisa J. 2007. "Classic Maya Temples, Politics, and the Voice of the People." *Latin American Antiquity* 18 (4): 407–27. http://dx.doi.org/10.2307/25478195.

Macri, Martha. 1988. "A Descriptive Grammar of Palenque Mayan." PhD diss., University of California, Berkeley.

Maler, Teobert. 1903. "Researches in the Central Portion of the Usumatsintla Valley." *Memoirs of the Peabody Museum* 2 (2).

Mann, Michael. 1986. *The Sources of Social Power*. Cambridge: Cambridge University Press. http://dx.doi.org/10.1017/CBO9780511570896.

Maran, Joseph, and Philipp W. Stockhammer. 2012. Introduction to *Materiality and Social Practice: Transformative Capacities of Intercultural Encounters*, edited by Joseph Maran and Philipp W. Stockhammer, 1–3. Oxford, UK: Oxbow Books.

Marcus, Joyce. 1973. "Territorial Organization of the Lowland Classic Maya." *Science* 180 (4089): 911–16. http://dx.doi.org/10.1126/science.180.4089.911.

Marcus, Joyce. 1976. *Emblem and State in the Classic May Lowlands*. Washington, DC: Dumbarton Oaks Research Library and Collection.

Marcus, Joyce. 1978. "Archaeology and Religion: A Comparison of the Zapotec and Maya." *World Archaeology* 10 (2): 172–91. http://dx.doi.org/10.1080/00438243.1978.9979729.

Marcus, Joyce. 1983a. "Zapotec Religion." In *The Cloud People*, edited by Kent V. Flannery and Joyce Marcus, 345–51. Ann Arbor: Museum of Anthropology, University of Michigan.

Marcus, Joyce. 1983b. "Lowland Maya Archaeology at the Crossroads." *American Antiquity* 48 (3): 454–88. http://dx.doi.org/10.2307/280556.

Marcus, Joyce. 1992. *Mesoamerican Writing Systems: Propaganda, Myth, and History in Four Ancient Civilizations*. Princeton: Princeton University Press.

Marcus, Joyce. 1998. "The Peaks and Valleys of Ancient States: An Extension of the Dynamic Model." In *Archaic States*, edited by Gary M. Feinman and Joyce Marcus, 59–94. School of American Research Advanced Seminar Series. Santa Fe: School of American Research Press.

Marken, Damien. 2010. "Programa de Mapeo PRALC 2009: Trabajos en la Zona Este y Oeste de La Corona y el Sitio La Cariba." In *Proyecto Regional Arqueológico*

La Corona: Informe Final Temporada 2009, edited by Marcello A. Canuto and Tomás Barrientos, 25–38. Guatemala City: Report submitted to the Instituto de Antropología e Historia, Guatemala.

Martin, Simon. 1993. "Site Q: The Case for a Classic Maya Super-Polity." Unpublished manuscript. http://www.mesoweb.com/articles/martin/SiteQ.pdf.

Martin, Simon. 1996. "Tikal's 'Star War' Against Naranjo." In *Eighth Palenque Roundtable, 1993*, edited by Martha Macri and Jan McHargue, 223–36. San Francisco: Pre-Columbian Art Research Institute.

Martin, Simon. 2000a. "Nuevos Datos Epigraficos Sobre la Guerra Maya del Clásico." In *La Guerra entre los Antiguos Mayas: Memoria de la Primera Mesa Redonda de Palenque*, edited by Silvia Trejo, 107–24. Mexico City: Instituto Nacional de Antropología e Historia, Consejo Nacional para la Cultura y las Artes.

Martin, Simon. 2000b. "Los Senores de Calakmul." *Arqueología Mexicana* 7 (42): 40–45.

Martin, Simon. 2000c. "At the Periphery: The Movement, Modification, and Re-Use of Early Monuments in the Environs of Tikal." In *The Sacred and the Profane: Architecture and Identity in the Maya Lowlands: 3rd European Maya Conference, University of Hamburg, November 1998*, edited by Pierre Robert Colas, Kai Delvendahl, Marcus Kuhnert, and Annette Schubart, 51–61. Acta Mesoamericana, vol. 10. Markt Schwaben, Germany: Verlag Anton Saurwein.

Martin, Simon. 2001. "Court and Realm: Architectural Signatures in the Classic Maya Southern Lowlands." In *Royal Courts of the Ancient Maya. Vol. 1, Theory, Comparison, and Synthesis*, edited by Takeshi Inomata and Stephen D. Houston, 168–94. Boulder, CO: Westview Press.

Martin, Simon. 2003. "Line of the Founder: A View of Dynastic Politics at Tikal." In *Tikal: Dynasties, Foreigners, and Affairs of State*, edited by Richard Leventhal, 3–45. Santa Fe: School of American Research Press.

Martin, Simon. 2005a. "Treasures from the Underworld: Cacao and the Realm of the Black Gods." Paper presented at the University of Pennsylvania Maya Weekend, Philadelphia.

Martin, Simon. 2005b. "Of Snakes and Bats: Shifting Identities at Calakmul." *PARI Journal* 6 (2): 5–15.

Martin, Simon. 2006. "Cacao in Ancient Maya Religion: First Fruit from the Maize Tree and Other Tales from the Underworld." In *Chocolate in Mesoamerica: A Cultural History of Cacao*, edited by Cameron McNeil, 154–83. Gainesville: University Press of Florida.

Martin, Simon. 2007. "Theosynthesis in Ancient Maya Religion." Paper presented at the 12th European Maya Conference, Geneva.

Martin, Simon. 2008a. "Reading Calakmul: Recent Epigraphic Finds of the Proyecto Arqueolgico de Calakmul." Paper presented at the VI Mesa Redonda de Palenque, Palenque, Chiapas, Mexico.

Martin, Simon. 2008b. "Wives and Daughters on the Dallas Altar." Mesoweb. http://www.mesoweb.com/articles/martin/Wives&Daughters.pdf.

Martin, Simon. 2009. "On the Trail of the Serpent State: The Unusual History of the Kan Polity." Paper presented at the Maya Meetings, Austin, TX.

Martin, Simon. 2014. "Early Classic Co-Rulers on Tikal Temple VI. Maya Decipherment: A Weblog on the Ancient Maya Script." http://decipherment.wordpress.com/2013/01/23/new-drawing-of-a-la-corona-panel/.

Martin, Simon. 2015. "The Dedication of Tikal Temple VI: A Revised Chronology." *PARI Journal* 15 (3): 1–10.

Martin, Simon, and Nikolai Grube. 1994. "Evidence for Macro-Political Organization amongst Classic Maya Lowland States."

Martin, Simon, and Nikolai Grube. 1995. "Maya Superstates." *Archaeology* 48 (6): 41–46.

Martin, Simon, and Nikolai Grube. 2000. *Chronicle of the Maya Kings and Queens*. New York: Thames and Hudson.

Martin, Simon, and Nikolai Grube. 2008. *Chronicle of the Maya Kings and Queens*. 2nd ed. New York: Thames and Hudson.

Martin, Simon, and Mary Miller. 2004. *Courtly Art of the Ancient Maya*. New York: Thames and Hudson.

Marx, Karl. 1998. "The German Ideology." In *Literary Theory: An Anthology*, edited by Julie Rivkin and Michael Ryans, 250–55. Malden, MA: Blackwell Publishers.

Masson, Marilyn A., and Heather Orr. 1998. "The Writing on the Wall: Political Representation and Sacred Geography at Monte Alban." In *The Sowing and the Dawning: Termination, Dedication, and Transformation in the Archaeological and Ethnographic Record of Mesoamerica*, edited by Shirley Boteler Mock, 165–75. Albuquerque: University of New Mexico Press.

Mathews, Peter. 1979. "Notes on the Inscriptions of 'Site Q.'" Manuscript on file. Calgary: University of Calgary.

Mathews, Peter. 1985. "Maya Early Classic Monuments and Inscriptions." In *A Consideration of the Early Classic Period Maya Lowlands*, edited by Gordon R. Willey and Peter Mathews, 5–54. Albany: Institute for Mesoamerican Studies, SUNY.

Mathews, Peter. 1991. "Classic Maya Emblem Glyphs." In *Classic Maya Political History: Hieroglyphic and Archaeological Evidence*, edited by Patrick T. Culbert, 19–29. Cambridge: Cambridge University Press.

Mathews, Peter. 1998. "Site Q Sculptures." *Archaeology Magazine Online Features*. http://www.archaeology.org/online/features/siteq/index.html.

Mathews, Peter, and John Justeson. 1984. "Patterns of Sign Subsitution in Maya Hieroglyphic Writing: The Affix Cluster." In *Phoneticism in Maya Hieroglyphic Writing*, edited by John Justeson and Lyle Campbell, 185–231. Albany: Institute for Mesoamerican Studies, SUNY.

Maudslay, Alfred P. 1889b. *Biologia Centrali-Americana: Archaeology*. Vol. 2. London: R. H. Porter and Dulau & Company.

Maudslay, Alfred P. 1889a. *Biologia Centrali-Americana: Archaeology*. Vol. 4. London: R. H. Porter and Dulau & Company.

McAnany, Patricia A. 1995. *Living with the Ancestors*. Austin: University of Texas Press.

McGee, Jon R. 2002. *Watching Lacandon Maya Lives*. Boston: Allyn and Bacon.

Means, Philip Ainsworth. 1917. *History of the Spanish Conquest of Yucatan and of the Itzas*. Papers of the Peabody Museum of American Archaeology and Ethnology, vol. 7. Cambridge, MA: Peabody Museum of Archaeology and Ethnology, Harvard University.

Miller, Arthur G. 1973. *The Mural Painting of Teotihuacan*. Washington, DC: Dumbarton Oaks, Trustees for Harvard University.

Miller, Daniel. 1982. "Artifacts as Products of Human Categorization." In *Symbolic and Structural Archaeology*, edited by Ian Hodder, 17–25. Cambridge: Cambridge University Press. http://dx.doi.org/10.1017/CBO9780511558252.003.

Miller, Daniel, ed. 2005. *Materiality*. Durham: Duke University Press. http://dx.doi.org/10.1215/9780822386711.

Moholy-Nagy, Huttula. 1997. "Middens, Construction Fill, and Offerings: Evidence for the Organization of Classic Period Craft Production at Tikal, Guatemala." *Journal of Field Archaeology* 24 (3): 293–313.

Morley, Sylvanus G. 1925. "Archaeology." *Carnegie Institution of Washington Year Book* 24:247–51.

Nehammer Knub, Julie, Simone Thun, and Christophe Helmke. 2009. "The Divine Rite of Kings: An Analysis of Classic Maya Impersonation Statements." *Acta Mesoamericana* 20:177–95.

Nicholson, Henry B. 1971. "Religion in Pre-Hispanic Central Mexico." In *Handbook of Middle American Indians*, vol. 10, edited by Robert Wauchope, 395–446. Austin: University of Texas Press.

Nutini, Hugo G. 1976. "Syncretism and Acculturation: The Historical Development of the Cult of the Patron Saint in Tlaxcala, Mexico (1519–1679)." *Ethnology* 15 (3): 301–21. http://dx.doi.org/10.2307/3773137.

O'Mansky, Matt, and Nicholas Dunning. 2004. "Settlement and Late Classic Political Disintegration in the Petexbatun Region, Guatemala." In *The Terminal Classic in the Maya Lowlands: Collapse, Transition, and Transformation*, edited by Arthur A.

Demarest, Prudence M. Rice, and Don S. Rice, 83–101. Boulder: University Press of Colorado.

Oakes, Maud. 1951. *The Two Crosses of Todos Santos: Survivals of Mayan Religious Ritual*. New York: Pantheon Books.

Olsen, Bjørnar. 2003. "Material Culture after Text: Re-Membering Things." *Norwegian Archaeological Review* 36 (2): 87–104. http://dx.doi.org/10.1080/002936503 10000650.

Olsen, Bjørnar. 2010. *In Defense of Things: Archaeology and the Ontology of Objects*. Lanham, MD: AltaMira Press.

Olsen, Bjørnar, Michael Shanks, Timothy Webmoor, and Christopher L. Witmore. 2012. *Archaeology: The Discipline of Things*. Berkeley: University of California Press. http://dx.doi.org/10.1525/california/9780520274167.001.0001.

Orellana, Sandra L. 1981. "Idols and Idolatry in Highland Guatemala." *Ethnohistory* (Columbus, OH) 28 (2): 157–77. http://dx.doi.org/10.2307/481116.

Orme, Bryony. 1981. *Anthropology for Archaeologists: An Introduction*. Ithaca, NY: Cornell University Press.

Otzoy, Simón. 1999. *Memorial de Sololá: Edición Facsimilar del Manuscrito Original*. Guatemala City: Comisión Interuniversitaria Guatemalteca de Conmemoración del Quinto Centenario del Descubrimiento de América.

Palka, Joel W. 2005. *Unconquered Lacandon Maya: Ethnohistory and Archaeology of Indigenous Culture Change*. Gainesville: University Press of Florida.

Parmentier, Richard. 1997. "The Pragmatic Semiotics of Cultures." *Semiotica* 116 (1): 1–115.

Parris, Caroline. 2014. "Refitting Refuse: An Assessment of Late Classic Maya Depositional Behavior." Paper presented at the Society for American Archaeology annual meeting, Austin, TX, April 25.

Patterson, Erin. 2011. "Análisis Preliminar de Los Restos Oseos Humanos de La Corona." In *Proyecto Regional Arqueológico La Corona: Informe Final Temporada 2010*, edited by Tomás Barrientos, Marcello A. Canuto, and Mary Jane Acuña, 375–84. Guatemala City: Report submitted to the Instituto de Antropología e Historia, Guatemala.

Patterson, Erin. 2012. "Analásis de Restos Óseos: Temporada 2011." In *Proyecto Regional Arqueológico La Corona: Informe Final Temporada 2011*, edited by Tomás Barrientos, Marcello A. Canuto, and Jocelyne Ponce, 373–89. Guatemala City: Report submitted to the Instituto de Antropología e Historia, Guatemala.

Patterson, Erin, Elisandro Garza, and Leticia Miguel. 2012. "Operaciones CR18 y CR19: Excavaciones en el Patio Norte del Grupo 13R-II." In *Proyecto Regional Arqueológico La Corona: Informe Final Temporada 2011*, edited by Marcello A. Canuto and Jocelyne Ponce, 319–34. Guatemala City: Report submitted to the Instituto de Antropología e Historia, Guatemala.

Pauketat, Timothy R. 2007. *Chiefdoms and Other Archeological Delusions*. Lanham, MD: AltaMira Press.

Peirce, Charles S. 1998. *The Essential Peirce*, vol. 2. Edited by Nathan Houser, Jonathan R. Eller, Albert C. Lewis, André De Tienne, and D. Bront Davis. Bloomington: Indiana University Press.

Pérez, Griselda, Stanley Guenter, David Freidel, Francisco Castañeda, and Olivia Navarro. 2014. "El Descubrimiento de la Estela 44 de El Perú-Waka': Un Nuevo Capítulo en la Historia de los Mayas Antiguos del Noroeste de Petén, Guatemala." In *XXVII Simposio de Investigaciones Arqueológicas en Guatemala, 2013*, edited by B. Arroyo, L. Méndez Salinas, and A. Rojas, 117–24. Guatemala City: Ministerio de Cultura y Deportes, Instituto de Antropología e Historia, Asociación Tikal.

Perla Barrera, Divina. 2013. "Operación CR117: Excavaciones en la Estructura 13R-7, Temporada 2012." In *Proyecto Regional Arqueológico La Corona: Informe Final Temporada 2012*, edited by Tomás Barrientos Q., Marcello A. Canuto, and Jocelyne Ponce, 221–50. Guatemala City: Report submitted to the Instituto de Antropología e Historia, Guatemala.

Plank, Shannon E. 2004. *Maya Dwellings in Hieroglyphs and Archaeology: An Integrative Approach to Ancient Architecture and Spatial Cognition*. BAR International Series 1324. Oxford: British Archaeological Reports and Archaeopress.

Ponce, Jocelyne, and María Antonieta Cajas. 2012. "El Grupo 13R-II de La Corona: el Contexto Arqueológico de la Escalinata Glífica 2." Paper presented at the XXVI Simposio de Investigaciones Arqueológicas en Guatemala, Guatemala City, July 16.

Ponce Stokvis, Jocelyne. 2013. "Operación CR16: Excavaciones en la Estructura 13R-10, Temporada 2012." In *Proyecto Regional Arqueológico La Corona: Informe Final Temporada 2012*, edited by Tomás Barrientos Q., Marcello A. Canuto, and Jocelyne Ponce, 141–86. Guatemala City: Report submitted to the Instituto de Antropología e Historia, Guatemala.

Ponce Stokvis, Jocelyne, and Camilo Nájera. 2012. "Operación CR16: Excavaciones en la Estructura 13R-10, Temporada 2011." In *Proyecto Regional Arqueológico La Corona: Informe Final Temporada 2011*, edited by Tomás Barrientos, Marcello A. Canuto, and Jocelyne Ponce Stokvis, 305–16. Guatemala City: Report submitted to the Instituto de Antropología e Historia, Guatemala.

Poole, Stafford. 1994. "Some Observations on Mission Methods and Native Reactions in Sixteenth-Century New Spain." *Americas* 50 (3): 337–49. http://dx.doi.org/10.2307/1007164.

Prager, Christian. 2013. "Übernatürliche Akteure in der Klassischen Maya-Religion: Eine Untersuchung zu intrakultureller Variation und Stabilität am Beispiel des K'uh 'Götter'-Konzepts in den Religiösen Vorstellungen und Überzeugungen

Klassischer Maya-Eliten (250–900 n.Chr.)." PhD diss., Rheinischen Friedrich-Wilhelms-Universität zu Bonn.

Preucel, Robert W. 2010. *Archaeological Semiotics*. Malden, MA: Wiley-Blackwell.

Preucel, Robert W. 2013. "The Epistemic Status of Words and Things: Archaeological Perspectives." Comments on the AAA Session "Signifying the Social: Language, Objects and Materiality," Chicago, November 20.

Preucel, Robert W., and Alexander A. Bauer. 2001. "Archaeological Pragmatics." *Norwegian Archaeological Review* 34 (2): 85–96. http://dx.doi.org/10.1080/00293650127469.

Price, Barbara J. 1974. "The Burden of the Cargo: Ethnographical Models and Archaeological Inference." In *Mesoamerican Archaeology: New Approaches*, edited by Norman Hammond, 445–65. Austin: University of Texas Press.

Proskouriakoff, Tatiana. 1978. "Olmec God and Maya God-Glyphs." In *Codex Wauchope: A Tribute Roll*, edited by Marco Giardino, Barbara Edmonson, and Winifred Creamer, 113–17. New Orleans: Tulane University.

Proskouriakoff, Tatiana. 1993. *Maya History*. Austin: University of Texas Press.

Pugh, Daniel. 2013. "Scenes of Exclusion: Historical Transformation and Material Limitations to Pawnee Gender Representation." *Journal of Material Culture* 18 (1): 53–67. http://dx.doi.org/10.1177/1359183512473559.

Rathje, William L. 1970. "Socio-Political Implications of Lowland Maya Burials: Methodology and Tentative Hypotheses." *World Archaeology* 1 (3): 359–74. http://dx.doi.org/10.1080/00438243.1970.9979453.

Redfield, Robert, and Alfonso Villa Rojas. 1962. *Chan Kom: A Maya Village*. Chicago: University of Chicago Press.

Reilly, Kent F. 1994. "Visions to Another World: Art, Shamanism, and Political Power in Middle Formative Mesoamerica." PhD diss., University of Texas at Austin.

Reina, Ruben. 1966. *The Law of the Saints*. New York: Bobbs-Merrill Company.

Renfrew, Colin. 1994. "Towards a Cognitive Archaeology." In *The Ancient Mind: Elements of a Cognitive Archaeology*, edited by Colin Renfrew and Ezra B. W. Zubrow, 3–12. Cambridge: Cambridge University Press. http://dx.doi.org/10.1017/CBO9780511598388.002.

Ricketson, Oliver G. 1925. "Report of O. G. Ricketson Jr. on the Temple of the Four Lintels (Station 7)." *Carnegie Institution of Washington Year Book* 24:267–69.

Ringle, William. 1985. "Notes on Two Tablets of Unknown Provenance." In *Fifth Palenque Round Table, 1983*, edited by Virginia M. Fields and Merle Green Robertson, 151–58. Palenque Round Table Series. San Francisco: Pre-Columbian Art Research Institute.

Ringle, William. 1988. *Of Mice and Monkeys: The Value and Meaning of T1016, the God C Hieroglyph*. Research Reports on Ancient Maya Writing 18. Washington, DC: Center for Maya Research.

Ruppert, Karl. 1943. "Number 43: The Mercado: Chichen Itza, Yucatan." In *Contributions to American Anthropology and History*, 223–60. Publication 546. Washington, DC: Carnegie Institution of Washington.
Ruppert, Karl. 1952. *Chichen Itza: Architectural Notes and Plans*. Publication 595. Washington, DC: Carnegie Institution of Washington.
Rus, Jan, and Robert Wasserstrom. 1980. "Civil-Religious Hierarchies in Central Chiapas: A Critical Perspective." *American Ethnologist* 7 (3): 466–78. http://dx.doi.org/10.1525/ae.1980.7.3.02a00050.
Ruz Lhuiller, Alberto. 1977. "Gerontocracy at Palenque?" In *Social Process in Maya Prehistory: Studies in Honor of Sir Eric Thompson*, edited by Norman Hammond, 287–95. London: Academic Press.
Sabloff, Jeremy A. 2015. "Remarks on the Symposium 'Contextualizing Maya History and Archaeology: Reflections on the 25th Anniversary of Forest of Kings.'" Paper presented at the 80th Annual Meeting of the Society for American Archaeology, April 15–19, San Francisco.
Sachse, Frauke. 2004. "Interpreting Maya Religion: Methodological Remarks on Understanding Continuity and Change in Maya Religious Practices." In *Continuity and Change: Maya Religious Practices in Temporal Perspective*, edited by Daniel Graña Behrens, Nikolai Grube, Christian Prager, Frauke Sachse, Stefanie Teufel, and Elizabeth Wagner, 1–21. Fifth European Maya Conference, University of Bonn, December 2000. Acta Mesoamericana 14. Markt Schwaben, Germany: Verlag Anton Saurwein.
Sáenz, Cesar A. 1956. *Exploraciones en el Pirámide de la Cruz Foliada*. Mexico City: Instituto Nacional de Antropología e Historia.
Sahagún, Fray Barnardino. 1969a. *Historia General de las Cosas de Nueva España*, vol. 1. Edited by Angel María Garirbay. Mexico City: Editorial Porrua.
Sahagún, Fray Barnardino. 1969b. *Historia General de las Cosas de Nueva España*, vol. 3. Edited by Angel María Garirbay. Mexico City: Editorial Porrua.
Sanders, William, and David Webster. 1988. "The Mesoamerican Urban Tradition." *American Anthropologist* 90 (3): 521–46. http://dx.doi.org/10.1525/aa.1988.90.3.02a00010.
Sanford, J. B. 1911. "Argument against Senate Constitutional Amendment No. 8." California State Archives, Secretary of State Elections Papers. http://sfpl.org/pdf/libraries/main/sfhistory/suffrageagainst.pdf.
Saturno, William A., David Stuart, and Boris Beltran. 2006. "Early Maya Writing at San Bartolo, Guatemala." *Science* 311 (5765): 1281–83. http://dx.doi.org/10.1126/science.1121745.
Saussure, Ferdinand de. 1966. *Course in General Linguistics*. Edited by Charles Bally, Albert Sechehaye, and Albert Riedlinger. New York: McGraw-Hill.

Schele, Linda. 1979. "The Palenque Triad: A Visual and Glyphic Approach." *Actes du XLIIe Congrès International des Americanistes* 7:407–23.

Schele, Linda. 1986. "The Founders of Lineages at Copan and Other Maya Sites." Copan Note 8.

Schele, Linda. 1987. "New Data on the Paddlers from Butz'-Chan of Copan." Copan Note 29.

Schele, Linda. 1989. *Workbook for the XIIIth Maya Hieroglyphic Workshop at Texas.* Austin: Art Department, University of Texas.

Schele, Linda. 1991. *Proceedings of the Maya Hieroglyphic Workshop.* Edited by Phil Wanyerka. Austin: University of Texas.

Schele, Linda. 1992. *Notebook for the XVIth Maya Hieroglyphic Workshop at Texas.* Austin: Art Department, University of Texas.

Schele, Linda. 1993. "The Texts of Group 10L-2: A New Interpretation." Copan Note 118.

Schele, Linda, and David A. Freidel. 1990. *A Forest of Kings: The Untold Story of the Ancient Maya.* New York: William Morrow.

Schele, Linda, and Nikolai Grube. 1990. "A Preliminary Inventory of Place Names in the Copan Inscriptions." Copan Note 93.

Schele, Linda, and Nikolai Grube. 1994. "Tlaloc-Venus Warfare: The Peten Wars 8.17.0.0.0–9.15.13.0.0." In *Notebook for the XVIIIth Maya Hieroglyphic Workshop at Texas*, edited by Timothy Albright, 79–165. Austin: University of Texas.

Schele, Linda, and Peter Mathews. 1998. *The Code of Kings: The Language of Seven Sacred Maya Temples and Tombs.* New York: Touchstone.

Schellhas, Paul. 1904. *Representations of Deities of the Maya Manuscripts.* Papers of the Peabody Museum of Archaeology and Ethnology, vol. 4, no. 1. Cambridge, MA: Harvard University.

Scholes, France V., and Ralph Roys. 1968. *The Maya Chontal Indians of Acalan-Tixchel: A Contribution to the History and Ethnography of the Yucatan Peninsula.* Norman: University of Oklahoma Press.

Schuster, Angela M. H. 1997. "The Search for Site Q." *Archaeology Magazine* 50 (5): 42–45.

Shanks, Michael. 2007. "Symmetrical Archaeology." *World Archaeology* 39 (4): 589–96. http://dx.doi.org/10.1080/00438240701679676.

Shanks, Michael, and Christopher Tilley. 1987. *Re-Constructing Archaeology.* Cambridge: Cambridge University Press.

Sharer, Robert J., William L. Fash, David W. Sedat, Loa P. Traxler, and Richard V. Williamson. 1999. "Continuities and Contrasts in Early Classic Architecture of Central Copan." In *Mesoamerican Architecture as Cultural Symbol*, edited by Jeff K. Kowalski, 220–49. Oxford: Oxford University Press.

Sharer, Robert J., and David W. Sedat. 1987. *Archaeological Investigations in the Northern Maya Highlands, Guatemala: Interaction and Development of Maya Civilization.* University Museum Monograph 59. Philadelphia: University Museum, University of Pennsylvania.

Sharer, Robert J., Loa P. Traxler, David W. Sedat, Ellen E. Bell, Marcello A. Canuto, and Christopher Powell. 1999. "Early Classic Architecture beneath the Copan Acropolis: A Research Update." *Ancient Mesoamerica* 10 (01): 3–23. http://dx.doi.org/10.1017/S0956536199101056.

Siebers, Hans. 1999. *"We Are Children of the Mountain," Creolization and Modernization among the Q'eqchi'es.* Latin American Studies 82. Amsterdam: Centre for Latin American Research and Documentation.

Siegel, Morris. 1941. "Religion in Western Guatemala: A Product of Acculturation." *American Anthropologist* 43 (1): 62–76. http://dx.doi.org/10.1525/aa.1941.43.1.02a00080.

Silverstein, Michael. 1976. "Shifters, Linguistic Categories, and Cultural Description." In *Meaning in Anthropology*, edited by Keith Basso and Henry Selby, 11–55. Albuquerque: University of New Mexico Press.

Silverstein, Michael. 1993. "Metapragmatic Discourse and Metapragmatic Function." In *Reflexive Language: Reported Speech and Metapragmatics*, edited by John A. Lucy, 33–58. Cambridge: Cambridge University Press. http://dx.doi.org/10.1017/CBO9780511621031.004.

Silverstein, Michael, and Greg Urban. 1996. "The Natural History of Discourse." In *Natural Histories of Discourse,* edited by Michael Silverstein and Greg Urban, 1–17. Chicago: University of Chicago Press.

Smith, Adam T. 2003. *The Political Landscape: Constellations of Authority in Early Complex Polities.* Berkeley: University of California Press.

Smith, Adam T. 2011. "Archaeologies of Sovereignty." *Annual Review of Anthropology* 40 (1): 415–32. http://dx.doi.org/10.1146/annurev-anthro-081309-145754.

Smith, Michael E. 2012. *The Aztecs.* 3rd ed. Malden, MA: Wiley-Blackwell.

Southall, Aidan. 1956. *Alur Society: A Study in Progress and Types of Domination.* Cambridge: Heffer.

Spores, Ronald. 1983. "Mixtec Religion." In *The Cloud People*, edited by Kent V. Flannery and Joyce Marcus, 342–45. Ann Arbor: Museum of Anthropology, University of Michigan.

State of Mississippi. 1861. "A Declaration of the Immediate Causes Which Induce and Justify the Secession of the State of Mississippi from the Federal Union." http://www.civilwar.org/education/history/primarysources/declarationofcauses.html#Mississippi.

Stone, Andrea, and Marc Zender. 2011. *Reading Maya Art: A Hieroglyphic Guide to Ancient Maya Painting and Sculpture.* London: Thames and Hudson.

Straight, Kirk D. 2007. "A House of Cards: Construction, Proportion, and Form at Temple XIX, Palenque, Chiapas, Mexico." In *Palenque: Recent Investigations at the Classic Maya Center*, edited by Damien Marken, 175–204. Lanham, MD: AltaMira Press.

Stuart, David. 1984a. "Epigraphic Evidence of Political Organization in the Usumacinta Drainage."

Stuart, David. 1984b. "Royal Auto-Sacrifice among the Maya: A Study of Image and Meaning." *Res: Anthropology and Aesthetics* 7/8:6–20.

Stuart, David. 1986. "The Hieroglyphic Name of Altar U." Copan Note 4.

Stuart, David. 1987. *Ten Phonetic Syllables*. Research Reports on Ancient Maya Writing 14. Washington, DC: Center for Maya Research.

Stuart, David. 1988. "Blood Symbolism in Maya Iconography." In *Maya Iconography*, edited by Elizabeth P. Benson and Gillett G. Griffin, 173–221. Princeton: Princeton University Press.

Stuart, David. 1995. "A Study of Maya Inscriptions." PhD diss., Vanderbilt University, Nashville.

Stuart, David. 1996. "Kings of Stone." *Res: Anthropology and Aesthetics* 29/30:149–71.

Stuart, David. 1997. "Kinship Terms in Maya Inscriptions." In *The Language of Maya Hieroglyphs*, edited by Martha Macri and Anabel Ford, 1–11. San Francisco: Pre-Columbian Art Research Institute.

Stuart, David. 2000. "The Arrival of Strangers." In *Mesoamerica's Classic Heritage*, edited by David Carrasco, Lindsay Jones, and Scott Sessions, 465–513. Boulder: University Press of Colorado.

Stuart, David. 2001. "Las Ruinas de La Corona, Petén, y La Identificación del 'Sitio Q.'" Paper presented at the XV Simposio de Investigaciones Arqueológicas en Guatemala, Guatemala City.

Stuart, David. 2003. "The Beginnings of the Copan Dynasty: A Review of the Hieroglyphic and Historical Evidence." In *Understanding Early Classic Copan*, edited by Ellen Bell, Marcello Canuto, and Robert Sharer, 215–48. Philadelphia: University of Pennsylvania Museum of Archaeology and Anthropology.

Stuart, David. 2005. "Ideology and Classic Maya Kingship." In *A Catalyst for Ideas: Anthropological Archaeology and the Legacy of Douglas Schwartz*, edited by Vernon L. Scarborough, 257–85. Santa Fe: School of American Research Press.

Stuart, David. 2006a. *The Inscriptions from Temple XIX at Palenque*. San Francisco: Pre-Columbian Art Research Institute.

Stuart, David. 2006b. *Sourcebook for the 30th Maya Meetings, March 14–19, 2006*. Austin: Mesoamerican Center, Department of Art and Art History, University of Texas.

Stuart, David. 2007a. "'White Owl Jaguar': A Tikal Royal Ancestor. Maya Decipherment: A Weblog on the Ancient Maya Script." decipherment.wordpress.com/2007/11/04/white-owl-jaguar-a-tikal-royal-ancestor/.

Stuart, David. 2007b. "Gods and Histories: Mythology and Dynastic Succession at Temples XIX and XXI at Palenque." In *Palenque: Recent Investigations at the Classic Maya Center*, edited by Damien Marken, 207–32. Lanham, MD: AltaMira Press.

Stuart, David. 2008. "Three Panels from La Corona? /Site Q K9126, K9127, K9128: Commentary from David Stuart." http://www.mayavase.com/corona/La_Corona.html.

Stuart, David. 2011. Comment on Blog Post "More on Tortuguero's Monument 6 and the Prophesy That Wasn't." *On Maya Decipherment: A Weblog on the Ancient Maya Script*. http://decipherment.wordpress.com/2011/10/04/more-on-tortugueros-monument-6-and-the-prophecy-that-wasnt/.

Stuart, David. 2012a. "On Effigies of Ancestors and Gods." *Maya Decipherment: A Weblog on the Ancient Maya Script*. https://decipherment.wordpress.com/2012/01/20/on-effigies-of-ancestors-and-gods/

Stuart, David. 2012b. "Notes on a New Text from La Corona." *Maya Decipherment: A Weblog on the Ancient Maya Script*. http://decipherment.wordpress.com/2012/06/30/notes-on-a-new-text-from-la-corona/.

Stuart, David. 2013. "Report: Two Inscribed Bones from Yaxchilan." *Maya Decipherment: A Weblog on the Ancient Maya Script*. https://decipherment.wordpress.com/2013/05/16/report-two-inscribed-bones-from-yaxchilan/.

Stuart, David. 2014. "A Possible Sign for Metate." *Maya Decipherment: A Weblog on the Ancient Maya Script*. http://decipherment.wordpress.com/2013/01/23/new-drawing-of-a-la-corona-panel/.

Stuart, David. 2015. "Preliminary Notes on Two Recently Discovered Inscriptions from La Corona, Guatemala." *On Maya Decipherment: A Weblog on the Ancient Maya Script*. http://decipherment.wordpress.com.

Stuart, David, and Joanne Baron. 2013. "Análisis Preliminar de las Inscripciones de la Escalinata Jeroglífica 2 de La Corona." In *Proyecto Regional Arqueológico La Corona: Informe Final Temporada 2012*, edited by Tomás Barrientos, Marcello A. Canuto, and Jocelyne Ponce, 187–220. Guatemala City: Report submitted to the Instituto de Antropología e Historia, Guatemala.

Stuart, David, Marcello Canuto, Tomás Barrientos, and Alejandro González. 2018. "A Preliminary Analysis of Altar 5 from La Corona." *PARI Journal* 19 (2): 1–13.

Stuart, David, and Ian Graham. 2003. *1: Piedras Negras*, vol. 9. Corpus of Maya Hieroglyphic Inscriptions. Cambridge, MA: Peabody Museum of Archaeology and Ethnology, Harvard University.

Stuart, David, and Stephen Houston. 1994. *Classic Maya Place Names*. Studies in Pre-Columbian Art and Archaeology 33. Washington, DC: Dumbarton Oaks Research Library and Collection.

Stuart, David, Stephen D. Houston, and John Robertson. 1999. "Recovering the Past Classic Maya Language and Classic Maya Gods." In *Notebook for the XXIIIrd*

Maya Hieroglyphic Forum at Texas. Austin, TX: Department of Art and Art History, College of Fine Arts, and the Institute of Latin American Studies.

Sullivan, Paul. 1989. *Unfinished Conversations: Mayas and Foreigners between Two Wars*. New York: Alfred A. Knopf.

Tambiah, Stanley. 1976. *World Conquerer and World Renouncer*. Cambridge: Cambridge University Press. http://dx.doi.org/10.1017/CBO9780511558184.

Tambiah, Stanley. 1985. "A Performative Approach to Ritual." In *Culture, Thought, and Social Action: An Anthropological Perspective*, edited by Stanley Tambiah, 123–166. Cambridge, MA: Harvard University Press. http://dx.doi.org/10.4159/harvard.9780674433748.c6.

Taube, Karl. 1992. *The Major Gods of Ancient Yucatan*. Studies in Pre-Columbian Art and Archaeology 32. Washington, DC: Dumbarton Oaks Research Library and Collection.

Taube, Karl. 2000. "The Turquoise Hearth: Fire, Self Sacrifice, and the Central Mexican Cult of War." In *Mesoamerica's Classic Heritage*, edited by David Carrasco, Lindsay Jones, and Scott Sessions, 269–340. Boulder: University Press of Colorado.

Thompson, Donald E. 1960. "Maya Paganism and Christianity." In *Nativism and Syncretism*, edited by Margaret Harrison and Robert Wauchope, 1–35. Middle American Research Institute Publication 19. New Orleans: Tulane University.

Thompson, J. Eric S. 1950. *Maya Hieroglyphic Writing: An Introduction*. Washington, DC: Carnegie Institution of Washington.

Tilley, Christopher. 1991. *Material Culture and Text: The Art of Ambiguity*. New York: Routledge.

Tilley, Christopher. 2007. "Materiality in Materials." *Archaeological Dialogues* 14 (1): 16–20. http://dx.doi.org/10.1017/S1380203807002139.

Tokovinine, Alexandre. 2008. "The Power of Place: Political Landscapes and Identity in Classic Maya Inscriptions, Imagery, and Architecture." Ph diss., Harvard University, Cambridge, MA.

Tokovinine, Alexandre, and Vilma Fialko. 2007. "Stela 45 of Naranjo and the Early Classic Lords of Sa'aal." *PARI Journal* 7 (4): 1–14.

Tokovinine, Alexandre, and Vilma Fialko. 2019. "El Cerro de los Colibríes: El Patrón Divino y el Paisaje Sagrado de la Ciudad de Naranjo." In *XXXII Simposio de Investigaciones Arqueólogicas en Guatemala*, 2018, 825–38. Guatemala City: Ministerio de Cultura y Deportes, Instituto de Antropología e Historia, Asociación Tikal.

Townsend, Richard. 1979. *State and Cosmos in the Art of Tenochtitlan*. Studies in Pre-Columbian Art and Archaeology 20. Washington, DC: Dumbarton Oaks, Trustees for Harvard University.

Tsukamoto, Kenichiro. 2014. "Politics in Plazas: Classic Maya Ritual Performance at El Palmar, Campeche, Mexico." PhD diss., University of Arizona, Tucson.

Valladares, León. 1957. *El Hombre y el Maíz: Etnografía y Etnopsicología de Colotenango*. 2nd ed. Mexico City: B. Costa-Amic.

Velásquez García, Erik. 2004. "Los Escalones Jeroglíficos de Dzibanche." In *Los Cautivos de Dzibanche*, edited by Enrique Nalda, 79–104. Mexico City: Instituto Nacional de Antropología e Historia.

Villagutierre Soto-Mayor, Juan de. 1983. *History of the Conquest of the Province of the Itza: Subjugation and Events of the Lacondon and Other Nations of Uncivilized Indians in the Lands from the Kingdom of Guatemala to the Provinces of Yucatan in North America*. Edited by Frank E. Comparato. Translated by Robert D. Wood. Culver City, CA: Labyrinthos.

Vogt, Evon Z. 1965. "Ceremonial Organization in Zinacantan." *Ethnology* 4 (1): 39–52. http://dx.doi.org/10.2307/3772997.

Vogt, Evon Z. 1969. *Zinacantan: A Maya Community in the Highlands of Chiapas*. Cambridge, MA: Harvard University Press. http://dx.doi.org/10.4159/harvard.9780674436886.

Vogt, Evon Z. 1973. "Gods and Politics in Zinacantan and Chamula." *Ethnology* 12 (2): 99–113. http://dx.doi.org/10.2307/3773340.

Vogt, Evon Z. 1993. *Tortillas for the Gods: A Symbolic Analysis of Zinacanteco Rituals*. Norman: University of Oklahoma Press.

Warren, Kay B. 1978. *The Symbolism of Subordination*. Austin: University of Texas Press.

Watanabe, John. 1990. "Saints to Shibboleths: Image, Structure, and Identity in Maya Religious Syncretism." *American Ethnologist* 17 (1): 131–50. http://dx.doi.org/10.1525/ae.1990.17.1.02a00080.

Watanabe, John. 1992. *Maya Saints and Souls in a Changing World*. Austin: University of Texas Press.

Watts, Christopher M. 2008. "On Mediation and Material Agency in the Peircian Semeiotic." In *Material Agency: Towards a Non-Anthropocentric Approach*, edited by Carl Knappett and Lambros Malafouris, 187–207. New York: Springer. http://dx.doi.org/10.1007/978-0-387-74711-8_10.

Weber, Max. 1978. *Economy and Society*. Edited by Guenther Roth and Claus Wittich. Berkeley: University of California Press.

Webmoor, Timothy. 2007. "What about 'One More Turn after the Social' in Archaeological Reasoning? Taking Things Seriously." *World Archaeology* 39 (4): 563–78. http://dx.doi.org/10.1080/00438240701679619.

Whitecotton, Joseph W. 1977. *The Zapotecs: Princes, Priests, and Peasants*. Norman: University of Oklahoma Press.

Wichmann, Soren. 2006. "A New Look at Linguistic Interaction in the Lowlands as a Background for the Study of Maya Codices." In *Sacred Books, Sacred Languages: Two Thousand Years of Ritual and Religious Maya Literature*, edited by Rogelio Valencia Rivera and Genevieve LeFort, 45–64. Acta Mesoamericana. Markt Schwaben, Germany: Verlag Anton Saurwein.

Willey, Gordon R. 1977. "A Consideration of Archaeology." *Daedalus* 106 (3): 81–96.

Wisdom, Charles. 1940. *The Chorti Indians of Guatemala*. Chicago: University of Chicago Press.

Witmore, Christopher L. 2007. "Symmetrical Archaeology: Excerpts of a Manifesto." *World Archaeology* 39 (4): 546–62. http://dx.doi.org/10.1080/00438240701679411.

Wright, Mark A. 2011. "A Study of Classic Maya Rulership." PhD diss., University of California, Riverside.

Wylie, Alison. 1982. "Epistemological Issues Raised by a Structuralist Archaeology." In *Symbolic and Structural Archaeology*, edited by Ian Hodder, 39–46. Cambridge: Cambridge University Press. http://dx.doi.org/10.1017/CBO9780511558252.005.

Wylie, Alison. 1985. "The Reaction against Analogy." *Advances in Archaeological Method and Theory* 8:63–111.

Wynn, Thomas. 1993. "Two Developments in the Mind of Early Homo." *Journal of Anthropological Archaeology* 12 (3): 299–322. http://dx.doi.org/10.1006/jaar.1993.1009.

Yoffee, Norman. 2005. *Myths of the Archaic State: The Evolution of the Earliest Cities, States, and Civilizations*. Cambridge: Cambridge University Press. http://dx.doi.org/10.1017/CBO9780511489662.

Zender, Marc. 2004. "A Study of Classic Maya Priesthood." PhD diss., University of Calgary.

Zender, Marc. 2007. "Mexican Associations of the Early Classic Dynasty of Turtle Tooth I of Piedras Negras." Paper presented at the XXXIst Maya Meetings, Austin, TX, March 9, 2011. La Corona Panel 1, Comments and Chronology. Unpublished paper in possession of the author.

Zender, Marc. 2011. "La Corona Panel 1, Comments and Chronology." Unpublished paper in possession of the author.

Zender, Marc, and Stanley Guenter. 2003. "The Names of the Lords of Xib'alb'a in the Maya Hieroglyphic Script." In *Eduard y Caecili Seler: Sistematización de Los Estudios Americanistas y Sus Repercusiones*, edited by Renata von Hanffstengel and Cecilia Tercero Vasconcelos, 91–126. Mexico City: Universidad Nacional Autónoma de México, Instituto Nacional de Antropología e Historia, Instituto de Investigaciones Interculturales Germano-Mexicanas, Ediciones y Gráficos Eon.

Zender, Marc, and Joel Skidmore. n.d. Maya. Mesoweb Encyclopedia. http://mesoweb.com/encyc/index.asp.

Index

Acalan Chontal, 96
agency, agents, 34, 35, 118
agriculture, 6, 10, 13
Aguas Calientes, 90
Aguateca, 78; and GI-K'awiil, 88, 90, 91
Ahuitzotl, 99
ajaws. *See* rulers
Aj K'ahk' O' Chaak, 111
Aj Wosal, 58–59
Akan, 76, 84
alcohol, 105
alliances, patron deities and, 76–78
Altar 1 (Naranjo), 58–59
Ana, Santa, 101
analogy, 43(n1); in semiotic archaeology, 40–42
ancestors, 53, 72(n6), 73(n7), 114(n6), 147; founding, 30, 59–60; veneration of, 57–59, 65, 112, 144, 160–61
animals, as offerings, 159–60
Annals of the Kaqchikels, 93, 94, 95, 160
archaeology, and epigraphy, 19–20
Archaic period, 7
architecture, political hierarchy in, 11–12
argument, signs and, 24
artifacts, high-status portable, 19
Atapan, 96

Auilix, 93
autosacrifice, 99
Avendaño, Fr., 96
Aztecs, 98–99, 111, 114(n9)

Balakbal, 173
Balam Acab, 94
Balam Quitze, 93
ballgames, and alliances, 140–42
baptismal events, naming and, 29–30
Béjar, Diego de, 96
B'eleje' Toj, 94
Belize, 6
Bernardino, Juan Diego, 102
Bernardino, San, 101
blood, 48, 99
Bolon K'awiil, 77
Bourdieu, Pierre, on *habitus*, 34–35
burials, in Coronitas, 127–28, 131–36, 139

Cabtanilcabtan, 96
cacao, 63
Calakmul, 18, 80, 84; Kaan polity at, 76–77, 119, 140, 168; and La Corona, 125–26, 145–46, 153; patron gods at, 56, 169, 173; political control, 14, 17; Yajaw Maan at, 58, 82
calendars: Catholic, 100, 105; long-count, 8
Camaxtli, 101

Campeche, 6
Cancuen, 56, 76, 88, 168–69
candles, as food, 105
captives, sacrifice of, 99
capture: of deities, 78–79, 84, *86*; of saints, 107
Caracol, 13, 53, 76, 87, 168, 169; patron deities of, 62, 173–74; PDIG at, *54*, 56; rulers at, 60, 73(n7)
cargo systems, 108
Catholicism, Spanish folk, 100–101
ceramics, 7, 39; in La Corona structures, 133–35, 143–44, *145*, 157, 158–59
Chablekal Fine Gray, 156–57, 159
Chak Ak', 152, 163(n15, n17)
Chakaw Nahb Chan, 3, 142, 144–45, 147, 150, 161, 167
Chalchuapa, 8
Chalco, 99
Chan Te'Ajaw, 77, 78
Chan Ujol K'uh, 79
Chay Ab'äj, 94
chert, in La Corona burials, 135–36
Chiapas, 6
Chiautempan, 101
Chichen Itza, 10, 57, *64*, 70; captured and subordinated gods at, 79, 169; patron deities of, 174–75; temples at, 65–67
Chimalkan, 94
Chinamitas, 97
Chinautla, 107
Chinikiha, 175
Ch'olti'an, 9, 55
Ch'orti', 11
chronologies, dynastic, 60
ch'ulel, 47
churches, deity iconography in, 101
Classic period, 33, 36, 107, 112; geopolitics, 9–10; *k'uh* glyph in 46–48; political organization, 11–14, 110–13, 170–72
cofradia system, 108
Comalcalco, 175–76
commoners, 36; patron god veneration, 85, 88
communication, 28, 37
Conay, Dioniso José, 93
condensation (fusion), of ritual, 32

conspicuous consumption, at La Corona, 146, 158, 159–60
context, in semiotic archaeology, 39–40
Copan, 12, 19, 47, 58, 62, 65, 72(n5), 137; patron deities, 53, 71, 77, 79, 87, 88, 91, 91, 176–78
coronation ceremonies, 32
Coronitas group, *121*, 142; burials in, *127*–28, 131–35; construction stages of, 122–23, 128–31, 145–46, 157; K'inich [?] Yook's inscriptions at, 146–52; as necropolis, 136–37; rituals at, 157–61. *See also individual structures*
Cortes, Hernán, 97
Course in General Linguistics (Saussure), 21
craft specialization, 13
Cross Group (Palenque), 61–62, 69, 70
Cuchumatan Mountains, 7
Cukulchan, 96
cults, 5, 76, 102; patron saint, 100, 101
Cumarcah, 95
Curicaueri, 98

Davis, Kim, 36–37
deities: capture and subordination of, 61–62, 79–80, 84, 169; dual nature of, 51–53; terms for, 46–47. *See also* patron deities
descendant communities, ethnographic analogy, 41–42
destruction, of patron gods, 78–79
devotions, Catholic, 100, 101
domestication: of conquered deities, 80, 82; of saints, 103, 113(n2)
Dos Caobas, 50
Dos Pilas, 88, 90, 179; attack on Seibal, 78–79; Stela 15 at, 61, 62
Dresden Codex, 54
drinking, of patron deities, 63
droplets, in water group iconography, 47–50
dualism, duality, of deities, 51–53
dual-processual theory, 14–15
Durán, Diego, 98, 99
dynasties: at Dos Pilas, 90–91; founders of, 59–60; Kaan, 137, 139, 140
Dzibanche, 62, 139, 140, 168

Early Classic period, Dzibanche, 168
Early Preclassic period, 7

Earth Lords, 104
Eastern Ch'olan, 55
effigies, 51, 72(n6), 75, 80, 95, 106, 167, 169; building and maintaining, 61–63, 66; capture and destruction of, 78–79; as gifts, 76, 93, 94; maintenance of saint, 104–5; patron deity, 71, 84–87, 170
effigy pots, gods in, 114(n9)
El Baúl, 8
El Encanto, 60, 61, 87
elites, 9, 14, 19, 36
El Mirador, 8, 9
El Palmar (Campeche), stairway at, 77, 79
El Peru, 57, 60, 82, 119; and Kaan dynasty, 76–77; patron deities at, 71, 84, 87, 169, 179; Tikal's conquest of, 85, 155
El Peru-Waka' archaeological project, 120
El Portón, 63, 64; temple building, 65–70
El Salvador, 6
El Zapote, 179
emblem glyphs, 12–13, 119
entitlements, manipulation of, 36–37
epigraphy, 162(n1); and archaeology, 19–20
Escobedo, Héctor, 120
ethnic identity, 106; patron deities and, 88, 90–91
ethnographers, 32
ethnographic analogy, 75; patron deity veneration, 92–93; in semiotic archaeology, 40–42
exile, ritual, 99

families, royal, 13
farming, 4, 10
fasting, by ritual specialists, 105
feasting, at La Corona, 146, 158, 161–62
feathered serpents, at Tikal, 84
feathers, quetzal, 140
feeding: of patron deities, 62–63, 166; of patron saints, 105
fertility, gods associated with, 52
fiestas, patron saint, 105
fire, Tohil and, 94–95
Firstborn Lord, 3
Foliated Ajaw, 9
folk Catholicism, patron saints, 100–101
food, for patron deities, 63

food preparation, at Coronitas group, 159–60
food sharing, and patron saints, 105
formality (conventionality), of ritual, 32
Freidel, David, 120
Fuensalida, Fr, 97

Galactic polity, 13
GI (Palenque), 52, 53, 56, 58, 69
gifting, 76; of gods, 93–94
GI-K'awiil, 113(n5); in Petexbatun, 88–90, 91
GII (Palenque), 52, 56, 69, 72(n5)
GIII (Palenque), 52, 56, 69
God C, 47
God D, 46
god lists, Patron Deity Introductory Glyph and, 53, 56
God N, 46
gods. *See* deities; patron deities
grave goods, in La Corona Burial 6, 132–36
Greater Tzeltalan, 7
Great Temple Rain God, 3
greenness, in *k'uh* and water group glyph, 47, 48
guardians, deities as, 88
Guatemala, 6, 7, 11, 104. *See also various regions; sites*

habitus, 34–35
Hakavitz, 93, 94
Hayward, Chris, 120
heredity, ancestor veneration and, 57–58
Hexchunchan, 97
hierarchies, sociopolitical, 11–12
hieroglyphic stairways: La Corona, *141*, 147–52; Naranjo, 62, 87; Tamarindito, 92; Yaxchilan, 111
hieroglyphic writing, 8, 9, 10, 42, 72(n3), 92; in La Corona texts, 118–19
historical events, at La Corona, 123–25
historical records, and semiotic archaeology, 42–43
histories, mythical, 69
Hojacastro, Fr., 102
Honduras, 6, 11
houses: ancestors buried under, 57; patron deity temples as, 65–67
Huitzilopochtli, 98, 99, 106, 111, 170

INDEX 221

iconography: god and saint, 101, 102; of *k'uh* glyph, 47–50
identity, community, 88, 90–91, 107
ideology, and ritual, 31–33
Ikiiy, *141*, 147, 161
Ilocab, 106
impersonation, 51
incense, as food, 105
indexicality, 24, 26; of signs, 28–29, 35–36
institutions, 30, 31, 32
interpretant(s), signs and, 23, 29, 39
Itza Maya, 96, 97, 114(n6)
Itzamkanac, 96, 97
Itzamna K'awiil, 88
Ixchel, 96
[?] Ixim Muwaan Maat, 59, 60
Ixlu, 60–61, 88

jaguar effigy, at Tikal, 80
Jaguar God of the Underworld, 59, 67, 78, 86
James, Saint. *See* Santiago
Jasaw Chan K'awiil, 80, *81*, 82, *83*
journeys, of La Corona leaders, 151
Juan, San, 101
Juan Diego, 102
Jun Tijax, 94
justice system, 29

Kaan emblem glyph, 119
Kaan polity, 62, 137, 168; clients of, 76–77; and La Corona leaders, 137, 140–42, 145, 152–55
k'ab'awil, 94
K'ahk'Chaak, 111
K'ahk' Tiliw Chan Yopaat, 73(n7), 79
Kaminaljuyu, 8, 9
K'an II, 87
K'an Tuun Chaak, 88
Kaqchikels, 93, 94, 95
K'awiil, 72(n5), destruction of, 78–79
K'awiil Chan K'inich, 90
K'axtok', 94
K'iche', 93; political authority, 108–9; and Tohil, 94–95, 106, 169
kingship, 15, 52
K'inich Ahkal Mo'Nahb, 69
K'inich Janahb Pakal, 72(n5), 73(n7)

K'inich Kan Bahlam, 68–69
K'inich Lakamtuun, 78
K'inich Yo'nal Ahk II, 73(n7)
K'inich [?] Yook, 145–46, 150–51, 152–53, 161, 167
k'uh glyph, 46–47, 52, 70; and *ku'hul*, 50–51; water group and, 47–50
K'uh Stage, at La Corona, 142–44, 158
k'uhul glyph, in rulers' titles, 50–51, 170
K'uk' Ajaw, 142, 163(n10)
K'uy Nik? Ajaw, 77, 78

La Amelia, 88, 90, 91
Lacandon Maya, 114–15(n10)
La Cariba, 155
La Corona, 3, 18, 68, 71, 112; and Calakmul, 125–26; construction history, 117–18, 122–23; discovery of, 119–20; feasting at, 158; hieroglyphic texts from 118–19; historical events at, 123–25; historical figures in, 126–27; inscriptions in, 137–39; K'uh Stage, 142–44; Main Group, 120–21; Mam Stage, 128–30; Muk Stage, 130–36; patron deities, 53, 62, *64*, 85, 87, 146–51, 160–62, 166, 167, 179; patron deity temples, 65, 67; rituals at, 161–62; royal burials in, 127–28, 131–35; rulers at, 60, 137–42; Ub Stage, 145–46, 151–52; Unen Stage, *154*, *155*, 156–58; Yajawte'e K'inich at, 153–55
La Corona Burial 1, 127–28
La Corona Burial 2, 131
La Corona Burial 6, offerings in, 132–36
La Corona Regional Archaeology Project, 120, 125
Lady Methuselah. *See* [?] Ixim Muwaan Maat
La Mar, 179–80
landscape, patron saints and, 100
language, 26
langue, 21
Late Classic period, Calakmul, 168
Late Preclassic period, 7–8
law, 29
Lee, Dan, 119
Levi-Strauss, Claude, sign and cultural phenomena, 22, 25

lineages: K'iche' ruling, 93; La Corona, 139–40, 150–51, 152-55, 160, 167
linguistics, 20, 38; sign in, 21–23
Lintel 10 (Yaxchilan Temple 3), 68
liquids: ritual use of, 63, 70, 105, 144, 148, 158–59, 161, 166
lithics, in La Corona burials, 135–36
looting, from La Corona, 118–19
lowlands, Classic period geopolitics, 9–10
Luis, San, 107
luut, loot, in PDIG, 55, 56

Maguey Grinding Stone, 9
Main Group (La Corona), 120–21
Maize God, 58, 72(n5)
Malinalco, 106
Malinalxochitl, 106
mam, 58
Mamom ceramics, 7
Mam Stage, 157, 158; construction at, 128–30, 139
Marx, Karl, 34
material culture, 20, 26
materiality, 38
Mayan languages, 6, 42
Mayapan, 6, 18(n1)
meaning, of objects, 38
mediators, signs as, 23
Memorial de Sololá, 93
Mesoamerica: interactions in, 5–6; semiotic networks in, 97–98
metapragmatics, 26–27, 39, 41, 43, 45, 75, 92; and indexicality, 28–29; and social norms, 34–35
Mexica, 114(n9), 115(n11); and Huitzilopochtli, 98–99, 106
Middle Preclassic period, 8
missionaries, and local beliefs, 101
Mississippi, 31
Mixtecs, 98
Monjas Complex, Las (Chichen Itza), 64, 65, 66
Monument 6 (Tortuguero), 62–63
Moon Goddess, 58
Moral Reforma, 180
Muk Stage, construction during, 130–36

Naah Ek', at La Corona, 137–39
Naranjo, 78, 82, 150, 155; Aj Wosal, 58–59; patron deities in, 87, 180; patron deity effigies, 62, 84, 86; Square Nosed Beastie, 59, 60
naming, 29–30
Nations, Jim, 119
necropolis, Coronitas group as, 136–37
networks, naming and, 30
New Archaeology, 4
Nicacah, 94
nobility, 13; hereditary, 108
Noh Peten, temples, 96–97

Oaxaca, deity effigies, 98
objects, 23; and signs, 24, 38, 75
object-sign-interpretant relationships, 24–25
obligations, to patron saints, 100–101
obsidian, 140; in La Corona burials, 135–36
offerings, 63, 95, 98, 105, 106; at Coronitas, 133–36, 157–60; to deities, 114–15(n10), 166; from K'inich [?] Yook, 147–48
Olmec, shamanistic figurines, 16
otoot (house), 70; for patron deities, 65, 66

Paddler Gods, 56–57, 88
Pakoc, 97
palanquins, and patron deity effigies, 62, 80, 84
Palenque, 58, 72(n5), 73(n7), 79, 95, 113(n5); god lists at, 53, 56; [?] Ixim Muwaan Maat, 59, 60; patron deities in, 87, 104, 180–82; patron deity effigies, 62, 85–86; patron deity temples, 64, 65, 68–70; PDIG at, 54–55; Sun God in, 51–52; temple dedications, 61–62
Panel 1 (Cancuen), 56, 76, 168–69
parole, 21, 22
patron deities, 17, 46, 71, 171; alliances and, 76–78; care and protection of, 84–87; Classic period, 173–85; effigies of, 61–63; ethnographic analogies, 92–93; geographic and ethnic identity, 88, 90–91; as gifts, 93–94; groupings of, 56–57; introduction of, 52–56; La Corona, 146–52, 160–62;

maintenance of, 165–66, 170; physical embodiment of, 51–52; as rulers, 58–59; rulers' care and protection of, 87–88; social relationships and, 166–67; at Tikal, 60–61; war and, 78–84
Patron Deity Introductory Glyph (PDIG), 53, 72(n4); parts of, 54–56
Paxbolon, Pablo, 96
Paxbolon-Moldonado Papers, 96
PDIG. *See* Patron Deity Introductory Glyph
Peirce, Charles S., 23
performative elements, 33
Petén Itza, Lake, 96
Petexbatun region, 183; GI-K'awiil, 88–90, 113(n5); ruling dynasty in, 90–91
pibnaah, 65, 68–69, 70, 73(n9)
Piedras Negras, 49, 62, 68, 73(n7), 182
place, patron deities and, 88, 90–91
place-names, Six Nothing lineage, 150
plantation owners, in Guatemala, 104
political authority: Classic Maya, 110–13; and supernatural power, 109–10
political organization/systems, 4–5, 17, 29, 104; ceremonies, 77–78; Classic period, 11–14, 170–72
Pomun Chaak, 67
Popol Vuh, 93–94, 95, 106, 107, 169; political authority in, 108–9
Postclassic, 46, 94
pottery. *See* ceramics
power, 37, 75; narratives of, 8–9; political and supernatural, 109–10
practice, 22
pragmatics, 45, 75
pragmatism, 25, 26
Preclassic period, 9, 10, 16
Principal Bird Deity, 46
privilege, 36; ancestor veneration, 57–58; ritualization and, 32–33
protection: by gods, 111; by saints, 107
Proto-Ch'olan, 55
Proto-Mayan speakers, 6–7
public works, and centralized states, 13
pulque, 63, 148
p'uluut, 54–55

Quebec Liberal Party, 30
Quiet Revolution, 30
Quintana Roo, 6
Quirigua, 73(n7), 79

reciprocity, 109, 170
redundancy (repetition), of ritual, 32
regalia, royal, 16
registers, semiotic, 35–36
Relación de Michoacán, 98
ritualization: and establishment of privilege, 32–33; of political ceremonies, 77–78
rituals, 13, 45, 85, 104, 113; archaeological identification of, 70–71; conjuring/capturing, 61–62; deity subordination, 79–80; ideology and, 31–33; liquids used in, 158; patron deity feeding, 62–63
ritual specialists, 16, 33; and saints, 105, 107–8
Roman Catholic Church, 30; patron saints, 100–101
royal court, 10, 13, 30, 88; ancestor veneration, 57–58
rulers (*ajaw*), 12, 13, 15, 16, 17, 18(n2), 60, 68, 72(n2), 73(n7, n8), 76, 79, 93, 110, 111, 112, 161–62; ancestor veneration and, 57–58; care for patron deities, 84–88; deities as, 58–59; responsibilities of, 170–71; at Tikal, 80–82, 90–91; titles of, 50–51, 150

sacred places, 100
sacrifices, 95, 98, 99
Sacul/Ixkun, 182
Sahagún, Bernardo de, 102
saints: effigies of, 104–5; patron, 100–101; as replacements for gods, 101–2; as supernatural entities, 103–4; visiting by, 106–7
sajal (*cahal*), 12
Sak Hix Muut, 59, 60–61, 68
Sak Maas, 147, 161, 163(n10); as ruler, 140–41
Sak Nikte', 147
Sak Tz'i', 65, 183
Sak Wahyis glyphs, 150
Salama Valley (Guatemala), 63
San Antonio (British Honduras), capture of saints, 107
San Bartolo, 8

San Luis (Petén), 107
Santa Elena, 79
Santiago (Saint James), 103, 104
Santiago Atitlan, community ancestors, 60
Santiago Chimaltenango, 103, 104, 107
Santiago Chiquito, 104
Santiago Patrón, 104
Saussure, Ferdinand de, *Course in General Linguistics*, 21
Second Vatican Council, 30
segmentary state, 13
Seibal, 12, 62; attack on, 78–79; GI-K'awiil and, 90, 91; patron deities of, 88, 183
semantic properties, 26, 75; and hieroglyphic texts, 42–43; of *k'uh*, 46–47
semiotic anthropology, 5, 25–27
semiotic archaeology, 38; analogy in, 40–42; context in, 39–40; historical records in, 42–43
semiotic chains, 23–24, 33, 82, 106; ethnographic analogy and, 41–42; signs and interpretants, 29, 39
semiotic network, Mesoamerican, 97–98
semiotics, 39; Peircian, 23–25; registers, 35–36; Saussurean, 21–23; and social norms, 27–28
semiotic theory, 20–21
serpent deities, 80
serpents, feathered, 84
Sever, Tom, 119
shamanism, 15–16
shrines, 69, 102; funerary, 136, 146
signifiers and signified, 21, 22
sign(s), 5, 25, 39; indexical meaning of, 28–29; and objects, 24, 38, 75; Saussurean model, 21–23; sets of, 35–36
sign-object relationships, indexical and symbolic, 24
Site Q: La Corona as, 119–20; search for, 118–19
sites, size and architecture of, 11–12
Six Earth Place, 150
Six Nothing lineage, 125–26, 137–40, 150–52, 161, 167
Six Nothing Place, 150
sky gods, 57
SNB. *See* Square Nosed Beastie

socialization process, 34–35
social structure, 5, 25, 27–28; entitlements in, 30, 36–37; patron gods in, 166–67; rules/norms in, 33–34
Sojuel, Francisco, 60
southern lowlands, 11; geopolitics, 9–10
Spain, hierarchy of patron saints, 101
Spanish conquest era, 93; patron saints and, 100–103
Spearthrower Owl, death of, 80, 82
spondylus shells, in *k'uh* and water group glyph, 47, 48
Square Nosed Beastie (SNB), as founding ancestor, 59–60
stairways, El Palmar, 77, 79
Stanford, J. B., on women, 31–32
states, strong vs. weak, 12–13
status, and effigies, 75
stelae, 17; Calakmul, 56, 62, 80; Caracol, *54*, 62, 87; Copan, 12, 72(n5), 87, 91; Dos Pilas, 61, 88, 90; El Encanto, 60, 61; El Peru, 57; La Corona, 137; Naranjo, 62, 78; Piedras Negras, *49*, 73(n7); Quirigua, 79; Seibal, 12, 91; Tikal, 57, 72(n4), 91–92; Tortuguero, 73(n9); Yaxchilan, 48, *49*; Yaxha, 78, 92
stereotypy (rigidity), of ritual, 32
structure, and practice, 23
Structure 1 (Yula), 66, 67
Structure J7-4B-2, 63
Structure 13R-2 (Coronitas group), 122, 136–37, 156, 158; K'uh Stage, 142, 143–44; Mam Stage, 128–30; Muk Stage construction, 130–36
Structure 13R-3 (Coronitas group), 122, 128, 129, 136–37, 156, 158; K'uh Stage, 142, 143–44; Muk Stage construction, 130–36
Structure 13R-4 (Coronitas group), 122, 137, 156, 158; K'uh Stage, 142, 143–44; Mam Stage, 128–30; Muk Stage construction, 130–36
Structure 13R-5 (Coronitas group), 122, 137, 156–57; dedication of, 152; inscriptions in, 127, 143, 150; Tahn K'inich Lajua burial in, 127–28; Ub Stage construction, 146
Structure 13R-9 (Coronitas group), 146, 159; Unen Stage modifications, 156–57

Structure 13R-10 (Coronitas group), 146–47, 159–60; Unen Stage modifications, 156–57
Stuart, David, 120
Sun God: ancestor as, 58; physical embodiments of, 51–52
supernatural entities, 45, 59–61; saints as, 103–4
supernatural power, and politics, 109–10
superstate (hegemonic) model, 13–14
supracommunity networks, 168–69
sweat baths, symbolic, 69
symbolic, 24, 26
symbolism, semantic function of language, 26
symmetrical archaeology, 38

Tabasco, 6
Tablet of the Foliated cross (Palenque), 61
Tablet of the 96 Glyphs (Palenque), 73(n7)
Taçato, 96
Tachabte, 96
Tadzunun, 96
Tahn K'inich Lajua (Alaan Tahn K'inich), 144, 161; burial chamber of, 127–28, 136; funerary temple for, 151–52; lineage, 139–40, 156; role of, 150–51
Tak'alik Ab'aj, 8
Tamarandito, 88, 90, 92
Tarascans, 98, 99
temple models, glyphs on, 47
Temple of the Cross (Palenque), 69
Temple of the Four Lintels (Chichen Itza), 66–67; captured and subordinated gods at, 79–80
Temple of the Hieroglyphic Jambs (Chichen Itza), 65–66
Temple of the Inscriptions (Palenque), *54*, 62, 63, 69, 87, 95
Temple of the Inscriptions (Temple VI; Tikal), 68; Sak Hix Muut and, 60, 61
temples, *64*; at Chichen Itza, 65–67; at Copan, 58, 88; Cumarcah, 95; dedications of, 61–62; to Huitzilopochtli, 99; at La Corona, 3; Noh Peten, 96–97; *pibnaab*, 68–69; at Tikal, 80, *81*, *83*. *See also* Coronitas group
Tenochtitlan, and Huitzilopochtli, 98, 99
Teotihuacan, 137; and Tikal, 73(n8), 80, 82, 168; water group iconography in, 48, *49*

Tepantitla, water group iconography at, *49*
Tepeyac, 102
Terminal Classic period, 10, 162
texts, 19, 20; on ruler-patron god relationships, 86–87
Tezcatlipoca, 101
theater state, 13
Thiessen Polygons, 11–12
Tianguismanalco, 101
Tikal, 18, 53, 57, 62, 70, 72(n4), 73(n8), *85*, *88*, 99, 169, 140; attacks by, 155, 156; calendar and gods at, 91–92; dynastic rulership at, 90–91; patron deities of, 168, 184–85; patron deity temples, *64*, 65, 67; political control by, 13, 14, 17; rulers at, 80–84; Sak Hix Muut, 59, 60–61; Temple I at, *81*, *83*
Tila, 185
time, and semiosis, 41
Titulo de Totonicapan, 93, 94, 95
Tixchel, 96
Tlaxcala, patron saints in, 101–2
Toci, 101
Tohil, and K'iche', 93, 94–95, 106, 169
tokens, qualities of, 24
tombs, in Coronitas, *127*–28, 131–33, 143
Tonina, 62, 72(n2), 185
Tortuguero: Monument 6, 62–63, 148; patron deities, 185–86; patron deity temple, 65, 73(n9)
trade, regional, 13
tradition, timelessness of, 31–32
tree resin, in droplet iconography, 48
Triad Progenitor. *See* [?] Ixim Muwaan Maat
tribute, 109, 110
Tulan, 93, 94, 106
Tuun K'ab Hix, 137
Tziminchak (Thunder Tapir), 97
Tz'utujil, 60

Ub Stage, 122; at La Corona, 145–46, 149, 158
Ucanal, 91, 186
Uchoch Yokpuy, at Chichen Itza, 67, 79
Uen Stage, 122
Unen Stage, at La Corona, *154*, *155*, 156–57
Ursua, General, 96

Vase of the Eleven Gods, 53, 56
Vase of the Seven Gods, 53; PDIG on, *54*, 56
verbs, mediopassive, 76–77
Virgin Mary cults, 100
Virgin of Guadalupe, 102
Virgin of Ocoltán, 101–2
visiting, by saints and gods, 106–7
Vulture, as La Corona leader, 137, 160–61

wahy glyphs, 16, 150, 162–63(n6)
warfare, 99, 109; and patron deities, 78–84; in Petexbatun, 88, 90
water, in droplet iconography, 48
water group, in *k'uh* glyphs, 47–50
Water Lily Serpent, at Chichen Itza, 67, 79
Waxaklajun Ubaah Kaan, at Tikal, 80, 82, *83*, 84, 168
Waxaklajun Ubaah K'awiil, 79
wayib, 65, 67, 70
[?] Winik Ub, 145, 150, 151–52, 163(n16)
women, Stanford on, 31–32
World Tree/axis mundi, 16

Ximenez, Francisco, 93
Xochiqutezalli, 102
Xultun, 86, 186

Yajaw Maan, 58, 62, 76, 80, *81*, 82, 84
Yajawte' K'inich, 73(n7), 145, 153–55
Yalbac, 117, 118
Yaxal Ajaw, 142, 148
Yax Chich Kan, 79
Yaxchilan, 48, 50, 62, 63, 70, 111; patron deities, 186–87; patron deity temples, 65, 67, 68; water group symbols in, 47, *49*
Yaxha, 78, 92, 187
Yax Ha'al Chaak, 67, 79
Yax Pasaj Chan Yopaat, 53
yellowness, in *k'uh* and water group glyph, 47, 48
Yellow Rain God, 3
Yihk'in Chan K'awiil, 68, 82, 84, *85*, 86
Ykchua, 96
Yucatan Peninsula, 6, 10, 96
Yucatec Mayan, 10
Yuknoom Ch'een, 140–42
Yula, 66, 67

Zacahuitzco, 102
Zapotecs, 98, 99, 114(n8)
Zinacantan, 47

www.ingramcontent.com/pod-product-compliance
Lightning Source LLC
Chambersburg PA
CBHW070921030426
42336CB00014BA/2485